Judy Garland
Splendor and Downfall of a Legend

by

Bertrand Tessier

Translation and Foreword by Lawrence Schulman

BearManor Media

2023

Published in the USA by
BearManor Media
1317 Edgewater Dr. #110
Orlando, FL 32804
www.BearManorMedia.com

Printed in the United States of America
ISBN-10:
ISBN-13: 979-8-88771-117-1

Book & cover design and layout by Sarah Joseph
Edited by Stone Wallace

"The truth is that movie making, though offering a small tax on the mind, is of all human endeavors, the most dangerous to the nervous system."

Ben Hecht, *I Hate Actors!*

Table of Contents

Table of Contents

Acknowledgments

From Bertrand Tessier:

I would like to thank Norbert Balit d'Adamis, producer of my documentary devoted to Judy Garland and Vincente Minnelli in the series "Mythical Movie Couples," which was the starting point of this book.

I would also like to thank Myriam Brough for her research in Los Angeles and New York and her attentive proofreading.

Thank you to those who told me their memories of Judy Garland: Stevie Philips, Randy Schmitt, Meredith Ponedel, Marc Wanamaker, Daniel Selznick, Mark Griffin, Joe McElhaney, Jeanine Basinger, and Steven Bingen.

Thank you to Gerald Clarke, whose biography of Judy Garland, *Get Happy*, was of precious help.

Thank you to Alain Pons for his fidelity.

A nod to Stella, my writing partner, and to Rocky, forever in my heart.

From Lawrence Schulman:

I would like to thank John Meyer, my good friend whose passion for Judy Garland is undiminished to this day, for the new information he provided me during the translation. Our times in Paris, New York, and Glens Falls, NY will always be fond memories. I would also like to thank the late Sid Luft, whom I met with on two occasions in California, and who took the time to enlighten me on many subjects relating to his late wife.

A big thanks too to my dear friend Kim Palmerston Lundgreen, whose collection of Garland photographs is second to none on the planet, for providing so many rare photos, the rest of which come from my collection and those of Bertrand Tessier, John Meyer, Gerald Waters, and Raphael Geroni, to Alain Lucien Falasse for his advice in solving seemingly insolvable translating problems, and to James Fisher for his vast knowledge of all things Garland. Kim, Alain, and James also agreed to proofread the translation, for which I am infinitely grateful. Many thanks too to Walter Frisch for his kind assistance in obtaining information about the filming of "Over the Rainbow," and to John H. Haley for his legal advice. Finally, I would like to thank Will Richter, Director of Library Services at the Grand Rapids Area Library, Lilah J. Crowe, Executive Director of the Itasca County Historical Society, and Janie Heitz, Executive Director of the Judy Garland Museum, for their assistance in researching information about the New Grand theater in Grand Rapids, Minnesota.

Fond thanks also go out to my late aunt Irene Feldherr, who attended Garland's show at the Palace in the early 1950s and told me it was one of the greatest experiences of her life. A thought too for my late mother, Sylvia Schulman, who took me, a boy of 15, to Garland's 1965 concert at the Forest Hills Stadium in Queens, New York. Let me not forget Deena Hurwitz, Jodie Hurwitz, and Dan Luria either for their kind assistance.

Finally, thank you to all those who opened their doors to me in Paris a half century ago, thereby enabling me to learn French and discover a new world.

The young Frances Ethel Gumm, circa 1928. Photo by Walter Rose, Hollywood. From the collection of Raphael Geroni.

Foreword

by Lawrence Schulman

With over forty biographies about her in English by such distinguished authors as Christopher Finch, Gerald Clarke, Gerald Frank, Anne Edwards and Scott Schechter, a half dozen original biographies in French, Italian, Swedish, and German, book-size studies of such films as *The Wizard of Oz* (1939) authored by Salman Rushdie, *Meet Me in St. Louis* (1944), *Summer Stock* (1950) and *A Star Is Born* (1955) written by Ronald Haver, CD liner notes by Emily Coleman and Ron O'Brien, LGBTQ studies by Camille Paglia in The New York Times and by Richard Dyer in his book *Heavenly Bodies: Film Stars and Society*, numerous memoirs including ones by Sid Luft, John Meyer, Mickey Deans, Mel Tormé and Stevie Phillips, a handful of plays and three films based on her life, several non-fiction works around her, published collections of her interviews, writings and articles about her, poems, songs, a disco "The Man That Got Away" remix based on her 1961 Carnegie Hall performance, to which an entire book by Manuel Betancourt was devoted and which was reperformed in its entirety by Rufus Wainwright in 2006 at Carnegie Hall, in-depth television documentaries on the BBC, PBS, A&E and Showtime, exhibits about her at the New York Public Library for the Performing Arts at Lincoln Center, London's Museum of the Moving Image and Los Angeles' Wilshire Ebell Theatre, posthumous duets with Lorna Luft and Barry Manilow, and over a score of CDs, high-resolution downloads and Blu-rays to mark what would have been her 100th birthday in 2022, Judy Garland's (1922-1969) life is, at this point in time, perhaps "overexamined," as *The New York Times* put it in 2000. But is it?

Judy Garland lived her life in the 20th century, but what does she mean in the 21st? A product of the golden era of classic American pop, and a pillar of the Great American Songbook, Garland sold sincerity and vulnerability in an age when such commodities were appreciable. Today, when celebrity and its self-promotion are the motors of an entertainment industry more and more interested in the bottom line, Garland would seem to be an anachronism. She would have loved to fill stadiums (and often did) on multi-city tours in the way Paul McCartney or The Rolling Stones do today, but her short-lived career was marked by artistic striving, and not economic success. Judy died broke and couldn't even cover her own funeral expenses. Although she was able to rent a house in London at the time of her death, she lived a life of a wanderer, sometimes able to own homes, sometimes able to stay in hotels, but often – especially near the end of her life – a houseguest of others. Indeed, at the end, she had to count on the kindness of friends, lovers, and strangers just to avoid the street. Homelessness is not a word one associates with celebrity, but Judy, had it not been for her reputation, would have been on the street towards the end. This incongruous situation is sad, and incomprehensible to most, but has meaning in the 21st century, when success is measured by millions in a bank account. No longer a part of the Hollywood machine, and unreliable to the extreme insofar as whether or not she could even show up for a booking, Garland's vagabond spirit is as much a part of her biography as *The Wizard of Oz*, *A Star Is Born*, or *Carnegie Hall*. It is strange to see her with Duke Ellington, Count Basie or Ray Bolger towards the end of her life because, although once part of the Hollywood elite, she was part of it no more, and very much diminished while on the arm of such famous colleagues and cohorts. On the decline, hooked on prescription drugs, an outcast from the industry, she was barely hanging on. Is this the Judy Garland one wants to know about? How could it be? The success of the Tony-nominated play *End of the Rainbow* and the Oscar-winning film *Judy* depicts the ravages time had inflicted on the once jubilant Judy Garland, but in some quarters microscoping the distasteful end of Garland's life is the equivalent of examining squalor, something better left under the rug. Is squalor open to discussion? Is a wandering soul open to discussion? These are not glamorous discussions, nor are they easy. Like the plague, they are to be avoided. Judy Garland makes people uncomfortable. How could such a talent have wasted away so young? Such wealth squandered? Such innocence wizened? Garland, in the 21st century, attracts us because she doesn't fit the model of success – certainly not financial – as we know it.

Judy Garland did not fit in the mold of 20th-century celebrity either. 20th-century celebrities died in Beverly Hills, not on toilet seats in modest cottages in London. Had it not been for mismanagement, drug addiction, and wanderlust, Garland might very well have continued to function. But she spent herself in a short life that was a long suicide. This is hardly success. Certainly, artistically, Garland in her brief time captured a longing and vulnerability that few entertainers achieve. Her disheveled success makes Judy Garland a heroic, modern, Don Quixotic hero of some kind of story gone wrong. A story where the happy ending is interrupted by forces beyond the hero's control. But "the end" is not unhappy either. For, Garland thrived on disorder. Only in disorder was she in her element. She mocked it, tempted it. Whether things happened to her or she brought them on becomes moot: this was her life. She would have had it no other way. Hers was a life in ruins that, for her, was right as the rain. No comfy fade-to-black for her. She went her way, by herself, alone. She thumbed her nose at convention and turned her back to the world if and when she wanted. She wrote the rules. As life galloped out of control, she enjoyed the ride. However the world perceived her was the world's problem. She was a misfit, and proud of it. Such a personality is the stuff that makes us want to learn more about her in the new century.

Intensity is another word that could be applied to Garland throughout her life and career. On screen, on record, or in the concert hall, her voice was like an arrow that broke your heart, or made you rejoice you had one. This direct emotion was far from cool. It was disturbing. It jolted you from the day-to-day into a realm of hyper-emotion, life at its fullest. This hyper-emotion fit mid-century American pop, which spoke from the heart in tunes one could hum. This hyper-emotion is too raw for comfort in the 21st century, wherein "I love you" is a common everyday pronouncement that has come to mean nothing. When Garland sang of love and longing, it made you pause. The faster pace of modern life is just the opposite of that pause that Garland gives you. We are stopped in our tracks when listening to her, and this stopping of time is out of sync with the 21st century. And that is why today we pay attention – surely more than at the time of her death – to Garland. Our fast pace stops as Garland's old-world intensity invades us, and we realize that her soaring voice can stop time itself. We recognize her today for her remarkable difference. Who would even use the word intensity today to describe a mere "entertainer"? Again, Garland is out of step. She was so in the 20th century and is even more so in the 21st. We are drawn to her even more today than yesterday because her intense inner life is something few today would dare to live. Judy Garland reminds us we are alive.

Finally, we in the 21st century are attracted to Garland because she was more than an entertainer. Today, people need to be entertained. They need to be amused. What they fail to see is that Garland was not a wind-up doll who could entertain you, and make you get happy. Garland spoke to the soul. She scared you by the power of her artistry. She was not simple. Garland can indeed be admired for her ability to take our minds off things, but she can also be admired for her ability to speak of the human condition through the songs she interpreted. That today she is still attracting new listeners is the sign that she has something to say, something complex that speaks to the complex 21st century.

To know anything about Judy Garland requires one to know everything about Judy Garland. This is what the French biography by Bertrand Tessier in your hands attempts to do, succinctly and without pretention. It is not yet another encyclopedic exegesis of her life and career that attempts to explain Judy Garland. Because Judy Garland, a complex cultural character if ever there were one, cannot be explained. As Tessier has stated: "I must say that the originality of the book is to be a European biography. In comparison to the American biographies, which are remarkable works of precision that accumulate details and archives, I preferred a precise book, historically irrefutable, but which seeks above all to give an impression of the character I am treating. A kind of intimate inquiry allowing us to discover the inner truth beyond the career. In a certain way, it is a bit like a novel, or rather, since the term novel would leave one to believe that passages are invented, like a biopic for the movies which is scrupulous with reality. That is what I try to do through my books, whether they be devoted to Judy Garland, Steve McQueen, Grace Kelly, Jean-Pierre Melville, etc.: make the character palpable by taking the essential of his or her career in order to give it flesh and life…" Revisiting works by Mozart, Beethoven, or Bruckner is an essential endeavor to getting at their musical truth. Revisiting Judy Garland is an essential endeavor to getting at the heart of a musical enigma and an infinitely bewildering life. What cannot be easily explained can never be overly examined.

Prologue

New York, an apartment with a panoramic view of Central Park. Stevie Philips is a legend of American show business. She was one of the first women to become an agent. She worked with Liza Minnelli, Robert Redford, Al Pacino, Bob Fosse and David Bowie, who owe her a part of their careers.

Stevie began as a simple assistant at the CMA agency at the beginning of the 1960s. In the Manhattan of the *Mad Men* era, she, by default, was assigned Judy Garland. "She needed someone to take care of her twenty-four hours a day, seven days a week. My bosses didn't have the time for that. They gave me this role. I became her shadow."

At the time, the former queen of the Hollywood musical had just succeeded in making a spectacular comeback. She had become the superstar of American song, giving concerts one after the other. Her show at Carnegie Hall in April 1961 became the stuff of legend: "I have never seen such an impressive concert," remembers Stevie Philips. "Onstage, she was always magnificent; but, on that night, she was more so than usual. After each song, the crowd gave her a standing ovation, in total communion with her. It was exalting."

Stevie Philips discovered the other side, the hellish side, of Judy Garland, icon of an America which had seen her grow up on screen and recognized itself in her combat to exist. "During her shows, she didn't cheat. She gave 100%. But, as soon as she left the stage, 98% of her disappeared. She only truly existed when she was practicing her art."

Stevie Philips doesn't beat about the bush. For years, she kept quiet. Today, since she is talking, it is best to tell the truth, however disturbing. She evokes Judy's suicide attempts, which were cries for help. She remembers a woman who was weak. She recalls the loneliness of a star surrounded by flatterers, but also and above all by profiteers whose only thought was to exploit her sick need to be loved. "It was horrible to see."

Starting from her MGM years, Judy Garland was addicted to medications – amphetamines to keep her thin, sleeping pills to sleep. She never managed to escape this self-destructive spiral. "I had a little black book where were noted all the doctors who could prescribe her tranquilizers, stimulants, and other barbiturates she needed at any hour of the day or night," recalls Stevie Philips. "I wasn't comfortable doing it, but each time I tried to persuade her to give them up, she refused to talk about it. In her eyes, I became the enemy. She believed herself to be invulnerable, which was of course a tragic error."

Without her pills, Judy Garland could behave unreasonably, to say the least. Stevie Philips never forgot the aftermath of a concert at the Sahara Hotel in Las Vegas. Back in her room, tottering due to the mix of alcohol and pills, the star collapsed, hurting herself on a corner of a coffee table. Blood flowed from her gashed eyebrow. She lay on the floor, not moving. Stevie Philips called for a doctor, who tried to be reassuring: "She isn't unconscious, she's sleeping. There is only one thing to do: wait for her to come to." Then, seeing dozens of capsules and pills on her night table, he took the initiative of confiscating them. A few hours later, she awoke. She looked around the suite, looking for her pills, before barging into Stevie Philips room. "She had a knife in her hand and threatened to kill me…"

Film is the art of illusion. In her films, Judy Garland forever embodied carefreeness, lightness, the joy of life. But, behind the legend, the backyard was rarely glorious. Deprived of her childhood, crushed by Hollywood, exploited by all, Judy Garland accumulated disasters. Ten times, a hundred times, she fell. She always picked herself up. But one can't live on a high wire with impunity, a tightrope walker balancing one's imbalances. Her demons got the best of her: on June 22, 1969, at the age of 47, she died of an overdose of barbiturates, in a sordid house in the suburbs of London. Wasted by life, physically destroyed, psychologically broken, financially ruined, dramatically alone, despite a final marriage that was as derisory as it was pathetic.

If her life had been a novel or film, one would have said: enough is enough. But, as Mark Twain said, "Truth is always more surprising than fiction, for fiction must seem possible, whereas truth doesn't have this obligation."

1.

Papa's Movie Theater

A village far from everything, amidst lakes and forests, bears and wolves, near the source of the Mississippi River, midway between the Canadian frontier and Minneapolis. Summers were hot, winters harsh, with unending snowstorms – the famous blizzards. Grand Rapids was a small town like thousands of others in the United States. One could be in Fargo, the small town of neighboring North Dakota, popularized by the Coen brothers' film.

Grand Rapids counted barely three thousand residents when Judy Garland was born there on June 10, 1922. On her birth certificate, she was named Frances Ethel Gumm. Her parents had hoped for a boy – they already had two daughters – and had planned on naming him Frank Jr. They had to improvise a first name at the last minute. In fact, they always called her "Baby."

Frank and Ethel Gumm had met ten years earlier. Frank was born into a family of five children in the heart of Tennessee, in Murfreesboro, home to five thousand residents, half of whom were Niggers – at the time, no one was bothered in using the "N word." His father lived off the fortune of his handicapped wife. Frank was nine when she died. Money was in short supply, and it was the town's richest man who paid for his education in an Episcopalian college. Two years later, he interrupted his studies to take care of his family. Endowed with a beautiful voice, he sang in church, then in a quartet, before joining a group of traveling entertainers who crisscrossed rural America by playing in vaudeville, a mix of theater, burlesque, and musical comedy — an American specialty. In Cloquet, in Minnesota, he bought a theater he eventually sold to his older brother and returned to his life as an entertainer, before being hired in Superior, Wisconsin in a picture house, as they then called movie theaters. Between reels he sang songs of the day.

It was there tha nt he met Ethel Milne: she was the cashier and accompanied films on the piano. Born near Lake Superior, of Canadian parents originally from Scotland, she was the oldest in a family of eight children who lived in Michigamme, a small village of six hundred residents in Michigan. Her father participated in the construction of the railroad, which was the great adventure of the late 19th century. An amateur violinist, he transmitted his taste for music to Ethel. She decided to make it her career.

Frank Gumm and Ethel Gumm in undated photos.

He was tall, elegant, with dark hair, blue eyes. She was small, stocky, lively, strong-willed. From the start, he was fascinated by her dark brown eyes, almost black; she reveled in a constant smile that crossed her rounded face. They went out together, but just when she was already envisaging a ring on her finger, he disappeared: he went back on the road to play in vaudeville.

One year later, after having traveled to thirty-eight states, he was back in Superior, where he again found Ethel. They picked up their relation where it had last ended. She was stubborn: in January 1914, they got married before an Episcopalian priest. He was 27, she 20. After Frances' birth, Ethel took three years off her date of birth.

Together, they gave shows in the north under the name of "Jack and Virginia Lee, Sweet Southern Singers." He sang and played the ukulele, she accompanied him on the piano. Without a doubt, he would have preferred to play in bigger cities, such as Chicago, or even New York, but when three months later he was offered a fixed salary to manage the New Grand, one of the two movie theaters in Grand Rapids, he didn't hesitate. He had to be reasonable. Ethel accompanied the films on piano and provided the sound effects, an essential role at the time of silent movies. He continued to sing songs during the intermission. The public rushed to the New Grand to applaud them, and the box office of the competing theater, the Gem, eventually declined.

Jack and Virginia Lee, Sweet Southern Singers.

In September 1915, their first daughter was born, Mary Jane, whom they called Susie. In July 1917, their second daughter, Dorothy Virginia, nicknamed Jimmie, was born. On their days off, in order to increase their income, but also because they truly loved to perform, they gave shows in nearby towns. Ethel directed amateur musicals and played in a jazz quartet. Frank became the local correspondent for the weekly *Itasca County Independent*. People were happy to give him news tidbits; to thank them, he sang. His debonaire manner and perpetual joviality made him a local figure who was unanimously appreciated. He had a contagious laugh.

In the Fall of 1921, Ethel was again pregnant. Neither Frank nor Ethel wanted a third child. In order to abort, Ethel swallowed a large amount of castor oil and asked Frank to drive at high speed on the bumpy roads nearby. It didn't work. Frank then contacted a Minneapolis medical student, Marc Rabinowitz, whose father ran a movie theater in the county. Would he help Ethel abort? The young man refused. Too dangerous. Too risky.

As they euphemistically say, Judy Garland was an unwanted child.

The baby Frances Ethel Gumm.

The house at 2727 S. Pokegama Avenue, Grand Rapids, Minnesota where the Gumm family lived between 1922 and 1926. Still standing, it is today the Judy Garland Museum.

The New Grand's marquee can be seen on the lower right of this undated photo found at the Itasca County Historical Society. It is the only known photo of the Grand Rapids theater, which was owned by Frank Gumm.

★

"The first few years of my life were incredibly happy," she recalled years later in talking about her early youth in Grand Rapids. She, who mainly lived her life in Los Angeles and New York, would even romanticize this uneventful small town in the country. Everything seems bigger and more beautiful when one is a child. She saw this period of her life as paradise lost, a time of childlike innocence that was taken from her early on.

"It was the only time I saw my parents happy," she added. Frank and Ethel got used to her birth. Ethel made dresses and took care of her frequent ear infections by covering her ears with socks full of hot salt. During the day, while her sisters were at school, Frank took her with him in his activities around town, putting her in the front seat of his Ford. Each evening at bedtime, he went by her bedroom to sing songs to her. Lullabies, but also gospels. She was his little princess.

An early publicity still of The Gumm Sisters.

In Grand Rapids, her two sisters sang and danced on the New Grand stage. They adopted a number from *Uncle Tom's Cabin* by the Duncan Sisters, who were vaudeville stars. Thereon in, it wasn't a question of knowing if, one day, Baby would sing at the New Grand, but when. On December 26, 1924, before a showing of *Through the Back Door* with Mary Pickford, the three Gumm daughters took the stage together for the first time: Frances, 2-years old, Virginia, 7, and Mary Jane, 9. After accompanying her two older sisters for the opening number, Frances sang a solo of "Jingle Bells." After a roaring reception, she reprised the song several times. Her mother had to intervene and lead her backstage. She already had an inborn sense of show business.

With her two sisters, little Frances became the new attraction. They were called the "Gumdrops." But, between Frank and his wife, their love was slowly dying. Ethel took off more and more to visit her family in Minnesota, and that suited Frank just fine. He had no desire to divorce in that he wanted to stay close to his daughters. For his part, he led his own life. He was often seen with the high school's basketball star. They often went for walks, but no one was bothered. On the other hand, when an employee at the New Grand let it be known that Frank had made advances to him, the situation became embarrassing.

In Grand Rapids, this lost community in the middle of the vast expanses of Minnesota, people didn't like scandals. People preferred to resolve problems between themselves. All the more so in that, at heart, everyone liked Frank. They thus let him know they would ignore the whole issue. On condition that he leave town.

★

Everyone had dreams of the west. Since the gold rush, the American west had become a preoccupation. The poor, outcasts, pariahs, adventurers, everyone headed towards the Pacific looking for better times.

In June 1926, the Gumms also headed towards Los Angeles. Marc Rabinowitz, who had shortened his name to Rabin, worked in one of the city's hospitals. It was he who advised them to move to the film capital. The city instantly pleased them. They discovered the sandy beaches parched by the sun, the jacarandas and their mauve flowers, the flamboyant sunsets that went from orange to violet... But Frank soon became disillusioned: his savings weren't enough to buy a movie theater and he was forced to conclude that he would have to distance himself from Los Angeles.

In Lancaster, forty miles to the north, on the other side of the San Gabriel Mountains, on the outskirts of the Mojave Desert, he was able to find a 500-seat theater, the Valley Theatre, whose lease was available. In impeccable condition, the leather seats were like new. A good deal: it was the only movie theater in the Antelope Valley and the town was in full expansion, doubling in population every two years. But, for he who had tasted Los Angeles, it was like an exile. Founded near the Southern Pacific railway, Lancaster was in the middle of nowhere. A crossing point in the mountains that joined the Red Rock Canyon, its reddish cliffs and dried water beds already had served as the natural decors of westerns made in Hollywood. Sometimes, real cowboys came through and spent some time in the bars of the town: fiction and reality intertwined like a crossfade.

The Valley Theatre, with The Gumm Sisters on the marquee, in Lancaster, California in 1934, the year the film Limehouse Blues *was released.*

Frank had hardly taken possession of the theater before all the sisters sang, played, and danced onstage. Why change a winning act? The slogan was the same as at the New Grand: "It's our pleasure to please you." Soon enough, no occasion could take place in the county without the presence of the sisters. Frank knew how to ingratiate himself. A year after their arrival, the Gumms had awakened local life. They integrated so well into the town that "they are one of the assets of the town," wrote *The Antelope Valley Ledger Gazette*, the local daily newspaper.

The more she grew up, the more Frances became the principal attraction. Her voice had a little something extra. Every evening, the three girls appeared onstage at 9 P.M., and Frank congratulated all three. Ever fair play, he couldn't help showing his preference for Frances. But he wasn't presumptuous and knew better than anyone what his daughters brought to the Valley Theatre. He liked the town, which had adopted him, and didn't ask for anything more.

The house at 44665 Cedar Avenue, Lancaster, California, where the Gumm family lived between 1927 and 1934.

On the other hand, Ethel, who accompanied her daughters every night on the piano, quickly understood all the advantages she could get out of the situation. Los Angeles wasn't so far, and she knew well that it was there that everything happened. In August 1928, upon learning that the station

KFI was organizing an audition for its Wednesday afternoon children's program, *The Kiddies Hour,* she enrolled her offspring. Big Brother Ken, the show's host, was captivated and hired them for a once-a-week appearance. Every week, Ethel brought them there in her Buick, speeding on Interstate 14. She liked what went fast. And things soon took off.

Baby had just turned six, and her voice was already resounding on the radios of all of southern California.

★

In Los Angeles, Ethel became close to another Ethel: Ethel Meglin. A former showgirl in the Ziegfeld Follies in New York, she had just founded a dance school with the backing of the king of comedy and slapstick, Mack Sennett, who allowed her to use the locale.

An early publicity still of Frances Gumm.

As for singing lessons, the mother of the "Gumms" could be in charge. But, as for dancing, she knew her limits. To allow her daughters to move up a notch, she enrolled them in her new friend's classes. From then on, each weekend would be devoted to their new apprenticeship: departure Saturday morning at daybreak, night in a hotel in West Hollywood, return home late Sunday afternoon. To finance the operation, Ethel played the piano during the courses. Between school, her appearances on the stage of the Valley Theatre, and her roundtrips to Los Angeles, little Frances barely had the time to frequent the Jazz Candy Shop, her favorite in Lancaster. She who delighted in candy!

For Christmas, Ethel Meglin organized at the Slate Theatre, one of the most beautiful ones downtown, a show which brought together a hundred "Meglin Kiddies," as she called her students. In a few weeks, the Gumm Sisters had made lightening progress at dancing. They made a strong impression.

Hollywood was at the time in full upheaval. No one believed in the arrival of talkies when Vitaphone presented its new process. But, the success of *The Jazz Singer*, released on October 6, 1927, was a game changer. When Al Jolson cried out: "Wait a minute, wait a minute, I tell yer, you ain't heard nothin' yet," he didn't know the half of it. In a few months, the entire film industry took to talkies. Howard Hughes, who had spent a fortune making *Hell's Angels*, decided to redo all the dialogued scenes, even if he had to change the lead actress!

To respond to the demand, studios, big and small, were not satisfied with filming musical spectacles. Everything that sang and danced was worth filming. The Hollywood musical was being born, almost despite itself. From the 11th to the 13th of June 1929, Mayfair Pictures Corporation made a short at the Tec-Art Studio with the best elements of the Meglin Kiddies. The three Gumm Sisters of course were part of the adventure, interpreting "That's the Good Old Sunny South" in top hat and black-and-white miniskirt. What is most striking today is the contrast between Mary Jane and Virginia, the eldest girls, who seem hardworking, almost maladroit, and the ease and natural of small Frances.

In the following months, the Gumm Sisters followed up with three other shorts. Filmed on a theater stage, now demolished, all three Vitaphone soundtracks for *A Holiday in Storyland*, *The Wedding of Jack and Jill*, and *Bubbles* today survive, although *Bubbles*, filmed in Technicolor, survives in a black-and-white print only. In *A Holiday in Storyland*, Frances sang her first solo, "Blue Butterfly." But rather than make a career plan, Ethel wanted to make money. As soon as a contract was in view, she accepted. She cared little about the theater, only the fee counted. One could thus applaud the Gumm Sisters in Santa Barbara or San Diego, but also in such small towns as Tehachapi, north of Lancaster.

"Baby Gumm" on the Warner Bros./First National Studios backlot, circa 1929, with John Perri.

Since the stock market crash of 1929, America was in crisis; but the crisis never affected the Gumm Sisters. The more their notoriety grew, the more they were in demand. Each time, the presence of Babe, as even the public called her, was required. "Without her, the show would have been rather mediocre," commented the producer Maurice Kusell. She was growing up, and her irresistible innocence could have diminished. Not only did she continue to thrill the public with her spontaneity, but she was becoming an entertainer who was more and more a trooper and whose voice never stopped blossoming.

She had a small supplement that made all the difference: a gift.

Frances Gumm in 1931.

2.

The Child with an Adult's Voice

"When I was a child, I wanted to be loved by my parents more than anything," said Judy Garland later in life.

Frank Gumm.

On her father's side, she had no trouble getting his love. Frank adored her. He knew how to reassure her, console her, flatter her, cuddle her, spoil her, encourage her. He was like a mother. Ethel, on the other hand, was distant and cold. Never were there any compliments, kind words, signs of affection, even less any tenderness. She was demanding, obsessed, finicky. With her daughters, and in particular with Babe, she always found something to criticize. She was the queen of "don't do this, don't do that"!

In Lancaster, little Frances wanted to be a kid like any other. But other kids kept their distances from her: they were too afraid of having Ethel on their backs, this mother they wanted nothing to do with! It was impossible for Frances to play children's games in which one risked scratching an ankle: Ethel was always afraid she would hurt herself. Even for Halloween, disguised as a witch, she wasn't allowed to ring neighbors' doorbells to get candy.

In fact, Ethel behaved less like a mother and more like a manager. She devoted all her energy to her daughters' success. In the evening, after having put the girls to bed, Frank would reproach her for putting pressure on them, after which she would storm into Frances' room, wake her, and hurl:

"Let's go, we're leaving Papa!"

Invariably, small Frances would reply:

"No, I love him!"

"Then, you don't love me?" answered her mother.

This perverse game tore Babe between her loyalty towards her father and her guilt at not sufficiently loving her mother. So, she obeyed her. She accepted everything from her and was always ready to get into the Buick to give a show or go to an audition. But, as much as she loved being onstage – for, there she could enjoy the immediate contact with the public, its laughter, its smiles, its applause, its "bravos!", its "encores!" – she hated the casting calls where she had to perform in front of men who were unshakeable, blasé, peremptory. She loathed her mother's behavior in those moments: deferential and ingratiating. She didn't like to see her grovel to these guys who strutted with arrogance. All things considered, she took her as she knew her: dominating.

After each audition, Ethel asked the girls to leave and wait for her. Sometimes, that lasted more than an hour. What was she doing in that hour? Frances was convinced that her mother was having sex to get a contract. Nothing, ever, will ever prove it, but that mattered little to her: she was sure of it. For her girls' success, Ethel was ready to do anything.

★

Frank and Ethel shared a bedroom together but dreamt apart. They fought more and more often. In those moments, Babe took refuge under the garden trees and cried. Nothing frightened her more than their quarrels, which inflamed her greatest fear: that of having to choose between one or the other.

Ethel never liked Lancaster. She hadn't left Grand Rapids to be buried in the desert. As for Frank, he had made lots of friends. And he continued to be interested in young men: some of them said that he liked to sit next to them in the Valley Theatre, in the darkness of the back rows, and fondle them. For the time being, their parents knew nothing.

On her side, Ethel now had a lover: the married Will Gilmore, a water pump salesman, tall, thin, with wide shoulders, always well-dressed, but sullen, boorish, and who tended to be violent. All the opposite of Frank. Babe detested him: "I never saw a man who was as terrifying," she stated. "He disgusted me." Most surprising of all was that the Gumms and the Gilmores socialized together: they regularly dined and sometimes picnicked together nearby. Babe was a friend of their children. One day, while playing hide-and-seek at the Gilmore's, Frances discovered her mother and her lover embracing in a shed in the back of the garden…

Ethel's only concern was to move away. When one lived in Lancaster, one went down south to Los Angeles. But in those years of economic depression, where some Americans went west in search of the promised land, as in *The Grapes of Wrath* by Steinbeck, money was rare. The family lived on the profits from Frank's Valley Theatre. Everything changed in 1932, when Maurice Kusell, a young impresario who had hired the Gumm Sisters for the show *Stars of Tomorrow*, in a theater on Wilshire Boulevard, proposed that Ethel direct the orchestra's eight musicians, and then hired her to teach popular songs in his school of dance and music. From then on, she settled in Los Angeles. Two of her sisters came from Minnesota to help Frank take care of the girls; but when Mary Jane, the eldest, got her middle-school diploma in Lancaster, the three sisters joined Ethel in the house she rented in Silverlake, which was then not the fashionable neighborhood it is today.

In a Los Angeles entirely devoted to the movie industry, Ethel enrolled Babe and her sister Jimmie in the Lawlor School for Professional Children, on Hollywood Boulevard. The courses were grouped in the morning, and afternoons were free in order to allow students to go to auditions and casting calls. Little Frances no longer had classmates, but rather colleagues, even rivals. At least she no longer had the impression of being different from the others, as she was in Lancaster. She became friends with a boy who was two years older and whose energy was bursting: Mickey McGuire. She adored his vitality and humor. He brightened her days and stymied her tendency to be morose. Sometimes, when the Gumms played the Valley Theatre, he accompanied them… and leaped onto the stage to the public's great pleasure. He later became known as Mickey Rooney.

Babe liked to perform in Lancaster. Her father was her best audience. He wildly applauded, and when the curtain came down, he was there, full of compliments and hugs, to welcome her and her two sisters. Just the opposite of her mother, whose discretion always gave her the impression that she had done wrong.

In early 1934, Maurice Kussell had to close his dance and music studio. Ethel, unemployed, was not returning to Lancaster: more so than ever, she would take charge of the Gumm Sisters. Mrs. Lawford, the school director, little concerned about her students' attendance record, allowed the three sisters to leave in mid-February for a one-month tour in northern California. For the summer, Ethel had another tour in mind: cross the United States to New York. Frank was against it: he thought it was risky for three females to cross America alone. As usual, he gave in. Not without writing a $300 traveler's check to be cashed in case of an emergency…

After Denver, they left for Chicago, where they had been hired at the Old Mexico. Ethel obtained an advance, but she never saw the rest. She was made to understand that it was better not to insist: it was after all a town controlled by the mafia. The first check went through. Fortunately, an opportunity arose at the Oriental Theatre. Ethel made haste to get there with her daughters. George Jessel, the master of ceremonies and a renowned vaudeville actor, was not impressed by

Mary Jane and Jimmie. On the other hand, he was astounded by Babe. Although she had just turned twelve, her voice was that of an adult. He wanted to hire her alone, but at Ethel's insistence, accepted to sign a contract with the trio. Mary Jane and Jimmie suffered from being their sister's sidekicks, but separating them was out of the question, even if Ethel was financially in dire straits. Still, she accepted to change their name. Gumm sounded like bum, scum, crumb, or dumb: not the stuff of dreams. From then on, they would be called the Garland Sisters. It was well known: the public liked all that glittered. As for Frances, she would now be called "Judy," the title of a well-known 1934 song by Hoagy Carmichael and Sammy Lerner.

Mid-October, after a detour in Detroit, Milwaukee and Kansas City, the girls were back on the West Coast. It had been four months since Frances had seen her father. For her, the separation had been like a deprivation.

★

Frances Gumm, now renamed Judy Garland, in a publicity still, taken in Chicago, 1934, posing to sing "Bill," as she performed it onstage in the style of Helen Morgan.

Ethel Gumm (1893-1953) and The Gumm Sisters (Judy Garland furthest right) in a publicity still taken in 1934 for the Chicago World's Fair.

Back in Los Angeles, the Garland Sisters played a few of the town's best venues: the Beverly Wilshire Hotel, Grauman's Chinese Theatre, and the Orpheum, all downtown. Although the critics had their doubts about the trio, Babe was singled out. The *Los Angeles Evening Herald and Express* found her to be "prodigious" and hailed her scenic presence and the emotional power of her voice.

The only known photo of The Garland Sisters live onstage at the Paramount Theater in Los Angeles on March 7, 1935. From left to right, Mary Jane Gumm, aka Susie or Suzanne (1915-1964), Dorothy Virginia Gumm, aka Jimmie (1917-1977) and Frances Ethel Gumm, later Judy Garland (1922-1969).

The Paramount Theater marquee in Los Angeles in 1935 displaying the Garland Sisters on the bill.

At the same time, in Lancaster, nothing was going well for Frank. To finance Ethel and his daughters, he had to leave the house on Cedar Avenue and move to a simple studio – a dump, as he called it. Separated from his daughters, he was depressed and frenetically sought comfort with young high schoolers. As if on self-destruct, he did it less and less discretely. Quite quickly, what no one wanted to see became evident in the eyes of the residents of this small town which kept growing. When he walked down the street, people avoided him. Behind his back, people called him a pansy, a fairy. Parents forbade their children to go see films alone in his movie theater, whose earnings were withering. Lancaster's doctor, in addition to being responsible for the health of his patients, also acted as keeper of the town's good moral standards: at the head of a delegation, he made it known to Frank that he was no longer welcome. Frank played deaf. The final blow came when the owner of the Valley Theatre premises claimed a late payment on the rent in order to deliver an expulsion notice to him. He had three months to leave. He tried to stay, but it was no use.

On April 1, 1935, Frank Gumm left Lancaster for Los Angeles to find Ethel and his girls.

★

It was a strange paradox that whereas audiences and critics were unanimous about Babe's talent when onstage with the Garland Sisters, the studios that abound in Los Angeles weren't interested in her. At each audition – and she never stopped going to them – the response was the same: no. For the movies, one needed more than a good voice. They wanted a body, and Judy's was neither beautiful nor ugly, just ordinary. The girl next door… More troublesome was that her immoderate appetite for pistachio ice cream and hot dogs gave her a look that was somewhat plump. "What would we do with a little female Huckleberry Finn?" noted one of Columbia's producers in a memo. On balance, they wanted less talent and more a pretty girl.

One encounter was enough to change things dramatically. The right person at the right time, not to mention luck. For Judy, that person was Al Rosen.

During the summer of 1935, from June 15 to July 26, the Garland Sisters played the Cal Neva Lodge, a hotel on the edge of Lake Tahoe that Frank Sinatra purchased in the 1950s as a front man for mafioso Sam Giancana. At the same time, Al Rosen was there on vacation for a few days. He was a talent scout and soon remarked young Judy. From their very first conversation, there was little chemistry with Ethel. Al Rosen was inflexible: he wasn't signing the trio, just Judy interested him. But, deep down, Ethel knew she had to count on Judy alone. Furthermore, the eldest was soon to be married, which seriously compromised the idea of seeing the trio last on her watch. What's more, the rub was that Al Rosen wanted to be the one making decisions. It was out of the question that Ethel interfere one way or another: he immediately saw the degree to which she could be intrusive!

Ethel gave in: never up to then had any well-established agent manifested the least interest in her youngest daughter. As soon as the contract was signed, Al Rosen began making the rounds at the studios. Without success at first. But, at the Feist Music Company, a subdivision of MGM, they were rather taken. So much so that they asked Roger Edens for his advice. A man of taste, elegant and refined, always dressed up to the nines, he had just been hired at MGM, after having accompanied Ethel Merman in her film debut at Paramount. He asked Judy to interpret "Zing! Went the Strings of My Heart" three times: he wanted to be sure that his first impression, which was more than favorable, was right.

Convinced of Judy's potential, he contacted Ida Koverman. In the structure at Metro-Goldwyn-Mayer, she occupied a secondary role in appearance: secretary to Louis B. Mayer, the most emblematic of Hollywood moguls. But in fact, Ida was a key character: the magnate trusted her instinct. It was she who noticed, in a downtown theater, a young actor with protruding ears who became the studio star: Clark Gable.

On September 13, the telephone rang at 842 North Mariposa, at the Gumm's. It was Frank who answered. On the line Al Rosen shouted out:

"Go to MGM right away! Ida Koverman wants to see Judy…"

That day, Ethel was playing piano at the Pasadena Community Playhouse. It was impossible to reach her. Frank and Judy immediately dashed off to Culver City, where the MGM lot was located. She didn't even have the time to change and wore a simple blouse over gray pants. Who cared? Ida Koverman was won over and asked Louis B. Mayer to join them.

Born into a Jewish family from Minsk, in Belarus, Louis B. Mayer emigrated to the United States and wanted to be the most American of Americans. Not knowing his date of birth, he had the habit of celebrating his birthday on July 4th. Did he not embody the American dream? After having started out as an ironworker alongside his father, in 1910 he bought a nickelodeon, the ancestor of movie theaters. Having become a distributor, he moved to Los Angeles and founded Louis B. Mayer Pictures. In 1924, he associated with Samuel Goldwyn and the Metro

Pictures Corporation to create Metro-Goldwyn-Mayer. Ten years later, MGM was the most powerful studio in the city and brought together, to repeat his slogan, "more stars than there are in heaven." His credo: "A great star, a great director, a great subject, a great interpretation." Leave the detective movies to Warner Bros., the comedies to Paramount, and the horror films to Universal; he swore to make great films that attracted the whole family. He wasn't afraid of crying at a projection but ran the studio with an iron fist. Voluntarily moralizing, he could be bad-tempered, cynical, and bitter.

That day, Louis B. Mayer fixed his gaze on little Judy from head to toe. He listened attentively to her sing and was silent. Then, he slipped away without saying a word.

Judy thought she had flopped, once again. But, a few days later, Al Rosen received a contract of nineteen pages. A seven-year deal, with renewable options every six months the first year, every year thereafter. Judy had the right to negotiate her own contracts to do radio, but the studio had to give its green light before any engagement. Her salary was $100 a week at first. A small fortune for the Gumms, who were having the hardest time just squeaking out a living.

On September 27, the Los Angeles Superior Court validated Judy's contract, as was customary for a minor. An MGM photo immortalized the moment.

A star was born.

Judy Garland reports to work for her first day at MGM on October 1, 1935 after the Los Angeles Superior Court approved her contract on September 27, 1935.

3.

The Little Hunchback

For Judy, it was like starting a new school year in a new school. This October 1, 1935, the first day of her contract, she passed through the Metro-Goldwyn-Mayer gate by the service entrance.

Culver City, headquarters to the main cavalry regiment of California, was at the time a small town of at most seven thousand residents, in the middle of orange trees and horses. Situated between Washington Boulevard and Culver Boulevard, MGM was a series of numbered hangars: studios, set and wardrobe workshops, warehouses. One would have thought one was in a factory, which is not surprising in that films were made there non-stop just like cars were made at Ford. Two- or three-story buildings were home to a succession of offices for scriptwriters, composers, and arrangers, who were employed at fixed working hours. Facades lined the streets of great American cities, fake villages with a saloon and dirt streets had been built for westerns, a lake had been dug to film scenes that were supposed to take place at sea. It was the reign of artifice and illusion. MGM had its own symphonic orchestra, ballet company, post office, hospital, police, and transport network. The studio even had its own brothel so as to cozy up to theater owners who wanted to discover in-house production: it was run by a former actress and all the prostitutes were lookalikes of studio stars. Some said all that was missing was a morgue. In short, it was a state within a state, a kind of 185-acre principality where 4,500 people worked, of which 250 actors and actresses were under contract.

Of all the studios in Los Angeles, MGM was also the only one to have its own school, the Little Red Schoolhouse, which got its name from its red walls. It enabled children under contract to go from classroom to set without losing time: indeed, according to California law, they couldn't be taken out of the school system. Judy Garland could there join her buddy Mickey Rooney, who had also just been signed.

Every morning, from nine to noon, they attended grammar school taught by Mary McDonald, a stern woman whose hair was pulled back in a bun and whose pocket watch was attached to her belt. Judy showed herself be a curious and hardworking student, sensitive to poetry. The afternoon was devoted to the arts. Until then, Judy trusted her instinct. Meticulously concealing that she was something of a performance monkey, Roger Edens, her vocal coach, developed her technique while preserving the spontaneity that gave her incredible emotional power. Gertrude Fogler, a former British actress, gave her diction lessons. Dave Gould, the head of ballet, dance, and tap-dancing classes. She was also taught acting.

Mickey Rooney and Judy Garland in the Little Red Schoolhouse.

Louis B. Mayer watched over his child actors under contract like thoroughbreds in the racing stables he also possessed. He went to see them and never forgot to celebrate their birthdays. Ordinarily cold, authoritarian, and brusque, he was rather charming with them. There was a patriarchal side of him. But he never forgot that, above all, they were there to make movies. Finding Judy a bit chubby, slightly fat, so he ordered:

"Give her nothing but clear broth at lunch!"

The newly contracted Judy Garland eats broth in the MGM commissary under orders from studio head Louis B. Mayer.

According to legend, he insisted that the pockets of other students be regularly gone through in order to confiscate candy they might offer to Judy. Because of her pudgy figure, he named her "my little hunchback." Coming from him, it was affectionate: no one worried at the time about a child's psychology. He never imagined for a moment that she would forever be traumatized.

Before being hired, Judy made no screen test. Louis B. Mayer, seduced by her voice, didn't even want to know if she looked good on screen. When the make-up department discovered her, they wondered just what the magnate saw in her. Besides her pounds in surplus, she was tiny despite her long legs, she had no neck, her hair went everywhere, and her face was ordinary. In an era of glamor, she was far from cinematic. For several days, with their creams and pencils, MGM's make-up artists refashioned her features. They designed small rubber discs she had to insert into her nostrils to modify the form of her face and made caps to hide her teeth's irregularity.

For a while, MGM considered giving Judy a small role in *This Time It's Love*, with Robert Montgomery, but the project fell through. In the meantime, they asked her to sing at parties organized by MGM, and on October 26, 1935, she participated in a prestigious radio show, the *Shell Chateau Hour*, on NBC, hosted by Wallace Beery.

"We have a girl here whom I think is going to be the sensation of pictures!" he announced to listeners.

★

Since he was forced to leave Lancaster, Frank lived with Ethel in the *Mariposa* house. Living together was difficult, the atmosphere often heavy and electric. Professing that she was going out to play bridge, Ethel left regularly to see Will Gilmore. As for Frank, he had found work: he managed a movie theater in Lomita, in the south of Los Angeles. At the age of 50, he said he "felt old." Abandoning the Valley Theatre had hit him like a hammer blow. He had lost his luster and lightness. But he was happy to be with Judy, of whom he had so often been deprived the past two years. Every morning, it was he who drove her to the studio. Sometimes, he accompanied her to the door of the Little Red Schoolhouse…

On Friday, November 15, 1935, Frank woke up with an earache. He wasn't worried; like Judy, he was prone to ear infections. But during the night, his condition got worse. When called for help, Dr. Marc Rabwin, a family friend, ordered his emergency transfer to Cedars-Sinai Hospital, where his diagnosis was confirmed: life-threatening meningitis. Frank's chances of recovering were nil.

That Saturday night, Judy was scheduled to sing for the second time on the *Shell Chateau Hour* on NBC. Ethel accompanied her. Dr. Marc Rabwin managed to get through to her backstage:

"I put a radio on your father's night table. Sing for him!"

In fact, he was already in a coma. Judy would never see him again. He died late Sunday morning.

In a misunderstanding worthy of a third-rate comedy, that same night Ethel's girlfriends had rung at the Mariposa house, cheerful and bearing gifts: Ethel had organized a party to celebrate her birthday. She hadn't had the time to warn them…

In the days that followed, Judy was prostrate. Mute. Ethel was annoyed: What was MGM going to think?

"My father's death was the worst thing that ever happened to me," she later said. Her world came tumbling down. Never again would Frank be there to console her, encourage her, applaud her. He may have been weak, but he was always on her side.

It was the end of her childhood. The end of innocence.

All her life, Judy never stopped looking for a substitute father in men.

★

Until then, it was Frank who paid for the lifestyle of the Gumm family. From then on, it would be Judy. Even if Ethel continued to give piano lessons.

At the time, no law protected the income of children who worked in show business. It took until 1939 for that to change following a lawsuit filed by Jackie Coogan. Recognized in 1921 at the age of seven for his role in *The Kid*, by Charlie Chaplin, he did one film after the other, earning more than $4 million. His parents had always claimed that they had opened a special account he could have access to at adulthood; after the death of his father, he was able to confirm that that was in no way true and that his money had been used to buy the family home, which wasn't in his name. Bringing the suit to justice, he waited five years to recuperate $125,000, most of which was eaten up in lawyers' fees. His case, however, forced legislators to react and lead to the adoption of the California Child Actor's Bill, which obligated parents to reserve half the earnings of their children in protected accounts.

In early December, Ethel, Judy, and her sister Jimmie, who was then going out with the actor Frankie Darro, left the Mariposa house to move into 180 South McCadden Place, in the heart of Hollywood, near Hancock Park. "A house that was more respectable but hardly glamorous," remembered Judy, but with a small swimming pool in the garden. Ethel always saw things on a grand scale.

And yet, Judy's situation at MGM was hardly reassuring. In nearly six months, she hadn't made a single film. The studio had to soon exercise its first option, but before deciding engaged in a perverse game: have their two latest recruits, Judy and Deanna Durbin, compete with each other in a short entitled Every Sunday, the story of two young girls who decided to sing in their small town at a Sunday concert, which might have to be cancelled for lack of funding.

When Judy discovered the film, she was despondent. "I had thought that I would be photographed like a screen siren. When I saw this chubby girl with a snub nose and whose face was covered with freckles, I understood that it was me I was looking at on the screen. I went home and cried until I fell asleep."

A promotional photo of Judy Garland for the 1936 short Every Sunday, *her first assignment at MGM.*

Louis B. Mayer was in Europe at the time. Upon his return, debate was hot at the studio. Some remembered Deanna Durbin, others, like Ida Koverman, defended Judy. In the end, the boss had decided to keep both. But during his absence, the option on Deanna Durbin expired. However, the ex-director of casting at MGM, Rufus LeMaire, who had signed her MGM contract, proposed a new one at $300 a week at Universal, where he now worked. She immediately thereafter made *Three Smart Girls, One*

Hundred Men and a Girl and *That Certain Age*, three great successes which saved Universal from bankruptcy and made her the studio's biggest star.

"We'll make Judy a bigger star," stormed Louis B. Mayer, furious at having been double crossed by his former collaborator.

★

During the months that followed the renewal of her contract, Judy still remained confined to radio shows and appearances at private parties organized by MGM, for which she had become one the of the principal attractions. With no film to offer her, the studio loaned her out to Fox for five weeks: she would appear in a half-dozen scenes and interpret three songs in David Butler's *Pigskin Parade*, which did well. After the premiere, *The Hollywood Reporter* wrote: "One of the strong points of the movie is the presence of the young Judy, who delighted the opening-night audience with a handful of fine songs."

Everything changed on February 1, 1937. That evening, Judy was invited to celebrate Clark Gable's 36th birthday on the set where he was filming *Parnell* costarring Myrna Loy. The studio was often at odds with him because he was a world-class party animal. Eddie Mannix, Louis B. Mayer's henchman – the fixer, as he was called, spent a lot of time mopping up his escapades; but Gable was the studio's number one star at the time, the sex symbol the country fantasized about, so all was forgiven.

Judy thought about interpreting "Drums in My Heart," but the composer Roger Edens was opposed: "It's a song for a woman, not a young girl," he decided. Knowing that anybody who's anybody at MGM would be attending the little get-together, which would be a good occasion to get his protégé some attention, he decided to adapt a song called "You Made Me Love You." On the said day, Judy leapt out of the giant birthday cake, half-singing-half-talking, to sing and play a young girl addressing a fan letter to her idol:

Dear Mr. Gable, I am writing this to you
And I hope that you will read it so you'll know
My heart beats like a hammer

And I stutter and I stammer
Every time I see you at the picture show…

Moved to tears, the star had a charm bracelet brought to her a few days later in the form of a miniature book which opened with this inscription: "To Judy, my best girl, from her most ardent fan, Clark Gable." Everyone who attended the party was captivated by this young entertainer no one really knew what to do with. Subsequently, she was asked to reprise the song for an annual distributor's gala, which was a difficult public that wouldn't hesitate to ask for an encore of the song when Clark Gable appeared onstage.

The next day, Louis B. Mayer summoned Judy to his office: her number would be added to her next musical, the follow-up to *Broadway Melody of 1936*, which was the sequel to the first sound film, *The Broadway Melody*, to win an Oscar for the best picture of 1930. In it, she sang "Dear Mr. Gable" to a photo of the star.

Clark Gable embraces Judy Garland after singing "(Dear Mr. Gable) You Made Me
Love You" to him for his 36th birthday on the set of Parnell.

For whatever reasons, the film was released in August 1937 as *Broadway Melody of 1938*… no doubt because MGM always wanted to be one step ahead! Having come from New York for the opening, Jack Kapp, the head of Decca, made the most of the opportunity to have her sign a recording contract just as the newspapers outdid themselves in lauding her with compliments. "In view of the extraordinary performance by the young Judy Garland, one cannot help asking why she's been hiding all these months. Here is a unique personality who deserves a promotion," raved *The Hollywood Reporter*. Suddenly, she had become famous all over America. An overnight sensation, as they say in Hollywood.

Sure of itself, MGM didn't wait very long for press or public reactions to make Judy its new headliner. Even before the release of *Broadway Melody of 1938*, she began filming Alfred E. Green's *Thoroughbreds Don't Cry*, a trifle that took place in the horse racing world. She sang "Got a New Pair of New Shoes" in it. For the first time, she partnered with Mickey Rooney, whose career had also just taken off. It was the beginning of an association that was particularly fructuous: they made eight other films together. Ronald Sinclair played the other male role, which was first meant for 15-year-old Freddie Bartholomew, who had to withdraw from the movie so as to make his case in a sordid judicial procedure. Given up at birth and raised by an aunt, he traveled with her to the United States, where he was hired by David O. Selznick to interpret the title role in *David Copperfield*. His angelic air made him a star and, since then, he made one film after the other at MGM. It was at that point that his parents showed up to demand the custody of their child… and his earnings. After a long judicial battle, Freddie Bartholomew obtained the right to remain with his aunt, but had to pay 20% of his income to his parents!

Judy Garland sings "Swing Mr. Mendelssohn" in Everybody Sing.

Parallelly — for, at MGM actors sometimes made two films at the same time — Judy also played the main role in Edwin L. Marin's *Everybody Sing*. It was her first great role, that of the youngest daughter in an eccentric family where she becomes a famous Broadway star. Starting at 7 A.M. she had to be in makeup to be ready to film at 9 A.M. It was now out of the question that she attend Mary McDonald's classes: Judy now had a private professor, Rose Carter, who took advantage of pauses between two scenes to teach her algebra and geography. The whole enormous machine of MGM was now at her service. Howard Strickling, head of publicity, began to build her legend. This genial storyteller like no one else distilled anecdotes to the various newspapers, even inventing them. How can one not see his hand behind this article in the *Hollywood Reporter* asserting that little Judy Garland was prompting the anger of her neighbors when practicing the saxophone for the needs of her next picture? Judy never played the instrument, but any quote in the papers was good for the taking.

Louis B. Mayer continued to personally watch over her. Although Roger Edens, always in her corner, reminded her of Frank, the head of MGM in her eyes embodied authority in its strictest sense. And when Judy disobeyed her mother, hadn't she gotten into the habit of saying: "I will tell Mr. Mayer about it"?

Louis B. Mayer was obsessed with Judy's weight. Despite her diet of chicken soup, she was still plump. He decided to send her to the studio doctor, who, after having admitted that she had "the health of a horse," prescribed Benzedrine for her. Sold since 1932, it was first used as a bronchodilator. But this medication of the amphetamine family is also used for its side effects: it induced and cut hunger. Wasn't the studio playing God by administering such a treatment to her? In light of her youth, yes. But Benzedrine was available over the counter at the time. In the newspapers, pages of publicity extolled its power to help people lose weight: a few pills more for a few pounds less. All of Hollywood was using them: actors, scriptwriters, producers, all of them wanted to increase their productivity. For, Benzedrine was also a stimulant. During World War 2, it was widely used to fight fatigue and increase soldiers' stamina. No one at the time imagined its destructive effects. In the United States, it took until 1958 for Benzedrine to be available only by prescription.

The problem was that it didn't take long for Judy to complain she couldn't sleep. So what? The MGM doctor had a solution: take Seconal before bedtime. A powerful sleeping pill.

Without knowing it, Judy had just put her finger on the infernal spiral that would end up taking her life.

4.

In the Land of Oz

Inside MGM, one man had spotted Judy Garland: Arthur Freed. He was to become her guardian angel for the next fifteen years.

Arthur Freed, lyricist, MGM producer, and head of the Freed Unit.

Born into a family of Jewish musicians living in South Carolina, he had been a sheet-music salesman, piano player-singer in Chicago, vaudeville actor, author of revues and sketches, most notably for the Marx Brothers, before writing musicals on Broadway. Upon the advent of talkies, he found himself hired by MGM, where he wrote numerous hit songs in tandem with the composer Nacio Herb Brown, whose "Singin' in the Rain" was performed in 1929 by Cliff Edwards in *The Hollywood Revue of 1929* then reprised in multiple recordings before becoming the hit song of the eponymously titled film by Stanley Donen with Gene Kelly in 1952.

In appearance, Arthur Freed was rather drab. Neither tall nor short, thin nor fat, handsome nor ugly, he was an in-between. He had the art of convolutions: Alan Jay Lerner said of him jokingly that "he started a sentence on Wednesday and finished it on Friday." For some time, he had felt hemmed in as a composer. He had ideas about how to reinvent the musical and wanted to become a producer. He opened up about it to Louis B. Mayer, who held him in the highest esteem: Freed was one of the rare studio collaborators Mayer regularly invited on weekends to his beach house in Malibu, with a view on the Pacific.

"Find a good subject and we'll see," replied the MGM head.

A few weeks later, Arthur Freed brought him *The Wizard of Oz*, a novel by Lyman Frank Baum published in 1900 that he had read as a kid, just like all American children. It tells the story of Dorothy, a small orphan who lives on a Kansas farm with her uncle, aunt, and her dog Toto. Following a tornado, Dorothy finds herself propelled to an enchanted land. How would she return home? The good witch of the North advises her to speak with the Wizard of Oz, who lives in the Emerald City. To get there, she would have to follow a yellow-brick road. On it, she encounters a scarecrow who complains that he has no brain, a tin man who has no heart, and a cowardly lion…

For the role of Dorothy, Arthur Freed had one person in mind: Judy Garland. Louis B. Mayer was quickly interested in going forward with the project. With *Snow White and the Seven Dwarfs*, his first animated feature, Walt Disney had just achieved great success, one that had taken Hollywood by surprise. No one had imagined that a movie for children could make so much money. Since there was a market for such films, it was out of the question that MGM concede the monopoly to Walt Disney!

MGM bought the rights for $75,000 from Sam Goldwyn, who had purchased them three years earlier for $40,000, without following through on the project. Which very quickly took on the allures of a super production. Starting from the first cost estimates, it appeared that the picture would cost $2 million. The world of Oz would need to be created from scratch, and for that Technicolor would be required. In view of its cost, Louis B. Mayer's enthusiasm was dampened with caution. Judy Garland? She wasn't well-known enough to assign such an expensive movie to such fragile shoulders.

Backed by Nick Schenck, who held the purse strings in New York, Louis B. Mayer leaned towards Shirley Temple, the baby star *par excellence*. For the past five years, her dimples, her blond ringlets, her sunny way of dancing and singing had made the young girl the American ideal. Freed protested: Shirley didn't sing as well as Judy. Who cares, replied Mayer, she's a star who attracts audiences. MGM thus contacted Fox… which refused to loan out the child prodigy to make a film. Fox was teeming with projects for Shirley Temple, so why would they deprive themselves of her for a rival studio's profit? Even the idea of exchanging Shirley Temple and Clark Gable went nowhere…

Return to the starting gate: on February 24, 1938, *The Hollywood Reporter* disclosed that Judy Garland had been hired to play Dorothy in *The Wizard of Oz*. Meanwhile, Louis B. Mayer had been maneuvering for Ethel to get rid of Al Rosen and replace him with one of his employees, Frank Orsatti, a former gangster who supplied him with alcohol during Prohibition and with mistresses more recently. Judy's pay would of course be increased, but she would only make $500 a week, even though she had just been hired for the title role of the most expensive production ever at MGM. Part of her salary would be directly paid to Ethel, who was her daughter's assistant, according to the studio's official job description: a pernicious way of reminding her that in addition to being Judy's mother, she was also a studio employee.

Arthur Freed thus managed to impose his choice. But, on February 3, Mervyn LeRoy was named the film's producer. Louis B. Mayer had just hired him away from Warner Bros., where he was one of their star directors, for a salary of $5,000 a week. A real pillage: LeRoy was in effect married to Doris Warner, the daughter of Harry Warner, one of the founders of Warner Bros. Freed would have to be satisfied being his assistant. To justify himself, Louis B. Mayer explained that he could not put the production of such a costly picture in the hands of a beginner. As soon as *The Wizard of Oz* was completed, he swore, Freed would have a free hand to produce another film.

Promises bind only those who want to believe them, especially in Hollywood, but Arthur Freed soon enough understood the advantages of the strange teaming. Mervyn LeRoy was perhaps a reassuring name, but he was a specialist in gangster movies (*Little Caesar*) and knew nothing about musicals. Freed could thus leave his mark on the film while letting LeRoy do the dirty work: managing the details of a super production.

For Freed, the first thing to do was to define a musical style. Should they go for swing, which was then popular, or for opera, which had led to several hits with Jeanette MacDonald at MGM? Finally, he was aiming for something more traditional: melodies that got into your head and never left. With that in mind, he hired the lyricist Yip Harburg and the composer Harold Arlen, who had just arrived in Hollywood after having written numerous musicals on Broadway. At the same time, the screenwriting department got to work. Three writers were credited: Noel Langley, Florence Ryerson and Edgar Allan Woolf, but in all around fifteen screenwriters worked on it, including Herman J. Mankiewicz, who authored an initial script of 56 pages. At MGM, as at the other studios, everyone contributed ideas. With their 75 screenwriters under contract, it was one gigantic writing room that was ahead of its time…

★

The Wizard of Oz was set to be released for the end-of-year holidays in 1939. No one could deny it was the perfect Christmas movie. Unfortunately, even if the script were finished at the beginning of March, filming couldn't start before April, as planned.

Until then, movies had always been realistic. Now, it was necessary to conceive an imaginary world. Make costumes. Draw and build sets, which would occupy six soundstages. It would also be necessary — and this wasn't the least of their worries — to invent special effects in an era when computers didn't exist. How would one recreate a cyclone in Kansas on a Hollywood set?

MGM did its best to boost Judy Garland's fame by organizing a major tour to promote *Everybody Sing*: Miami, New York, Columbus, Chicago, Pittsburgh, Detroit. During this trip, she stopped for two days in Grand Rapids, where she was born and never again went back, although she returned to Minnesota in 1958 for the state's centennial, but not to Grand Rapids. Ethel accompanied her and, in view of the flood of fan mail — a hundred letters a day, hired a remote assistant to answer them two afternoons a week.

Because of accumulated delays, the studio in May assigned a small role for Judy in *Love Finds Andy Hardy*, the second installment of the adventures of a son who was mildly rebellious of a small-town judge. A forerunner of others to come, this soap opera, which exalted the virtues of family life, was going to become a real social phenomenon. Then, during the summer, Judy followed up with *Listen, Darling*, costarring Freddie Bartholomew and Mary Astor. Two minor films which would at least have the merit of ensconcing her a bit more in the public's mind.

(Left) Judy Garland during a prerecording session for the 1939 MGM musical The Wizard of Oz. *(Right) Judy Garland in a rare photo as a blond Dorothy on* The Wizard of Oz *set the first day of shooting, October 13, 1938.*

Starting in September, Judy recorded the songs for *The Wizard of Oz*. Then, filming MGM production 1060 began on October 13 under the direction of Richard Thorpe, one of the house directors, who was a good craftsman with a reputation of being at ease in any genre. He had been signed on three weeks earlier, which says a lot about the studio's low esteem for directors in the creative process — an MGM historian described directors of the era as efficient traffic cops.

Ten days later, Buddy Ebsen, who played the Tin Man, fell ill, poisoned by the aluminum powder in his makeup. He was hospitalized in critical condition and put on oxygen. While looking for a replacement — Jack Haley, a Fox loan-out — filming was interrupted. Mervyn LeRoy took advantage of the delay to see and re-see the rushes and concluded that Thorpe's direction lacked warmth and poetry. "He didn't have the necessary sensitivity," he said. "To tell a fairy tale, one must think like a child." Exit Thorpe, who was officially "ill"! Above all, the studio didn't want to give the impression that the film had problems. At the end of the day, no scenes filmed by Thorpe were used.

In the meantime, George Cukor, who was considered a "woman's director," was called to the rescue. Immediately distressed by Judy Garland's look, he demanded that her makeup be reduced and that her blond wig be removed in order to accentuate the freshness and innocence of Dorothy's character. For him, a farmer's daughter from Kansas must not be glamorous: the public must identify with her and discover the world of Oz through her eyes. He also asked Judy to act the most naturally possible. Two decisions which contributed to putting the film back on track.

Already contracted to direct *Gone with the Wind*, Cukor had to withdraw from the film after one week in favor of Victor Fleming, who was known for his adventure films (*Treasure Island*) and torrid romances (*Red Dust*), and was the only director named in the credits. Four months later, Fleming had to leave the film to replace George Cukor… who had just been fired from *Gone with the Wind*! There remained three weeks of filming, and it was King Vidor who completed the final sequences — or rather the first ones, in that the opening scenes on the farm were filmed last. A real directorial waltz, mirroring a chaotic shoot. The result was that upon filming the first scene in which the wicked witch disappeared in front of Dorothy, the actress Margaret Hamilton suffered from second-degree burns on the face and third-degree ones on the hand.

To play the Munchkins, the studio enlisted 120 dwarfs from around the world. Lodged in the Culver City Hotel, they were uncontrollable: they fought with knives and slid under women's skirts. They were never to be found when they were needed. Judy humorously recalled that studio security had to swoop them up "with butterfly nets"! "They participated in orgies at the hotel," recalled Mervyn LeRoy. "Everything sexual you can imagine, they did it." One of them even asked Judy to go out with her.

"No, I don't think my mother would approve," she eluded.

"Really? Ask her to come along," he replied.

The technicians, actors, and cameramen operating the projectors — all the more powerful than the ones used for black and white — had to endure punishing heat to make a color film. Furthermore, Technicolor, then in its infancy, tended to accentuate green. Filming had to be interrupted for a week in order for set designers to find the right paint for the yellow-brick road that led to the land of Oz. Everywhere, stress was evident. Furious over the film's delays, Nick Schenck found himself forced to go to Culver City to reproach Louis B. Mayer for having lost control of the movie…

In this electric atmosphere, Judy Garland kept steady, like a brave little soldier. Every day, she arrived at daybreak to have her makeup applied and wriggle into the girdle that hid her breasts, as her character was supposed to be eleven years old. On the set, she had a tense relationship with Victor Fleming, a roughneck who liked motorcycles, planes, and firearms. People said that Clark Gable modeled his manly and curt personage by observing him. Fleming behaved like a head general and hated losing his time. But, to evacuate the pressure of a film that rested on her shoulders, Judy frequently broke out in great big giggles, which seriously annoyed him. One day, he wound up slapping her and sending her back to her dressing room.

Judy Garland and some Munchkins take a break from filming The Wizard of Oz *in 1938.*

Taking advantage of moments when the technical team prepared scenes, Rose Carter continued to teach private courses to her. Was this a constraint? It was more a joy. In June, Judy would graduate, thus finishing her studies.

"I am finally going to be like everyone else," she told her costar Margaret Hamilton, who had worked in a kindergarten before becoming an actress. "Since I was four, I have been onstage and am the breadwinner. You can understand why this diploma is so important for me: that day, I will be a kid like the others, one of many in my class. I will have my small bouquet in my hand and will walk towards the principal…"

Unfortunately, Judy Garland was not able to get her diploma that year. At the time of her graduation, MGM sent her on a promotional tour. Furious, Margaret Hamilton called the head of the class and explained to him that it was inhuman to deprive Judy of this pleasure.

"It is a decision of Mr. Mayer in person," he replied to her.

Judy would have to wait another year to be "a young kid like the others"…

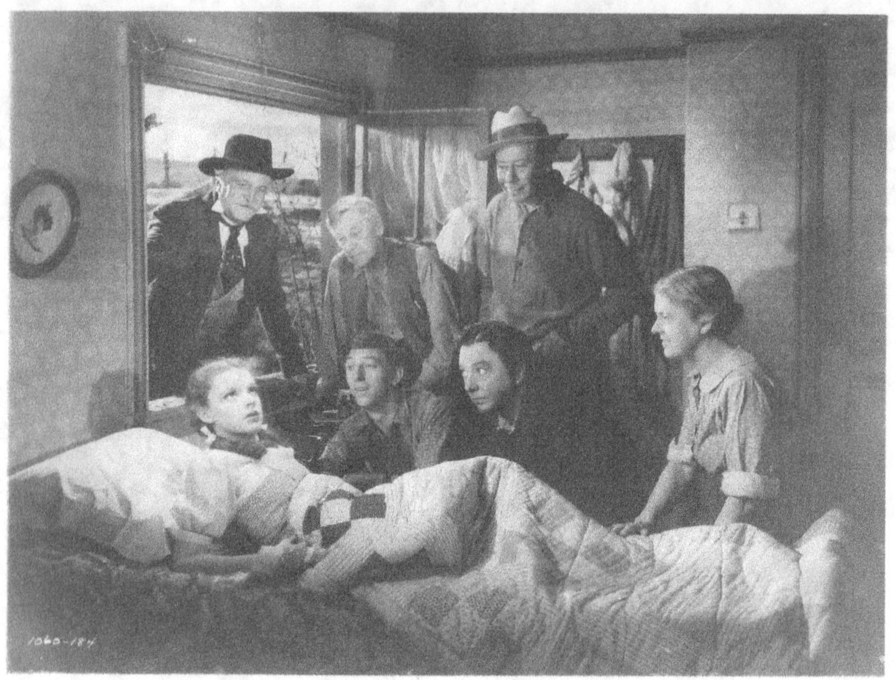

Judy Garland, in the final scene of The Wizard of Oz, *surrounded by Frank Morgan, Charley Grapewin, Bert Lahr, Ray Bolger, Jack Haley, and Clara Blandick.*

*

On March 26, 1939, the filming of *The Wizard of Oz* was completed. The first cut, which lasted two hours, had to be brought down to one hour forty-five minutes so that the number of daily showings not be reduced. A few scenes were cut, most notably ones with the wicked witch, out of fear they might traumatize some children. For studio executives, another cut was necessary: the song "Over the Rainbow," which they judged not rhythmic enough, and that slowed the picture down. Above all, it didn't conform to the studio approach. MGM had based its reputation on a lavish style. Further, it was out of the question to see Judy Garland sing in a barnyard in the middle of hens and pigs!

For Arthur Freed, it was a heresy: this song was an indispensable transition between the real world of Dorothy in Kansas in sepia and the wonderful world of Oz in color.

Somewhere over the rainbow
Way up high
There's a land that I heard of
Once in a lullaby

Somewhere over the rainbow
Skies are blue
And the dreams that you dare to dream
Really do come true

Someday I'll wish upon a star
And wake up where the clouds are far behind me
Where troubles melt like lemon drops
Away above the chimney tops
That's where you'll find me

Somewhere over the rainbow
Bluebirds fly
Birds fly over the rainbow
Why then, oh, why can't I?

If happy little bluebirds fly
Beyond the rainbow
Why, oh why can't I?

The music publisher Jack Robbins got involved:

"No one will remember this song! It's not made for a young audience!"

Freed was convinced of the contrary. To the point that he arranged to meet Louis B. Mayer and offered to resign if it weren't kept in the picture.

So much for "Over the Rainbow"… which would become Judy Garland's signature song! By the time she definitively abandoned the movies for concerts, she never gave a performance without singing it. And although she may have sometimes spoken ironically about the movies and songs she sang over the years, she never once denigrated "Over the Rainbow." To composer Harold Arlen she once wrote these words: "Over the Rainbow" is part of my life. This song symbolizes the dreams and hopes of people. That's why some have tears in their eyes when they hear it. I have sung it thousands of times and it will always be the song that is dearest to my heart."

A publicity still of Judy Garland and Toto from The Wizard of Oz.

5.

A Miniature Oscar

Even before the release of *The Wizard of Oz*, Judy Garland was back on the soundstages at MGM. Starting May 12, 1939, she began filming *Babes in Arms*.

Louis B. Mayer had kept his word: Arthur Freed had obtained the right to produce a musical on his own. He chose to adapt a musical by Richard Rodgers and Lorenz Hart, first performed in 1937, which told the story of a group of youngsters putting on a show in order to demonstrate to their parents, who were vaudevillians, what they were capable of.

The show had just triumphed on Broadway. Still, Freed cut most of the songs, except "Where or When," and himself wrote most of the new ones, including "Good Morning," which was reprised in *Singin' in the Rain*. In fact, what interested him was the starting point: right away, he saw the opportunity of reuniting Judy Garland and Mickey Rooney. True, they had already done two films together, but this time they would share star billing. Freed had noticed the degree to which they clicked together and wanted to play on this alchemy.

Barely 19 years old, Mickey Rooney established himself as one of the superstars of the moment with the Andy Hardy series. In 1937, the *Motion Picture Herald* ranked him 104 in its yearly popularity poll. One year later, he was in third place, behind Clark Gable and Shirley Temple. The same year, he received the Academy Juvenile Award and was from then on earning ten times more than Judy: $5,000 a week. Redheaded, with unruly locks, he compensated for his fresh-faced roundness and short stature – 5'1" – by his enthusiasm and vitality, like someone supercharged and in perpetual motion. He was a remedy again morosity: with him, one always felt great. He had pep and knew how to communicate it.

Reuniting Mickey and Judy was guaranteed dynamite. And, to guarantee that luck was on his side, Arthur Freed decided to sign Busby Berkeley as director. At Warner Bros. in the 1930s, Berkeley revolutionized musicals by filming dance sequences with vertiginous camera movements, whereas his colleagues were happy with a simpler filming style. With Berkeley, the camera was part of the choreography. A notorious alcoholic, he had been accused of having killed two people in a car accident, before being cleared. He had just come back to MGM looking for a new start. On the set, he was a tyrant: it was true that he had earlier supervised military parades during the First World War. Berkeley was obsessed with the details: his direction was millimetric, his traveling shots interested him more than his actors, whom he pushed to the limits. He barked at Judy non-stop:

"Your eyes, open them wide!"

All of Hollywood feared him. Under his direction, the days had no end. Mickey and Judy made the best of it: though a superstar, Mickey was also a hard worker, Judy was humble and obedient. And then too, Judy had her magic pills to recharge her batteries when she had slept little…

★

Mickey Rooney and Judy Garland in Babes in Arms.

Completed at the end of June, *Babes in Arms* was scheduled for theatrical release on September 15, barely one month after the release of *The Wizard of Oz*. Based on the assumption that Mickey Rooney was far better known than Judy Garland, MGM then chose a strategy that was audacious to say the least: promote both films at the same time, with Mickey Rooney giving Judy a leg up.

In early August, Judy Garland and Mickey Rooney arrived on the East Coast. After a few previews in Washington, New Haven, and Bridgeport, on August 14 at noon they arrived at Grand Central Station in New York. MGM had gotten the word out: they were welcomed by a crowd of 10,000 people in delirium. Two hundred fifty police officers had been mobilized for the occasion. Checked into the Waldorf Astoria, they gave a series of interviews for the newspapers and radios.

Three days later, for the first public showing of *The Wizard of Oz*, fifteen thousand patrons who had arrived at daybreak lined the block. The papers laid it on thick in stating that the film's release was the greatest event since the return of Charles Lindbergh, the first man to have crossed the Atlantic by plane. In the heat of the New York summer, each showing was like a riot. After one week, the film had already brought in $100,000: an unprecedented event! "See and re-see this movie as many times as you like, you will never get tired of its wonders," wrote the *Los Angeles Herald Examiner*.

Before each projection, five times a day, Judy and Mickey sang and danced for twenty-five minutes. Judy was small (4'11"), but with high heels was taller than Mickey. Starting from the first song, she took her shoes off so as not to dominate her partner. Scheduled to last a week, the show was extended a second, leaving Judy exhausted: she even fell ill, leaving Mickey alone onstage while she recovered.

On August 31, Mickey had to leave for Los Angeles, where he was expected for the filming of the umpteenth *Andy Hardy*. Despite Judy's fatigue, MGM decided to add a third week to the festivities: from then on, it was with two of her costars from *The Wizard of Oz*, Ray Bolger (the scarecrow) and Bert Lahr (the cowardly lion), that she sang and danced.

An ambulance, reserved by MGM, remained permanently parked near the stage door, just in case…

For her services at the Capitol Theatre, Judy Garland was paid $3,500 a week, thus $10,500 all told: more than for the nineteen weeks and two days of filming, which only earned her $9,650. From the West Coast to the East Coast, from the Canadian border to the Rio Grande, in the cities as in the countryside, *The Wizard of Oz* was a triumph. In view of the film's success, MGM gave Judy a one-time bonus of $10,600.

Promoting the film, the Cowardly Lion Bert Lahr, Dorothy/Judy Garland, and Scarecrow Ray Bolger perform "The Jitterbug," a number cut from The Wizard of Oz, *at the Capitol Theatre on Broadway in New York sometime between August 31 and September 6, 1939.*

In all, *The Wizard of Oz* thus garnered her a bit more than $30,000. A trifle when one knows the exceptional career of this feature film. But, at the time, actors got no royalties, neither on box-office earnings nor television airings.

Judy Garland, alongside Mickey Rooney, leaves her footprints and handprints at the forecourt of Grauman's Chinese Theatre in Los Angeles on October 10, 1939.

On October 10, Judy reunited with Mickey at Grauman's Chinese Theatre in Los Angeles, this time for the opening of *Babes in Arms*. Immediately after, she was invited to leave her footprints and handprints on the sidewalk: a tradition that became an institution ever since Norma Talmadge, a silent-film star and Buster Keaton's first wife, accidentally stepped into fresh cement when visiting the construction site in 1926. Since then, the Oscars crowned talent, the Chinese Theatre celebrity. For the occasion, Judy asked to wear a dress by Adrian, the studio costume designer, the prince of glamor, who made stars look sublime.

"You are too young to wear that kind of gown," thundered Louis B. Mayer, who had an eye on everything and wanted her to adhere to her image of a school kid.

She insisted, and he wound up giving in.

With its lightness, gaiety and optimism, *Babes in Arms* was in sharp contrast with the spirit of the times. America was worried about the situation overseas. France and England had declared war on Germany, after it invaded Poland. Twenty-one years after the First World War, were American soldiers going to once again have to come to the aid of Europe? In this context, Busby Berkeley's picture was more than a feel-good movie celebrating carefreeness: it was a hymn to youth in the form of a pressure valve:

We've got no Duce, we've got no Fuhrer,
But we've got Garbo and Norma Shearer…

As soon as it was released, the movie met lightening success. Paradoxically, for MGM it did much better than *The Wizard of Oz* — at least, in the short term. Filming Dorothy's adventures cost the studio $ 2.7 million, but if one takes into account the promotional and publicity costs the bill in the end amounted to $4 million. However, despite the public's enthusiasm, box office maxed out at $3 million. A large majority of the audience was children, at ten cents a seat, whereas the adult ticket was on average twenty-five cents. How many people saw the film? That's impossible to know precisely in that in the United States it wasn't the number of tickets sold that counted, but box office, business oblige. So much so that the movie made money only when MGM decided to rerelease it throughout the country in 1949. Thereafter, it became a veritable cash cow with its multiple airings on television Christmas nights.

For MGM, 1939 was a very good year, with the release at the end of the year of *Gone with the Wind*. At the Oscars, the adaptation of Margaret Mitchell's novel cleaned up with thirteen nominations and eight awards, whereas *The Wizard of Oz* had to settle for six nominations and two awards (Best Original Score and Best Original Song), at the end of a particularly fruitful year in which, among the other films in competition, were *Mr. Smith Goes to Washington* by Frank Capra, *Wuthering Heights* by William Wyler, *Love Affair* by Leo McCarey, *The Rains Came* by Clarence Brown, and *Ninotchka* by Ernst Lubitsch.

At the ceremony held at the Cocoanut Grove, a Juvenile Oscar was awarded to Judy Garland "for her remarkable interpretation as a young actress." Mickey Rooney, the previous year's winner, handed it to her:

there never could have been a finer handover. No doubt about it, this was an honorary trophy. This award was not the result of a vote by the members of the Academy, but a decision of the board. Designed to pay tribute to a performance by a minor, it was inaugurated in 1935 with Shirley Temple and given out now and then until 1960, before being definitively retired.

Curiously, this Juvenile Oscar was half the size of the usual trophy: around seven inches, instead of the 13-inch original. A "Munchkin Oscar," as Judy joked.

A "Munchkin Oscar" is awarded to Judy Garland, alongside Mickey Rooney, on February 29, 1940 for her performance in The Wizard of Oz.

6.

A Wedding on the Sly

Since she was a small girl, Judy Garland never stopped moving. From Grand Rapids to Los Angeles, with a detour in Lancaster, she was always in transit. She never really had a home sweet home. Shunted around from house to house due to the vicissitudes of her family and the whimsies of her mother, who never liked to stay in the same place for very long, she longed to settle down.

In the spring of 1939, while waiting for *The Wizard of Oz* to begin filming, it was Judy who pressured her mother to have a house built at 1231 Stone Canyon Road, in Bel-Air, a neighborhood in the hills, as chic as Beverly Hills but more discreet and less showy. It was hardly opulent, but a large structure surrounded by trees, in red brick, with a recessed entrance door protected by roofing, in the purest Connecticut style. In this true family home, Judy didn't just have a bedroom among others, but occupied a large part of the upper floor. She had a vast bedroom with a chimney and sofa, a dressing room, and a private bathroom. Since her marriage with Bobby Sherwood, Virginia had left the house and now had a little girl, Judaline, that everyone called "Little Judy." On the other hand, the eldest daughter, Mary Jane, divorced, shared the other rooms with Ethel and their maternal grandmother, who now lived with them.

With the acceleration of her career, Judy Garland had to learn to give interviews. "I have nothing to say," she declared each time the studio's promotional department asked her to bend to the exercise. What could she, whose life for years could be summed up by saying she had spent all her days at the studio, possibly tell them? The only thing she could talk about was her mother. And although rather mordant about her in private, Judy's public stance on her was far more guarded.

Judy Garland in front of her 1231 Stone Canyon Road, Bel-Air, home.

"Let it be said, my mother is the most remarkable of mothers," she assured the journalist Irving Wallace, the future screenwriter and renowned novelist. "She is so different from other mothers. When I am on set, she never intervenes. But if I turn to her, she advises me. Sometimes, I advise her. She never was a mother who drags their children from one hiring office to another."

Always put on a brave face. Always keep up appearances. The real truth of these interviews was that they were not the intimate truth, and one can get burned mixing truths. But even though mother and daughter had little in common, even though Ethel showed no tenderness towards Judy, and even though they couldn't really communicate, there was no conflict between the two. Judy did as she always did: she obeyed.

The clash occurred at the end of 1939, after the double triumph of *The Wizard of Oz* and *Babes in Arms*, when, to celebrate her 46th birthday,

Ethel decided to spend the weekend with Will Gilmore, in Yuma, Arizona. Since the death of his wife, they no longer needed to hide. But they intended to make the most of it and marry.

When they learned the news, the Gumm sisters were stunned. All three loathed Will Gilmore to the same degree. For Judy, it was as if her mother had defiled their father's tomb: for, if November 17 was their mother's birthday, in their eyes it remained the anniversary of Frank's death four years earlier. However much Judy and her sisters objected, Will Gilmore soon moved into the Stone Canyon house. All three were afraid he might get his hands on Judy's money. And soon enough, as feared, Gilmore asked to see the accounts of "his" new family.

"Like hell you'll do that!" coldly replied Ethel. "Judy's money? Not on your life! If you are greedy, I am greedier." Ethel hadn't done everything she had done to in the end be robbed. She nevertheless had to meet the needs of Will Gilmore and offer a car to one of her children. In a certain way, Ethel and Will were cut from the same cloth: cold, overbearing, bossy. They always wanted to dominate. The conflicts between them became more and more frequent, and they finally separated in March 1943.

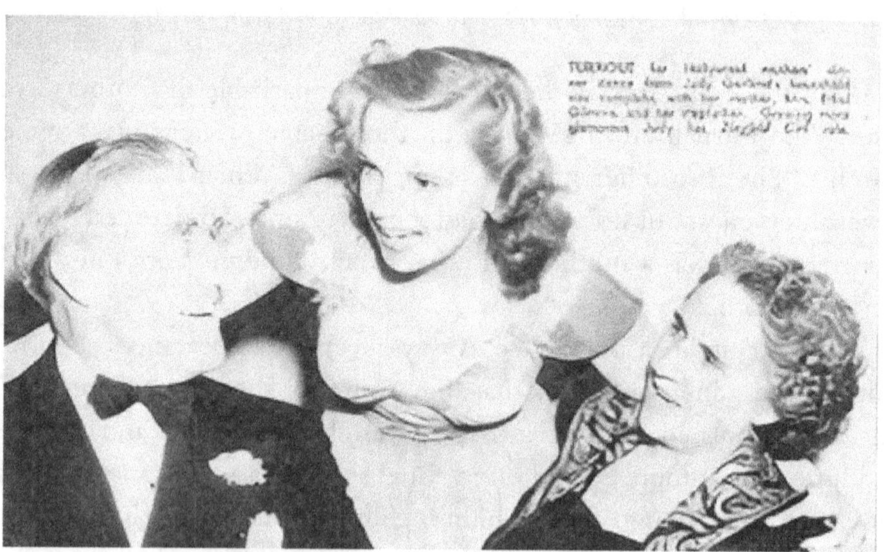

Will Gilmore, Judy Garland, and Ethel Gumm in the early 1940s.

★

In the Stone Canyon house, Judy did everything to avoid Will. For the first time, she thought about living alone. By early 1940, she was heading towards her eighteenth birthday, but MGM continued to lead people to believe she was sixteen. The studio was dead set on her continuing to play young girls — teenagers, as they would say today. In February, she costarred with Mickey Rooney in *Andy Hardy Meets Debutante*, the ninth episode of the series, the second they made together. Reprising her character of Betsy Booth, she helps Andy obtain a photo of a movie star he pretends to know to impress his friends, when in fact she had beforehand given him the boot...

In April, Judy returned to musicals, as ever with Mickey Rooney, in *Strike Up the Band* by Busby Berkeley, produced by Arthur Freed. The movie presents a high-school orchestra that participates in a contest backed by the king of "white jazz," Paul Whiteman, who plays himself. At first, it was a Broadway musical written by George and Ira Gershwin in 1927; but, with the exception of "Strike Up the Band," which provided the film's title, the songs in the film were replaced by compositions by Roger Edens. Still, Mickey Rooney declared:

"Gershwin's music is as good as Beethoven's or Bach's. But there's better: it's American."

While the war was raging in Europe, MGM catered to the patriotic fiber of the American public. The movie ends, for that matter, with a flag raising and the faces of Mickey and Judy merged with the star-spangled banner in order to impose their new stature: that of symbols of American youth.

Shooting the film, however, was grueling to the extreme. Busby Berkeley was more and more despotic. Not only did he relentlessly ask her to do retakes, but he reprimanded her. Judy took his orders "like a flogging" and sometimes asked herself "if she would survive to the end of the day," as she confided to Hedda Hopper. With him, workdays could last from 9 A.M. to 11 P.M., the limit set by the studios' unions. The technicians didn't object to the golden hours — overtime that was comfortably paid, but Judy was wiped out, physically and morally. For once on her side, Ethel wrote to Louis B. Mayer to demand that her schedule be lightened. His response was that Ethel was forbidden access to the studio for several weeks…

★

In an interview, Judy Garland played the game of the perfect babe in the woods:

"I won't get married before I'm twenty-four." No one thought of boys less than she, she insisted.

The lesson had been well absorbed. In reality, Judy thought about it all the time. With Mickey Rooney, there never was any question of romance: he was an incorrigible party-animal, a world-class Don Juan. Every week or almost, Louis B. Mayer in person admonished and implored him to behave. He was the brother she never had. "She and I, we came out of the same womb," he summed up. He was also the one who allowed her to express her share of fantasy. "With Judy, work and pleasure were inextricably related," he wrote in his memoir. "It was impossible to know when one began and the other ended. Our work was our pleasure and our pleasure was our work." More experienced than she, he gave her much advice. While singing was natural for Judy, she froze when she had to act. It was he who found the words that freed her:

"Play this scene as if you were singing."

As for Judy, she went out with other young actors — Jackie Cooper, Freddie Bartholomew, Buddy Pepper or Billy Halop, but the word "date" is vague: it applies to both flirtations as well as more intimate relations. "Who was the first to share the pleasures of sex with her, where and when? A question without an answer," writes her American biographer, Gerald Clarke. "What is sure is that she lost her virginity at fifteen. Insofar as sexuality, Judy was a free spirit, devoid of guilt or inhibition."

Sex was and would above all be a way of affirming herself. No doubt one must see in her behavior a way of compensating for her bodily complexes. On the MGM lot, when Lana Turner or Hedy Lamarr, two of the world's most beautiful women, went by, men stopped to admire them; whereas for her, men pat her on the back to say hello, as Judy told. Compared to these desirable women, Judy was uniquely different: no chichi, no games, she was natural. "She laughed more than anyone else and cried more too," said Buddy Pepper.

After having frequented boys her age, Judy Garland, during her stay in New York in the winter of 1938, met an older man. It was her first true unhappy love affair. Conductor and clarinetist, Artie Shaw, was establishing himself as the king of swing. He was tall, dark-haired, spirited, and charismatic. He was also irresistible. At twenty-eight, he was already divorced twice. In February 1939, when he came to give a concert in Los Angeles, Judy was in the first row. After a few songs, he fainted and had to be carried away. The next few days she visited him in the hospital; then, when his condition improved, they took long walks in the afternoon. Artie was impressed by her vocal talent. He admired her way of owning any song and never stopped reassuring her:

"But yes, you are beautiful!"

Artie Shaw.

For once, the first since her father's death, she had the impression that a man understood her. They embraced at length, but it never went any further. Back in New York, Artie didn't take long to vanish into thin air: he disbanded his orchestra, backed out of his already-signed contracts, and disappeared without leaving an address. Judy was next seen with the musician Oscar Levant.

"What do you think of me?" she asked him.

"You are like a Mozart symphony."

The next day, she ran to purchase all of Mozart. Oscar was thirty and their relation remained platonic.

A few months later, Artie Shaw returned to Los Angeles. They saw each other in February, but it took Judy little time to discover, when reading the newspaper, that he had just gotten married during an improvised escape in Las Vegas. The news was made worse by the fact that the new wife was none other than Lana Turner, nineteen years old, whom she knew from the Little Red Schoolhouse and who in her eyes embodied the glamorous woman she wanted to be. Judy was on the verge of a nervous breakdown. Ethel called Artie Shaw:

"How dare you run off with this woman and marry her?"

"Judy and I are good friends, we have a lot of affection for each other, but that's as far as it goes," he replied. "It is not at all what you think."

Later, he said: "We were like a brother and sister. Dating would have been incestuous… it was impossible."

Was Judy, the eternal best friend, delusional about their relationship? Did Artie Shaw play with fire by cultivating ambiguity? One thing is sure: he shaped her ideas about the perfect man. From then on, she would be drawn to men older than she.

Notwithstanding, young men sought her out. Sometimes to the point of obsession. On March 9, the Los Angeles police received a call: it was reported that there was a plan to kidnap Judy for a ransom of $50,000! A few days later, a young man was arrested. Robert Wilson was an enamored 19-year-old fan.

"Every time I see her move her little nose, I fall more in love with her. She's the girl of my dreams," he explained to the police.

The incident didn't stop Judy from going out. An insomniac, she liked to spend her evenings at Ciro's, at the Cocoanut Grove, at La Conga, and even at the Café Gala, which was mostly frequented by gay men and where she liked the sophisticated atmosphere. She was bored with people of her age and only appreciated the company of adults. But MGM kept an eye on her and reprimanded her regularly. "The boss of the effervescent Judy, who knows what is best for herself, has asked her to reduce her night-club outings," reports Louella Parsons, one of the Hollywood gossip columnists, who made and unmade reputations. The movie capital is a little world where everyone knows everything.

★

Ethel Gumm, Louis B. Mayer, and Judy Garland celebrate her 18th birthday on June 10, 1940.

On June 10, 1940, Judy Garland celebrated her eighteenth birthday. In his office on the third floor of the Thalberg Building, Louis B. Mayer sang the traditional "Happy Birthday" to her. He helped her cut the cake under the eye of a photographer. As a birthday present, MGM offered Judy her first car: another photo inside the studio was taken. The newspapers needed fodder. To build the legend.

Judy Garland with her car at MGM, 1940.

But the true gift Louis B. Mayer gave her was to accept to review their financial agreement. Frank Orsatti had sold his agent's contract to Leland Hayward in exchange for $25,000. Hayward subsequently negotiated a salary for her of $2,000 a week for the first three years, that is $104,000 a year, $2,500 the next three years, and $3,000 the last year. It was quite an operation: no actress her age had earned that much money up to then. Signed on August 28, validated immediately thereafter by the California Supreme Court because Judy was less than twenty-one years old, the document contained an article signed by Ethel stipulating that Judy "agreed to take care materially of her parents." When Leland Hayward proposed $125 a week to Ethel, deducted from Judy's salary and directly deposited by MGM, she thought best to add that she expected greater generosity, but the agent dryly sent her packing:

"No one needs $500 a month to live!"

Judy's career was burgeoning. Released in the fall, *Andy Hardy Meets Debutante* brought in $2.6 million, and *Strike Up the Band* $2 million, whereas they had cost no more than $700,000. During the summer, Judy had also made *Little Nellie Kelly* under the direction of Norman Taurog, a musical produced by Arthur Freed in which she interpreted the song "Singin' in the Rain." She played the role of a young wife who dies at the birth of her daughter, then that of the daughter in question.

"She can't have a baby in the film!" railed Louis B. Mayer at first.

That is, before he understood the advantage of this double role: which was to discover if the public was ready to accept her in the skin of an adult woman. In the studio system, governed by seven-year contracts, stars were long-term investments. One had to prepare for the future. For the first time, Judy therefore kissed a man — George Murphy — on the screen. The test was conclusive: *Little Nellie Kelly* crossed the $2 million mark.

By the end of 1940, Judy Garland had lived up to all her promises. When the *Motion Picture Herald* published the yearly list of stars who had earned the most money during the last twelve months, only two women figured among the first ten: Bette Davis and her.

★

Since the fall of 1939 and the release of *The Wizard of Oz*, Judy participated almost every week in the *Pepsodent Show*, one of the most popular radio shows, hosted by Bob Hope on NBC. This non-negligible source of supplementary income obligated her to do a double workday each Tuesday, but she never balked at working.

In February 1940, during recording sessions, she met David Rose, a more and more popular conductor and arranger, who was second to none in adding strings and wind instruments to popular songs. He wasn't as handsome as Artie Shaw. Rather short, brown-haired, he was calm, rather shy, a bit bland. And he collected electric trains. At parties, he kept his distances and spoke little. In private, he was rather deadpan. One hardly noticed him. Perhaps it was for that reason that no one saw their romance blossom in the spring of 1940. "Few would have believed that they would go out together," wrote a journalist, "until the moment when Hollywood became aware that they were at Ciro's sitting at the same table almost every evening for the past three months. Judy must be in love!"

Obsessed by Judy's image, MGM didn't take long to react. What made David Rose so attractive in the eyes of the actress, that is that he was thirty, was unacceptable in the eyes of the studio. To make matters worse, David Rose had already been married. Louis B. Mayer refused that Judy, who continued to embody innocence — not to say virginity — become the second wife. Being America's "little Valentine" had its requirements.

As for Ethel, she stepped on the brakes: her two older daughters had already married musicians and she concluded that they were not acceptable. In any case, even though she opposed it, she knew well enough that one day or the other Judy would get married, and she would no longer have any control over her.

But this time, rather than giving in, Judy took a stand. She was now eighteen and her birthday had been like an emancipation: the young woman, up to then so docile, no longer hesitated to affirm herself. She would not give David up. She intended to marry him.

"I don't see how a happy marriage could ruin my career," she asserted to Louis B. Mayer.

Who, based on the fact that David Rose was not yet officially divorced, decided to play out the clock:

"We'll talk about it again in a year."

Up until that time, Judy was asked to be discreet.

★

The last few months, she had ripened. She had become more attractive. The nondescript teenager had become a seductive young woman.

Early 1941, MGM hired her for *Ziegfeld Girl*, by Robert Z. Leonard, who five years before had made *The Great Ziegfeld*. Since the beginning of the century, the Ziegfeld Follies were successful on Broadway. They were New York's stage-show equivalent of the Paris Folies Bergère: a sumptuous revue, with magnificent dancers dressed in ultra-sophisticated gowns. A national monument.

For *Ziegfeld Girl*, Judy Garland shared the billing with two studio sex symbols: Lana Turner — already divorced from Artie Shaw, their marriage didn't last six months! — and the Austrian Hedy Lamarr, who had filmed in the nude in *Ecstasy* in 1933 and was considered one of the most beautiful women in the world, and was under contract to MGM since she emigrated to the United States. Here was a cast that should have rid her of her complexes, but Judy, shorter than her two costars, even in heels, had the impression that she was there to make them look good. When Lillian Burns, one of her dramatic arts teachers, with whom she continued to work one hour a day, congratulated her, she responded:

"What is this movie going to do for me? Nothing! All they could find for me to do was to throw me in a scene where I have to sob for the umpteenth time. Who has a real acting role? Lana. Who dies at the end? Lana. She is loved, desperately loved. The world hangs onto her every word. And Hedy Lamarr, let's talk about her: she is loved, the whole world fights over her!"

Judy Garland and Ethel Gumm in the early 1940s.

Hedy Lamarr, Judy Garland, and Lana Turner in the 1941 Ziegfeld Girl.

Immediately afterwards, Judy went straight into *Life Begins for Andy Hardy*, the latest episode and new hit of the series. During the first part of 1941, MGM tried to get her interested in Robert Stack, one of her leading men, but Judy found him dull, boring and, above all, too young. Secretly, she continued to see David Rose. In February, she asked him to accompany her to the Oscar ceremony. David's presence didn't escape Louella Parsons: "Frankly, Judy is in love with him. Whereas MGM continues to think it is a schoolgirl crush, if she decides to marry him, I don't see what they can do."

As soon as David Rose's divorce was finalized, Judy didn't want to hear about it anymore. Ethel and the studio had no other choice but to concede. In late May, the papers were notified, and on June 15, Ethel organized at Stone Canyon a "tea and cocktail," according to the words on the invitations, to celebrate Judy's nineteenth birthday and her engagement to David. Yellow parasols were set up on the lawn. Six hundred guests rushed to hear the rhythm of the new orchestra of Bobby Sherman, of which Virginia had become the songbird. Joan Crawford was photographed admiring Judy's engagement ring, set with a three-and-a-half carat diamond. James Stewart, who played one of the main leads in *Ziegfeld Girl* and had enrolled in the U.S. Air Force without waiting for Pearl Harbor, took advantage of a leave to congratulate the engaged couple in uniform. Judy wore a long gown of rose tulle and David, as usual, was smoking a pipe. They together cut the huge cake in the form of entwined hearts. "The most charming engagement party ever seen in Hollywood," commented a daily newspaper. The wedding of Deanna Durbin, Judy's old rival, took place on the very same day. No one noticed.

David Rose's and Judy Garland's engagement party, June 15, 1941.

One man was conspicuous by his absence: Louis B. Mayer. In Hollywood talk, the fact that he chose to miss such an occasion was simple to translate: he wanted to show his disapproval. Unable to veto Judy's matrimonial projects, he nonetheless succeeded in convincing her that the marriage not take place before September and the end of filming on *Babes on Broadway*, which would keep her busy the whole summer. This thinly disguised sequel (the characters didn't have the same name), as always with Mickey Rooney, marked Judy's return to an Arthur Freed production.

Impatience? Defiance? The engaged couple decided to precipitate things when they were at the Brown Derby in Beverly Hills, on Sunday, July 27. While there, Judy phoned her mother:

"Come join us right away!"

Ethel's protests were useless: Judy and David were determined. All three took the last flight to Las Vegas, where a justice of the peace married them at 1:20 in the morning. Forty minutes later, by naiveté or provocation, perhaps the two, Judy sent a telegram to Louis B. Mayer and Arthur Freed: "I am so pleased. Dave and I got married this morning. Please, give us a little time and I'll be back to finish the movie." The studio's reply was not long in coming: MGM summoned Judy to return to filming that very afternoon.

The happily married Rose-Garland couple.

7.

David's Boring Trains

In Los Angeles, the news of their marriage spread fast. "We haven't had a honeymoon," she explained to journalists who had come to greet them, "but we are the happiest people on earth."

The Garland-Rose home in Bel-Air with one of Rose's miniature trains in the foreground.

Since Ethel's marriage to Will Gilmore, leaving Stone Canyon had become Judy's obsession. Barely back from Las Vegas, the young married couple settled in downtown, at the Ambassador Hotel. After filming on *Babes on Broadway* had wrapped, they moved into a house at 10693 Chalon Road in Bel-Air in early October. David was able to set up his collection of miniature trains. Nine hundred eighty-four feet of tracks stretched out on the property's grounds, and for a wedding present, Judy offered him the replica of a western train station. As for decorating the house, she gave free rein to her fancies, transforming the dwelling into a bijou house, with replicas of 18th -century French furniture. She took care of it like the doll house she never had. As for its upkeep, however, she was quickly over her head. Never having cooked nor kept house, she turned to her mother, who lived a few streets away. Ethel hired two servants and supervised their work. She was free, but she couldn't cut the umbilical cord. She was not a woman who broke things off.

At the previews for *Babes on Broadway*, it was reported that the audience couldn't identify either Judy Garland or Mickey Rooney in the scene where, black faced, they performed a minstrel number, this typically American discipline where Whites disguised themselves as Blacks. Both were called in for an additional day of filming in November and the movie, which came out in December, once again thrilled the studio, taking in $3.8 million, four times more than it cost.

Judy Garland and Mickey Rooney in the 1941 Babes on Broadway, *directed by Busby Berkeley. Today politically incorrect, blackface was a 19th century racial stereotype that fortunately died in the 20th century.*

Director Busby Berkeley and Judy Garland rehearse "Yankee Doodle Boy" in Babes on Broadway.

For once, Judy Garland wouldn't have to make back-to-back movies. Her next picture was scheduled for February 20, which gave her two months to breathe. But, instead of taking advantage of this pause to savor her honeymoon, she decided to promote war bonds. Preoccupied by the war in Europe, the American government, despite its wait-and-see position, had begun to raise money and bet on the popularity of its movie stars. Judy would be the first to participate. On December 7, she visited the troops stationed at Fort Ord, in the Monterey Bay, south of San Francisco. The concert, which was broadcast by NBC, was periodically interrupted by news flashes: in the early morning, the Japanese air force had attacked the base at Pearl Harbor, which precipitated the United States' entry into the war. This crucial event eclipsed another: the same day, Judy Garland was promoted to the rank of corporal of the 1st medical regiment of Fort Ord. They pinned her star and regiment emblem onto her uniform.

All Hollywood rallied in the war effort and Judy Garland was one of the first, if not the first, to volunteer for a major tour to entertain the troops. On January 21, accompanied by David, she left for a series of concerts in Midwest training camps, while participating in meetings to sell war bonds. But winters were harsh in this part of America. Unheated trains, windy auditoriums, a packed schedule: the result was that Judy, suffering from a sore throat, had to interrupt her slog on February 7 after her stop at Camp Wolters in Texas.

"I'll come back," she promised.

1942, Rose and Garland arriving at Camp Wolters in Texas.

She kept her word: during the summer, as always accompanied by David, she went back on the road, visiting seven camps in seven different states. In the present as in the past, Judy was a good little soldier.

★

At MGM, they still hadn't digested her marriage. Louis B. Mayer was embittered. And petty: on February 26, 1941, at the Oscar ceremony at the Biltmore Hotel, he asked that Judy not be seated at his table among the studio's other stars, as she was the two preceding years. Accompanied by David Rose, she was thus relegated to the second fiddles. A humiliation that didn't go unnoticed by society columnist Hedda Hopper: "The studio behaved like a rattlesnake. They think that she belongs to them body and soul." Venomous as usual, she added: "They are trying to poison her relationship with David Rose by making her believe that he is using her fame to advance his own career." In her memoirs, she wrote that after she reproached Louis B. Mayer for his galling behavior he showed "neither shame nor compassion. I had wasted my saliva."

Fortunately, Judy could count on Arthur Freed, who, at the same time, gave her the lead in *For Me and My Gal*, a bittersweet musical whose story echoed geopolitical events, in that, in a tribute to vaudeville, it told the story of a singer married to an entertainer who, recruited during the First World War, chooses to voluntarily injure himself, before regretting his action. This was a true turning point in Judy Garland's career: she played an adult woman and, for once, Mickey Rooney would not be her partner. At first, MGM wanted to team her with George Murphy, but Freed insisted that the studio hire Gene Kelly, in his first screen role in Hollywood.

However, between Kelly and MGM, things began badly. After having noticed him on Broadway, Louis B. Mayer proposed a contract to him with a promise that he would not have to pass a screen test. But no sooner had he arrived in Los Angeles, the studio asked him to do one. Furious, Gene Kelly immediately returned to New York. "Sorry," he wrote to the mogul, "I won't work for you. I prefer to dance in a bar." Consequently, Gene Kelly signed with David O. Selznick. But after having seen him in New York in *Pal Joey*, in which he managed to make an unpleasant character likeable, Arthur Freed insisted on hiring him. To get him, MGM had to buy up his contract from Selznick, Mayer's son-in-law, who made a killing with the deal.

Judy Garland and Gene Kelly in a For Me and My Gal *rehearsal.*

On set, Gene Kelly was bewildered by Busby Berkeley. The director viewed him just like he viewed the other actors: an accessory. Judy, barely twenty, took him under her wing and initiated him to the basics of film making: how to place oneself in front of the camera, how to move between one's marks, how to not be too expressive — for, compared to theater, movies amplified the smallest movements of the face. As for Kelly, he consoled her when Busby Berkley verbally aggressed her. The result was an unfailing friendship that never ended.

For the first time, Judy Garland had top billing, above the film's title. And the studio had no complaints: released on November 20, 1942, the movie made $4.4 million on an investment of $800,000. She was thus capable of attracting the public just on her name.

Immediately thereafter, Judy worked again with Norman Taurog, who directed her in *Little Nellie Kelly*, for *Presenting Lily Mars*, the story of an unknown singer who falls in love with a Broadway producer. It was a musical produced by Joe Pasternak who, after having done great things at Universal, just re-signed with MGM. At first, it was to have been a drama played by Lana Turner. Stated Pasternak: "Nothing could convince her that she was anything but a second choice. She was persuaded she was ugly. In fact, she wasn't glamorous enough for women to be jealous of her, but she was pretty enough for men to fall in love with her. Ah, her eyes when she looked at you!"

Furthermore, the picture displayed a Judy Garland different from the one the public was used to seeing: hair pulled back and more feminine gowns created by Irene, one of the studio's great costume designers. Throughout filming, Pasternak was astonished by her professionalism. "When she discovered a song, she sang it one or two times with Roger Edens on the piano and the first take was the final take. She was perfect. The same with scenes with dialogue: everything went very fast."

MGM didn't give her an instant of time off. "Does Judy do anything else but work?" asked a magazine. To make matters worse, David was still at work when she came home. She waited patiently for him, but when he finally got home to get some sleep, it was already time for her to go to work. Of course, her Benzedrine pills gave her a pick-me-up, but they couldn't hide the dark circles under her eyes. Alarmed, the studio doctor asked Freed to rearrange her schedule to give her rest periods.

Scheduling questions were not the only obstacles in their relation. Obsessed by the idea of leaving Stone Canyon and her mother's stranglehold, Judy wanted to see only the good side of David. After a few months, she realized the degree to which they were different. Their differences, far from complementing each other, pushed them apart. Judy liked to go out, see people, talk, laugh, dance. She couldn't stand still. As for David, he revealed his true character: glum, dour, depressed. Instead of opening up, he took refuge in his daily grind, and all his free time was devoted to his miniature trains. Outside the moments when they made music together, she experienced a new feeling: boredom.

Worse, David was not the mentor she imagined. She wanted to be reassured, he destabilized her. She expected him to guide her, he was happy to put up with events. In the fall of 1942, when she told him she was pregnant, he reacted as usual: listlessly. Neither enthusiastic nor disheartened. As if it didn't concern him. When it was Ethel's turn to be informed of events, she reacted more predictably: she thought about the repercussions on her daughter's career.

"You can have as many children as you want, but not now," she said to her.

On her own initiative, she herself informed MGM of the situation. A crisis meeting was called on the third floor of the Thalberg Building, where strategic decisions were made. The verdict was irrevocable: Judy had to have an abortion.

At the time, abortions were illegal and severely punished in California, but MGM knew how to work things out in secret. Like all the other studios, MGM was persuaded that the status of a star was incompatible with that of a mother. From Jean Harlow to Joan Crawford, numerous actresses were pressured to go through with it. When Lana Turner, married to Artie Shaw, got pregnant, MGM's doctor practiced an abortion without anesthesia on a hotel bed in Hawaii where she was on a promotional tour. Her own mother had to put her hand on her mouth to stop her from crying.

At no time did David Rose support the idea that Judy should keep the child. His passiveness got the better of their relation. "After that, our couple was never again the same," she said. "Something broke." For Judy, it was quite obvious: David Rose was not the man she needed. By luck, Ethel had made sure that they got married with a prenuptial agreement. Faced with rumors, they published a press release in late January 1943: "We are separated. We both agree that that is the only way to resolve our mutual differences."

There would be no reconciliation. Their marriage hadn't lasted more than a year and a half: an achievement in itself in view of how little they were made for each other...

Hearing to divorce David Rose, 1944.

8.
Collateral Victim

MGM was obsessed with control and didn't hesitate to spy on its own stars. Every time a telegram was sent from the studio's post office, a copy just as quickly landed on the desk of Howard Strickling, head of public relations. Stars' private affairs were handled by the fearsome Eddie Mannix. Their obsession: always be a step ahead, first to muzzle the press, second to pay off the police, if necessary.

By the end of 1942, even before the announcement of her separation from David Rose, Judy Garland had left the Bel-Air house and moved to Westwood. From then on, Betty Asher lived with her pretty much permanently. Officially, she was her press secretary. Daughter of a Universal producer and five years older than Judy, she had taken care of the young star for two years. Unofficially, she was a sort of chaperone appointed by the studio, the Lion's watchful eye. Every week, Betty Asher prepared a report for Strickling on Judy's visitors and comings and goings. In order that she confide in Asher more easily, Mannix even suggested that Betty — who was his ex-lover — get Judy to drink, which would have devastating effects on the addictive profile of Judy, who was already hooked on sedatives and stimulants.

Judy knew nothing of all that. In her great naiveté, she made Betty her confidante, instead of keeping her distances. Shopping, parties, going to the movies: since her divorce, they did everything together and never left each other. Judy listened to her alone. She liked Betty's sophisticated elegance; in a certain way, she would have liked to resemble her. When, at the end of her ropes, Judy had a meltdown on a Culver City set, Betty alone knew how to calm her. On order of Louis B. Mayer in person, no one was authorized to disturb them, not even the director, if Betty was with the star.

Betty's brother, William Asher, a director and producer, later stated that his sister was a lesbian and that the two women had an affair. No documentation proves it, but nothing disproves it either. Several sources confirm that Judy sometimes flirted with women, a common practice among actresses in the permissive little colony called Tinseltown. The two women had a relationship for several years, up until Judy discovered her role as a "double agent" and excluded her from her company for treason. Betty Asher never overcame her bitterness at being repudiated and ended up killing herself…

★

To cheer herself up after her marital mishap, Judy Garland fell in love with another man: Tyrone Power. They met at a party in Brentwood, in the fall of 1942, when her marriage with David Rose was disintegrating. Since Henry King's *In Old Chicago*, Tyrone was the young male lead of the moment, the new star at Fox. He had unequivocal charm, both mysterious and mischievous. At first sight, they liked each other. There was one small problem: the star of *The Mark of Zorro* was married to a French actress who was androgenous-looking, Annabella, who had come to Hollywood at the beginning of the war to try her luck. For some time, this insatiable seducer had had numerous adventures with men and women — for, he was notoriously bisexual, as was his wife, but he had always made sure that they did not jeopardize his marriage.

Tyrone Power.

With her enthusiastic and naïve temperament, Judy was persuaded she could win him over. She was deluding herself. First, Tyrone Power was hindered by his military duties, like many actors. In those war times, there were not exemptions for stars: quite the contrary, they had to be exemplary. In early January 1943, the actor went back to the United States Marine Corps. Putting his career, his status and his relations on hold, Tyrone Power, who hated irreversible decisions, didn't want to deal with any stress. Annabella was his last anchor. He would not divorce her for now, he announced to Judy. Which didn't stop them from continuing to keep up a hot correspondence, with Tyrone's letters sometimes fifteen pages long.

But Judy was restless and could behave like a child. Believing she would cut him to the quick, she refused to see him on his first leave. In reality, it was first and foremost herself she was punishing in that she was exhausted from filming *Girl Crazy*, the adaptation of a musical by George and Ira Gershwin. Arthur Freed once again cast her with Mickey Rooney under the direction of Busby Berkeley, but the director showed himself to be even more lunatic than usual. In a megalomaniacal attack, he got it into his head to transform the opening scene — a simple rodeo number — into an elaborate super production. The more days that went by, the more the costs increased. After three weeks, he had already spent $100,000 more than budgeted. This time, it was too much: he was dismissed and replaced at short notice by Norman Taurog.

Between Busby Berkeley's harassment and her romantic tumult, Judy was morally and physically exhausted. In just a few weeks, she had gone from 110 to 95 pounds. Her family doctor, Marc Rabwin, prescribed five days off.

When Judy and Tyrone finally saw each other again, their passion hadn't diminished. Now, Tyrone opened up about his relationship with Annabella. Who refused a divorce and, the sly devil, gave her husband the freedom to continue to see his mistress. It was a total stalemate: Judy had no intention of settling for a secret liaison. Another obstacle was that Tyrone Power was assigned to the navy officers' school at Quantico, in Virginia, on the other side of the country.

Since the start, MGM's executives had been informed by Betty Asher of the Power-Garland affair. Their fear was to see Tyrone Power get a divorce to marry Garland: the papers never failed to call Judy a husband robber, which was catastrophic for her image. In that Power was busy far from Hollywood, the studio nevertheless decided not to confront Judy so as to strike the final blow in due time. Which happened soon enough when Tyrone suggested to Judy that she come meet him in New York on his next leave.

Overcoming her fear of flying, she went running, accompanied by Betty Asher, who did everything in her power to hijack the actor's messages. Persuaded he had stood her up, Judy returned home without having seen Tyrone. A few days later, Betty struck the deathblow: Tyrone Power was reading her love letters to his barracks buddies. A pure fabrication by Strickling — MGM was decidedly expert in scenarios, but it worked: humiliated, Judy thenceforth kept her distance from Tyrone Power, thereafter nicknamed "Tyroney the Phony."

A few years later, Power admitted that Judy Garland was still in his thoughts. His love was real. One more collateral victim of MGM's Machiavellianism…

9.

On the Couch

At MGM, Judy Garland made the acquaintance of an intellectual: Joseph L. Mankiewicz. An unidentified Hollywood object inside the studio, he was nicknamed "Harvard College" by Louis B. Mayer, even though had had studied at Columbia in New York.

Formerly a newspaper correspondent in Berlin, Mankiewicz broke into the film world by translating silent film subtitles from German to English, before joining in Hollywood his older brother, Herman, who was a screenwriter and had cowritten Orson Welles' *Citizen Kane*. Since being hired by MGM, he had written around thirty scripts, before producing some of the studio's biggest hits: Fritz Lang's *Fury*, Frank Borzage's *The Shining Hour*, and George Cukor's *The Philadelphia Story*, etc.

Tall, well–built, already in his thirties, always elegant with his tweed jackets with their leather elbows, pipe smoker Joseph Mankiewicz looked at the little Hollywood world with the typical distance of someone from the East Coast. For him, it was a zoo. Witty, voluntarily sardonic, never duped, he knew how to size things up for what they were worth. From Joan Crawford to Loretta Young, the studio's stars adored him. He knew how to make them believe he was interested in their intelligence more than their beauty or fame.

Joseph L. Mankiewicz.

Right off, Judy was seduced by this self-assured man, who listened to her as no one else had before. Her film credits didn't dazzle him: he didn't hesitate to tell her that she was wasting her time on rubbish that didn't bring out her acting talents. Both had the same biting irony. "We made each other laugh and we quickly became close," he commented. He introduced her to his friends — screenwriters, authors, directors, artists — and offered her a new world. And always, he uplifted her. He was the mentor she always dreamed of.

Between them, however, there was an obstacle: Joe Mankiewicz was married to the actress Rose Stradner, an Austrian who came to Hollywood to flee the Nazis and who gave him two sons. It was impossible for him to divorce her: the victim of a catatonia attack, Rose had been hospitalized for several months at the Karl Menninger Clinic, which was at the forefront of psychiatric treatments. He would never abandon her, and Judy knew it.

Known to penetrate the feminine psyche like an X-ray, Mankiewicz was the first to explore Judy's complexity. No, she wasn't a woman who was as simple as she seemed. "Everything Lana Turner ever thought, felt or wanted to say, you could write it down and put your pen down. It's an open book. But I do not think one can say everything has been said about Judy Garland," he stated.

Intrigued by the omnipresence of her mother, alarmed by her mood swings, worried about the disorders she displayed more and more frequently, appalled by the number of pills she took, Joe Mankiewicz advised Judy to undergo a psychoanalysis, as he had done. In his view, it was time for her to finally find out who she truly was, beyond the performing dog manipulated by her mother and the cash machine exploited by MGM. Until then, she had decided nothing, except her marriage with David Rose, which was bound to fail since it was the result of exasperation, and not a will to build something stable and lasting.

To advance, she had to stir up her past. Joe presented her to Karl Menninger, who was passing through Los Angeles. He confirmed to her that the answer to her problems was to be found in herself. Unable to attend to her daily—he felt she needed a one-year treatment, he recommended her to the neurologist Ernst Simmel. This old friend of Freud, formerly president of the Berlin Society of Psychoanalysts, had moved to Los Angeles after having fled Nazi Germany. Since then, he had founded the California Society of Psychoanalysts, of which he was president, and counted many members of the film industry among his patients.

Dr. Ernst Simmel.

Every morning, before going to the studio in Culver City, Judy lay down for three quarters of an hour on Simmel's couch. She had difficulty understanding his English, which had a strong German accent, but she was intimidated by the stiff and authoritarian side of the practitioner. Discovering the truth about oneself was a long road and sometimes necessitated taking the path less traveled. Sometimes even, she lied to him: a usual phase he was never fooled by.

If Judy was ready to sacrifice so much time to therapy, it was because she was at a decisive moment of her existence. She understood that she finally had to take control of her life. What truths, what gung-ho-come-what may attitude did her frenetic activity hide? Why did she always say yes? Where did her feeling of being ugly and perpetual doubt about her talent come from? What guilt ate away at her? Why did she have so little self-esteem?

When Ethel learned that her daughter had begun psychoanalysis, she choked. And ordered her to stop seeing Dr. Simmel. Joe Mankiewicz became the man to bring down, the one who had convinced her that her brain didn't run smoothly, and who sought to weaken her in order to better dominate her.

"I live my own life," replied Judy. "I do what I want to do. I have been married. Stop treating me like a baby."

In view of Judy's inflexibility, Ethel asked to see Louis B. Mayer. He was aware that several studio stars resorted to psychoanalysis, but he was a fierce critic of Dr. Freud's theories. He too didn't look favorably upon Judy Garland in the hands of a shrink: in his view, neuroses were always easier to take care of by yourself. How could he make her change her mind? Certainly not by confronting her, as her mother had done. Louis B. Mayer knew that only Joe Mankiewicz could discourage her to continue her therapy. He would have to speak to him.

★

God works in mysterious ways. In the following days, Mayer and Mankiewicz by chance found themselves in the same train, the Super Chief, a luxury hotel on rails, which crossed the United States from east to west. The MGM head was coming back from a meeting with his New York backers; as for the producer, he came onboard in Texas where he had gone to see his wife, who was still hospitalized in Dr. Menninger's clinic. In the middle of New Mexico, Mayer invited Mankiewicz to his compartment. They spoke small talk. Louis B. Mayer knew that he had to play it shrewdly. He knew Joe's character, and that he was not a man who gave in easily. When he finally decided to get to the point, Joe dryly replied:

"You're talking like a jealous old man, not like a studio head."

That was the end of the conversation. Louis B. Mayer called it quits. He knew he would never win the case. What's more, what use was it to get angry with one of his best producers?

But Ethel brought it up again. Worn down, Mayer summoned Mankiewicz to his third-floor office, in the presence of Judy's mother. He was appalled that Joe could insinuate that Judy was crazy. "Mayer asked me forcefully how I could get involved in Judy's life, when her mother's love was the only thing she needed," stated Mankiewicz. I replied: "Her mother's love, my ass." She was a fearsome bitch…She said: "I know what I have to do with my daughter," and all hell broke loose. "I was so fed up that I wound up saying: 'Obviously, Mr. Mayer, this studio isn't big enough for both of us.' One of us has to go."

A week later, Joe Mankiewicz resigned from MGM and signed with Fox, which paid him more and agreed to his most cherished wish: allow him to direct his own films. An opportunity which allowed him to become one of the most brilliant directors of his generation, author of such masterpieces as *A Letter to Three Wives*, *All About Eve*, *The Barefoot Contessa*, and *Suddenly, Last Summer*.

★

On June 10, 1943, Judy Garland celebrated her twenty-first birthday. Thereafter, she had the right to manage her own affairs.

As a birthday present, her friends offered her a record: the recording of a comedy that told her life story, interpreted by her sister Jimmie, Betty Asher, the producer Dore Schary, the actors Phil Silvers and Keenan Wynn, as well as the singer and dancer Danny Kaye.

In that MGM had no projects for her in view, Judy made the most of it by making her stage debut at the Robin Hood Dell in Philadelphia, accompanied by the philharmonic orchestra of the city under the direction of Andre Kostelanetz. More than thirty thousand spectators applauded her and gave her standing ovations: not only was every seat sold, but fans climbed trees, roofs, and the hills around to see their idol.

Judy Garland, in her very first concert, appears at the Robin Hood Dell in Philadelphia on July 1, 1943 with Andre Kostelanetz conducting the Philadelphia Symphony Orchestra.

Immediately after, Judy Garland performed in several U.S. Army camps in the East and Midwest. Then, after a month of vacation at home in Los Angeles, she once again devoted herself to the war effort. On September 8, in Washington, the Hollywood Bond Cavalcade got going. This train, with twelve stars on board — Fred Astaire, James Cagney, Lucille Ball…, crossed the United States and stopped in big cities to at each stop give a two-hour show in order to raise funds. Judy and Mickey Rooney came onstage just before the finale. In all, they traveled over nine thousand miles, appeared before seven million people, and collected more than a million dollars.

Judy Garland, farthest left, and a host of other stars embark on a multi-city tour around the country on September 4, 1943 selling War Bonds.

Judy couldn't have dreamt a better way of testing her popularity: at each stop, it was she, "America's sweetheart," who stole the show. The public deeply loved her: because of her films, her songs, her talent, but also for what she was: a girl who was simple, natural, sparkling, and emanated something positive. Only unhappy people knew how to play happy comedy so well...

Coming home in mid–September had a bitter taste. Rosa Mankiewicz, whose health had improved, had returned to Los Angeles. In a certain way, this return dealt the fatal blow to her affair with Joe. But Judy didn't want to give up on this man who had opened new horizons and taken care of her like no one else before. "I sincerely wanted to marry Joe," she later said to her daughter Liza. "I wanted him to leave his wife. I hated this compromise."

She chose to lie to him by announcing she was pregnant. Joe immediately understood that it was a bluff, a call for help; but, being a good psychologist, he avoided confronting her with her own lie. He knew that that would risk hurting her ego which was already so fragile. "It was up to her to tell me it wasn't true," he explained. As such, he played her game to the point of absurdity. By reminding her that he could not divorce his wife who had just left a clinic, he encouraged her to choose the only decision possible: abort. And suggested that the procedure be done in New York, far from curious eyes in Hollywood ever in search of gossip. Given that Judy was still in denial, they together took the train for Manhattan, where one of his friends welcomed them in his apartment. At a doctor's office, Judy took a pregnancy test. Negative, of course. "She was both happy and sad about the result," told Joe.

A trip for nothing? Not really. During this trip across America and these few days on the East Coast, Judy had had Joe for herself, one last time. Later on, she would talk about it nostalgically, as if this improbable trek had been nothing but a kind of honeymoon and not a farewell journey.

Back in Los Angeles, their encounters became less frequent. They phoned each other, but Joe always found an excuse not to see her. Too much work. His wife. His children. Judy spent her days at home, waiting for phone calls that were more and more rare, more and more brief, more and more colorless. "We didn't split up," he commented. "Things just died on their own…"

One day, he finally told her:

"You should be seeing other men."

A piece of advice she followed.

10.

The Pygmalion and His Muse

At MGM, Arthur Freed had gotten a promotion. In view of his productions' success, Louis B. Mayer gave him free rein where it came to musicals. In a few months, he put together a studio in the studio: the "Freed Unit."

Convinced that musicals were condemned to sclerosis if they couldn't be reinvented, Arthur Freed set about culling the most promising talents on Broadway. Gene Kelly, but also the singer and dancer Lena Horne, the choreographer Charles Walters, the set designer Oliver Smith, the costume designer Irene Sharaff, the composers Alan Jay Lerner, Betty Comden and Adolph Green. He was also going to bring new blood to his movies by hiring a director who was causing sparks to fly in New York: Vincente Minnelli.

Vincente Minnelli.

Born in Chicago into a family of vaudeville actors, Minnelli made his onstage debut at three, but quickly realized he preferred the wings. Gifted at drawing, he designed theater costumes and sets, while at the same time coming up with window displays for a Chicago department store. Set on trying his luck in New York, in 1933 he was named artistic director of the brand-new Radio City Music Hall, where before long he designed his first stage show. Color, lights, sets: his shows had a flamboyant side which differed from the usual productions. Soon enough, Paramount offered him a juicy contract as a producer and director. But, after a year, it led to nothing. He had only been able to direct a single sequence in a Raoul Walsh film. Frustrated, he decided to return to New York.

Freed and Minnelli met in the spring of 1940. At first sight, the two hit it off, but the director had gotten his fingers burnt by his first Hollywood experience. Arthur Freed shot back:

"Listen, I am proposing that you come and try my method for a year. You wouldn't have a specific title, but you would learn the ropes. You could read scripts, make suggestions, direct a few musical numbers, work in editing… If that doesn't please you, you are free to return to New York; but if you decide to stay, I already know that you would make an excellent director."

For $300 a week — whereas Paramount had offered him $2,500 two years earlier! — Minnelli thus returned to Hollywood in April 1940. During this observation period, which was an on-the-job training for the mysteries of filmmaking, one day Arthur Freed led him to the set of *Strike Up the Band*. Mickey Rooney was shooting the scene where he announced to Judy Garland that he wanted to become a great band leader.

"We need to improve this scene to make it more spectacular," Arthur Freed explained to him.

Sighting a fruit bowl on the set, Vincente Minnelli suggested:

"What if Mickey handled each fruit as if it were a musical instrument? Apples would be violins, oranges brass, bananas woodwinds. Mickey could be the band leader and the fruit would come to life one by one…"

Judy Garland and Vincente Minnelli met for the first time on this occasion. They barely spoke. "I was immediately seduced by her directness which was in contrast to my own shyness," he later stated.

★

From the day Arthur Freed read a series of articles by Sally Benson in *The New Yorker* that evoked her childhood memories at the beginning of the 20th century in St. Louis, he couldn't stop thinking about doing a film. In that war time, he thought that this glorification of the American heartland, an ideal counterpoint to current worries, would by its very nature move the public.

Unlike other musicals, apart from *The Wizard of Oz*, *Meet Me in St. Louis* was not adapted from a show. Everything had yet to be done: write an original script, compose the songs, write the lyrics. A meticulous job supervised by Arthur Freed, who couldn't afford to make a mistake in that such a film's budget would be big. But he wasn't a man who turned away from a challenge, all the more so here because he saw an opportunity of rejuvenating the musical. As ever on the lookout for new talent, he had the songs written by Hugh Martin and Ralph Blane, who had just triumphed on Broadway with *Best Foot Forward*. For once, they would not interrupt the story. They would not be "numbers," but real scenes which would advance the action and reveal the characters' psychology.

Arthur Freed first thought about hiring George Cukor as director, but he had joined the Signal Corps, the army's movie department. He then thought of Vincente Minnelli, to whom he had already assigned *Cabin in the Sky*, a musical cast in its entirety with African Americans. A bomb in an America that was still segregated: until then, the musical numbers interpreted by Lena Horne could in no way be indispensable to understanding the story, for in the southern states, they were cut pure and simple! On a small budget, Vincente Minnelli had worked wonders and *Cabin in the Sky* had brought in $1.7 million. Since then, Minnelli had come to the studio's rescue by taking over *I Dood It*, with Red Skelton and Eleanor Powell, on the fly.

Once again, Arthur Freed was taking a risk: Minnelli had never directed a super production, but his new approach would be a plus. Better yet: ever keen on giving his collaborators a maximum of creative freedom, Freed included Minnelli in the movie's preparation very early on. Minnelli reworked the script and got involved in the costume design, but also the sets. It was out of the question that he reuse those used in the *Andy Hardy* series, even though they depicted small-town America: he got permission to recreate inside the studio a street lined with eight Victorian houses surrounded by luxurious gardens. In all, the budget for the sets would be near $500,000.

For the lead, that of Esther Smith, the choice was unhesitatingly obvious: Judy Garland. But after having received the script, the star refused point-blank. Joe Mankiewicz had told her that she would be nothing but a foil to the little sister's character, Tootsie, attributed to Margaret O'Brien. Furthermore, her character was only seventeen: it was out of the question that she once again play a teenager in love with her neighbor! She was an adult and wanted adult roles. For that matter, why hadn't the role of the older daughter, Rose, been proposed to her? Well, because it had been given to Lucille Bremer, a former dancer at Radio City Music Hall, who happened to be Arthur Freed's mistress. Determined not to be taken in, Judy Garland went straight to Louis B. Mayer's office to plead her cause.

"I'll read the script," replied the boss.

After having read it, he expressed his concerns to Arthur Freed:

"There isn't any story…"

Which was true. *Meet Me in St. Louis* depicts a family, the Smiths, who live happily in St. Louis. One evening, the father announces that he had found a better-paying job in New York. They would have to move. But his wife, daughters and son are opposed. In the end, the Smiths remain in St. Louis and attend the World's Fair. True, there were more dramatic storylines to put MGM's money on, but Freed was sure that Louis B. Mayer would let him go ahead.

For the moment, it was out of the question to give up on Judy Garland. Freed, who could be obsequious with the powerful and delicious when he wanted to be persuasive, could also prove himself to be brutal. If Judy refused the role, he was offering her, he would apply MGM's habits and customs: her salary would be suspended until she accepted another movie. Financially, Judy was cornered. She had just discovered that her mother and Gilmore had made dangerous investments with her money and that they hadn't the funds to pay her taxes. She needed money.

She had no other choice but accept.

★

On the first day of rehearsals, Judy Garland arrived four hours late. That she wanted to show she had no desire to make *Meet Me in St. Louis* couldn't have been clearer. On the following days, she was at least twenty-five minutes late. On December 7, the first day of filming, everyone waited one hour and sixteen minutes. At MGM, star or not a star, everything was scrupulously noted, filed, classified, archived. Her costars were annoyed. One day, Mary Astor, who had been her costar six years earlier in *Listen, Darling*, took her aside:

"We waited for two hours for you to honor us with your company…"

"I don't sleep," she replied.

It was the period when she spent her nights waiting for phone calls from Joe Mankiewicz.

Judy didn't just lack punctuality, she made no effort at all. She hated her role and found her lines ridiculous. Vincente Minnelli handled her very gently. Not once did he raise his voice, not once did he lose his self-control. Just the opposite of Busby Berkeley, who shouted relentlessly and did retake after retake, but never because of her. This time, it was her acting that was a problem. "What seemed obvious to me left her totally in the dark," Minnelli later stated. What's more, she noticed that he was often happy with a single take with the beginner Lucille Bremer. Disconcerted, she complained about it to Mary Astor. Is this Minnelli experienced enough to direct such a movie?

"You know, I have been observing him since the beginning," she answered. "I can tell you one thing: he knows exactly what he's doing. He knows his job very well."

Up until then, Judy had always acted naturally. Instinctively. However, for this family saga, Minnelli didn't want her to act by herself, as she always did, but in unison with the other actors. He wanted her to give depth to her character. Without wanting to, he awoke in her an insidious doubt. One day, she asked Arthur Freed to come to her dressing room:

"I don't know how to act anymore…"

To make matters worse, the presence of Margaret O'Brien, seven years old, deeply disturbed her. The childhood she was cheated of all came back to haunt her: under contract to MGM since she was three, *Meet Me in St. Louis* was her tenth movie! Margaret O'Brien's mother, who was on set every day of filming, was a monster who reminded her of her own mother. One day when Minnelli asked Margaret's mother how to get her to cry, she replied without skipping a beat:

"You'll have to say someone is going to kill her dog!"

Frankly, this film displeased her. On set, she was in a rush for just one thing: go home. However, every day after filming, Minnelli liked to bring up the next day's scene with the actors. Judy tried to slip away. Sometimes, the director had to call the gate keeper at the studio entrance to try to stop her and to ask her to turn back…

And then, one day, the skies opened.

★

Judy Garland sings "The Boy Next Door," composed by Hugh Martin and Ralph Blane, in the 1944 musical Meet Me in St. Louis.

When viewing a few rushes, Judy understood why Minnelli was so demanding. She was just right. Most of all, for the first time, she thought she looked beautiful on screen. Because of his attention to lighting and the precision of his directing, Minnelli had known how to show her to her advantage. Another factor counted: Judy from then on benefited from the services of Dorothy Ponedel. A makeup legend, the queen of glamor. At Paramount, she had worked with Marlene Dietrich, Paulette Goddard, Carole Lombard and Barbara Stanwyck. When they first met, Judy arrived with her little rubber discs she put in her nostrils since the day she arrived at MGM.

"What the hell is that? Throw those away. You don't need them, you are very pretty."

With her brushes, tweezers and makeup, Dottie Ponedel literally remodeled her face. She brought out her eyebrows, broadened her lower lip, depilated her front hair to enlarge her forehead. Finally, Judy began to like herself. The two women were from then on inseparable, on set and in life. Dottie, twice as old as Judy, became a substitute mother, a counselor, a friend. Faithful among the faithful.

The one to whom Judy could tell all.

A Meet Me in St. Louis *Lobby Card on which can be seen Margaret O'Brien and Judy Garland performing the 1902 song "Under the Bamboo Tree," making it contemporary with the turn-of-century musical.*

★

Judy fell in love too easily. From the start of filming, in order to forget Mankiewicz, she fell for Tom Drake, in the role of John Truett, of whom she became enamored. Tall and square-jawed, he was a strapping young man who fascinated her from the start. They flirted, but their relationship ended the first night together: nothing happened. And understandably: Tom Drake preferred men. Judy hardly spoke to him again.

Seeing that Judy was on better terms with Vincente Minnelli, Don Loper, the costume designer, invited them to dinner along with his fiancée, Ruth Brady. Judy discovered that Minnelli was like her, from a theatrical family, trained in vaudeville. Both had been dragged from town to town by their parents. He discovered a woman with a sense of humor, always ready to make fun of others, but also of herself. She told a story about how Louis B. Mayer presented her to his friends, after her first films: "Do you see this little girl? Look at what I've made her into. She used to be a hunchback." In his autobiography, the filmmaker wrote about this first dinner as such: "I found Judy's self-deprecating wit disarming, and the vulnerability she disguised with it all the more touching. Like everyone else at the studio, I wanted to protect and love her. And Judy was affectionate and loving right back."

The foursome got into the habit of regularly meeting up outside the studio. But one evening, Don Loper was ill and asked Minnelli to phone Judy to postpone the evening.

"We don't need Don and Ruth all the time," Judy shot back. "What's the use of chaperons? We're old enough…"

★

Scriptwriters call it a narrative arc: two characters who despise each other wind up appreciating each other, then loving each other. For Judy Garland and Vincente Minnelli, it wouldn't be long before their lives turned into a romantic comedy. And as in all good romantic comedies, the two protagonists were radically different. Whereas Judy was exuberant and flirting, Vincente was introverted. As opposed to her being instinctive, impetuous, and impassioned, he was guardedly intellectual, shy, and collected.

There are those who look for a double in the one they love and those who look for their opposite. The former are as one, the latter complement each other. Between Judy Garland and Vincente Minnelli, it wasn't love at first sight: complicity transformed itself into tenderness, then into love. She was his muse, he was her Pygmalion. Forty-one years old, he was nineteen years older than she. On his side was life experience, culture, and refinement. Judy had only been with men who had dedicated their life to music and to movies. Minnelli was more than that: of course, he was a director, but he was an artist at heart. An esthete. In tribute to his absolute master, the painter Whistler, who always wore yellow gloves, Minnelli wore yellow shirts or sportscoats. In his Hollywood Hills home, where he lived with a Filipino butler and two poodles, one of his rooms, painted entirely in black, contained only white furniture. He collected porcelain objects, paintings, art books, and designer furniture. He introduced Judy to another world: that of beauty, far from Hollywood superficiality.

A few weeks after wrapping *Meet Me in St. Louis*, MGM brought them together again. Louis B. Mayer had an idea of making a musical which, for MGM's twentieth anniversary, would assemble the studio's greatest stars, from Judy Garland and Lucille Ball to Cyd Charisse and Esther Williams, not forgetting Gene Kelly and Fred Astaire, who would do their only duo. The pretext would be a new tribute to the Ziegfeld Follies, with William Powell reprising the role of Florenz Ziegfeld, which he had already played so successfully. Didn't the Freed Unit include the best singers, dancers, actors, and choreographers in Hollywood? He had pulled the rug out from under the other studios. Since Busby Berkeley's departure, Warner Bros. had dropped the genre. As for RKO, they had never gotten over the end of the Fred Astaire-Ginger Rogers coupling. Fox alone continued, but their productions centered on Betty Grable, American soldiers' favorite pin-up, were both less lavish and less inventive.

For Louis B. Mayer, *Ziegfeld Follies* had to be real fireworks. It was also an excellent way for the studio to make its human resources profitable: as soon as stars had a few days' break in their schedule, they could film their number. America hadn't invented Taylorism for nothing…

After George Sidney's withdrawal, Vincente Minnelli was the obvious first choice to supervise *Ziegfeld Follies* — with the understanding that if he were occupied with another film, he would delegate the direction to another house filmmaker.

It was thus that Judy Garland and Vincente Minnelli filmed their first sketch, brilliantly choreographed by Charles Walters, and titled "A Great Lady Has an Interview." It was an amusing self-deprecating number in which Judy, more glamorous than ever — pale blue dress and matching scarf, gives a press conference which didn't lack spice: for, if ever there was a star who behaved like a star, it was she!

On June 10, 1944, for her twenty-second birthday, Minnelli offered her a beautiful evening purse. She sent him a thank-you note:

Dear Vincente,

Your magnificent birthday gift has truly transformed me. I have always been very shy and very awkward just entering a room full of people. From now on, I only have to hold on to your purse well in view of all to dazzle them.

They considered getting married, but Judy was still not divorced. While initiating the procedure, in early July, they drifted apart. She had just gone back to Joe Mankiewicz. "An intellectual who was rather tormented," commented Minnelli. "She went back to him, fairly proud that such a brilliant man was interested in her."

What was missing between Judy and Vincente? Perhaps the heat of passion.

It was the movies that would once again reunite them.

Judy Garland sings "The Trolley Song" in the famous sequence from Meet Me in St. Louis, *with the boy next door, Tom Drake, by her side.*

Judy Garland, as photographed by George Hurrell for the June 1, 1944 Esquire *magazine.*

11.

The Boss' Blessing

On August 1, 1944, Judy began filming *The Clock*. There was one challenge: even though the producer's name was Arthur Freed, it was the first time a purely dramatic role was on her shoulders. To reassure herself, she called in an acting coach. She played a woman who meets a young corporal on leave, played by Robert Walker, in New York's Penn Station. She shows him the town, but they inadvertently become separated in the crowd. Not knowing the other's last name, they reunite where they had met near the escalator of Penn Station. They get married and say good-bye where they had met…

The seasoned Jack Conway was set to direct. Since his early days in 1912, he had made seventy silent movies and some of Jean Harlow's best films. Falling ill before shooting started, he was replaced at short notice by the studio's young hopeful, Fred Zinnemann. From the start of shooting, Judy got along poorly with him.

"We are incompatible," Judy let on.

No one was worried: at MGM, they were used to difficult relations with directors she didn't know. Then again, the first rushes disappointed the studio. After three weeks, it became apparent that his directing went every which way and that there was no unity between scenes. On August 24, Fred Zinnemann was abruptly fired — which didn't stop him from later making *High Noon*.

Judy Garland then insisted to Arthur Freed that Vincente Minnelli take over the movie. Not yet a couple, they had remained good friends. After reading the scenario, the filmmaker accepted to take up the challenge: on September 1, shooting restarted under his supervision. It was a new start: no shot filmed by Zinnemann was retained.

Confident in her talents as an actress, Minnelli asked Judy to give up her coach. To help her understand her character, he wrote her a memo summarizing his vision of the character that was punctuated with questions. Who is this young woman? What problems has she known? What magazines did she read? Who are her favorite stars? It was an extremely modern method for a film that could not be more classic: except for a few cutaway shots filmed in New York by a second unit, *The Clock* was entirely filmed in the studio. For the scenes in the train station, MGM hadn't hesitated to spend $66,450 to recreate Pennsylvania Station. Movies are decidedly the realm of illusion, for New York had rarely been better rendered: Minnelli knew how to make Manhattan more than a setting for a "brief encounter." It was a character in its own right.

Judy Garland and Robert Walker in a scene from the 1945 The Clock, *directed by Vincente Minnelli.*

★

Joe Mankiewicz and Judy Garland's reunion was brief. Although the physical and intellectual attraction was still there, Judy quickly understood that nothing had changed: Joe would not get a divorce. What was the use continuing a relation that was at a dead end?

On the other hand, the more she spent time with Minnelli on the set of *The Clock*, the more she said to herself that he was truly delicious. Always caring. Always charming. Always respectful. Better yet, he wasn't married. What if he was the man she was looking for? Of all the men she loved, he was the only who never made her suffer.

Not only did they get back together, but they no longer hid it. On the set, they could be seen cuddled up to each other. One day, at lunch break, three extras discovered them kissing in the corner of the set.

At the end of filming *The Clock*, Judy offered Vincente Minnelli an office clock, accompanied by this note:

My dear,

When you check the time on this clock, I hope that you will remember our movie. You know how much it has counted for me. You alone could give me the necessary confidence. If the film is successful, it is to my adored Vincente that we owe it. I thank you for everything, my angel.

In the meantime, it was *Meet Me in St. Louis* that had been released. To entice the public, Decca had put the album of Decca recordings from the film on sale a few weeks before its opening. The album peaked at number two on the April 7, 1945 *Billboard* Best-Selling Popular Record Albums chart.

On November 24, Judy and Vincente took the train to New York. On earlier trips to the Big Apple, Judy never had the time to visit Manhattan. Vincente let her discover this city that he knew so well. He showed her the places that had been recreated with the help of back projections in *The Clock*: the Metropolitan Museum, the Central Park zoo, an Italian restaurant in Times Square. For the first time, she attended a Broadway musical. He introduced her to a few of his friends.

They were all the more happy in that the reviews of *Meet Me in St. Louis* were excellent. All the papers lauded Minnelli's direction, his sense of color, movement, and rhythm. *The New York Times* raved over Judy: "Miss Garland is full of gay exuberance…and sings…with a rich voice that grows riper and more expressive in each new film. Her chortling of "The Trolley Song" puts fresh zip into that inescapable tune, and her romantic singing of a sweet one, "The Boy Next Door," is good for mooning folks." And *Life* magazine put her on its cover.

Meet Me in St. Louis was more than a success: it was one of those triumphs that made movie history. In a few weeks, it had brought in $6.6 million: more than double the gross of *The Wizard of Oz*. Never had MGM won such recognition — except for *Gone with the Wind*, but that was a Selznick production. Judy had no choice but to make a public apology to Freed, who had backed the project against all odds.

"Arthur," she said, "remind me to never again tell you what movies I should make."

Meet Me in St. Louis remained her favorite film till the day she died.

★

When Judy decided to move in with Vincente Minnelli, Ethel couldn't help but meddle by writing a furious letter to the filmmaker. She reproached him for not having wanted to wait and for not sufficiently taking care of her daughter's interests.

Their wedding, however, was taking shape. In early January, they announced their engagement and Judy sported the ring Vincente had offered her. A most singular piece of jewelry: a pink rose set on an onyx backdrop designed by the filmmaker himself. No one was surprised in that everyone had gotten used to seeing them together. But many people were perplexed. For, Vincente Minnelli could not be said to be perfect marrying material, the marrying kind, as they say. Why was he still a bachelor? Everyone in Hollywood had noticed his mannerisms and effeminate ways. When he got to MGM, he hadn't hesitated to wear makeup: mascara, eye shadow, makeup foundation. His collaborator Hank Moonjean said: "He was 98% woman and 2% man. I'm talking about the way he walked, the way he dressed, the way he smoked. But I never saw him make advances on anyone or anything inappropriate."

Was he gay? One thing is certain: he had been at some point. During his New York years, he was out of the closet. It was known that he had had a long-term relation with one of the figures on the arts scene, Lester Gaba, even though they had never shared the same apartment. But New York was New York. More anonymous, thus more liberated. Hollywood, on the other hand, was a micro-society where homosexuality remained frowned upon. Did Vincente Minnelli suppress this side of himself to give himself every chance of succeeding at the very conservative MGM, which didn't hesitate to arrange marriages in name only for its gay stars? Had he used Judy Garland to advance his own career, as the gossip had insinuated.

Even if two young Hollywood actors confided that they had had discreet affairs with him, Minnelli also had a fling with the African-American actress Lena Horne during the making of *Cabin in the Sky*. A secret romance it took until 1965 for her to reveal in her memoirs, for the United States, even in Los Angeles, was still segregated. In 1940, when Hattie McDaniel, the servant in *Gone with the Wind*, was nominated for an Oscar as best supporting actor, it was necessary to grant her an exemption in that the Ambassador Hotel where the ceremony took place was reserved for Whites only…

Was it Lena Horne who brought out his taste for women? In that he had just turned forty, might he have wanted to fall into line and start a family? But clearly, Vincente Minnelli never viewed his marriage to Judy as a last resort. But never did he ever talk about his homosexuality: his motivations will forever remain his secret. It was impossible, nonetheless, to believe that Judy wasn't in the know: do-gooders maintain they had warned her.

It is tempting, of course, to draw a parallel between the filmmaker and Frank Gumm. It is the wrong track: at the time, Judy knew nothing about her father's homosexual past. It was only at the end of the 1950s, getting wind of rumors about the matter, that she asked Dr. Marc Rabwin to tell her the truth. Who, considering that she was already rather fragile, preferred to deny it…

★

MGM, which up to then did its best to torpedo her romances, viewed the announcement of her engagement to Minnelli rather approvingly. Because Judy was now older. Because Vincente was a house director, which perpetuated the idea that the studio was a big family. Because they thought that Minnelli could bring her the stability she was short on. Last but not least, because Judy regularly let it be known that she was not going to renew her contract when it expired: she missed the contact with the public and she dreamed of a career on Broadway. She opened herself most notably up to Louella Parsons, who hastened to relate her conversation to Louis. B. Mayer. For MGM, this couple was insurance on the future. With a husband getting the very best out of her on screen, Judy would be less inclined to leave Hollywood. With MGM, cynicism was never far off.

In early June 1945, Judy had finished filming *The Harvey Girls*, a strange hybrid between a western and a musical, and Vincente had completed *Yolanda and the Thief*. *The Clock* had just been released and the reviews were glowing. "To say that Judy Garland is superb is a euphemism. She no longer needs to sing and dance," wrote the *New York Daily Mirror*, whereas as James Agee, in *The Nation*, deemed that "the film proves, for the first time, that she could be an actress who was full of sensitivity." With grosses close to $2.8 million for a cost of $1.3 million, the movie was profitable; but in that earnings were considerably less than those of her latest musicals, MGM never again asked her to do another purely dramatic role.

One week after her divorce from David Rose became official, the two lovebirds wed on Friday, June 15, at 3 P.M. The ceremony took place in the Wilshire neighborhood at the new house of Ethel, who had sold Stone Canyon. The witnesses were Betty Asher, for Judy, and Ira Gershwin, for Vincente. The bridegroom wore a gray dress, designed by Irene Gibbons, the head costume designer at the studio, with long sleeves decorated with pink pearls, which matched her engagement ring. All of MGM's higher-ups were there, from Arthur Freed to Howard Strickling, not to forget Ida Koverman. Louis B. Mayer had unambiguously asked to accompany Judy to the improvised altar where the Reverend William E. Roberts officiated. It was a way of reminding people that he had been, the last few years, like a father to her.

As Minnelli summed it up so well: "We were married before God, but also with the blessing of our boss, whom some feared much more than the Lord."

Louis B. Mayer, Judy Garland, and Vincente Minnelli at the couple's wedding on June 15, 1945.

Vincente Minnelli and Judy Garland, newlyweds.

12.

Vacation in New York

As a wedding present, MGM offered Judy Garland and Vincente Minnelli three months of time off.

For their honeymoon, the couple chose New York. "The most beautiful moment of our marriage," stated Minnelli. This time, she wouldn't have to go to a hotel. Vincente had sublet a three-floor penthouse on Sutton Place, between Midtown and the Upper East Side, with a servant and cook. It was a small paradise: from their plant-filled terrace, they could watch the sun rise over the East River.

Vincente Minnelli and Judy Garland in New York on their honeymoon.

It was summer, and it was hot, very hot, but Manhattan was more effervescent than ever: two days after arriving, the city was jubilant about celebrating the return of General Eisenhower, the man who had organized the Normandy landing and defeated Hitler's troops. Four million New Yorkers hailed him by waiving flags. In August, the surrender of Japan, flattened after the Hiroshima and Nagasaki bombardments, was met with cries of joy. World War II was over, and the boys would be coming home, so a wind of lightness and optimism had descended onto the city.

In Los Angeles, no one would ever ask for autographs of stars: they were a dime a dozen. In New York, on the other hand, Judy's fans were thrilled to cross paths with their idol on the street corner. They approached her head-on with the familiarity one reserves for those one saw grow up:

"Hi, Judy." "Is it really you?" "How's my little girl doing?"

Aware that in people's imagination she was still the little girl she no longer wanted to be, Judy always responded to greetings with warmth and generosity.

One evening, while parking in front of a night club, admirers gathered around their car. Frightened, Gobo, Vincente's poodle, escaped through the windows that were open because of the heat wave. Naturally, Judy's admirers joined in looking for him, but Gobo couldn't be found. Back at the apartment, Judy called the police, who also bent over backwards to find the animal… as if no one wanted to see Dorothy from *The Wizard of Oz* separated from her cherished Toto.

Every evening, Judy and Vincente attended a show or went out to dinner. Sometimes, they had guests. New York intellectuals, who were rather elitist, tended to look down their noses at moviemaking, contemptuous of an art that was too mainstream and out of bitterness at not having been sought after by rich Hollywood. Vincente was delighted at the welcome reserved for his young wife: "They were expecting to meet a rose-colored Judy, just like the studio had sold her. They discovered an explosive and corrosive personality. Her self-deprecation pleased them in particular." It was a dimension that was overlooked in Judy Garland: her humor and her insolence. She was fooled by nothing, above all not by her success.

More acrimonious, however, was her dinner with Lester Gaba. Vincente wanted to present his old buddy to Judy. However, he had not gotten over Vincente's departure for Hollywood, which precipitated their separation. He understood that he had become a stranger in his new life. Bringing up this dinner in front of friends brought tears to his eyes in later years. Vincente Minnelli had forever remained the love of his life.

Lester Gaba, sculptor, writer, and retail display designer, who is said to have had a relation with Vincente Minnelli before he went to Hollywood.

Far from Culver City, the young newlyweds still remained in contact with MGM. Arthur Freed informed them of the projects he had planned on their return. And one day, to their great surprise, they got a call from Nicholas Schenck. Formerly a newspaper salesman, he now presided over Loew's, which was the majority stockholder in MGM. He never intervened in artistic decisions, a domain reserved for Louis B. Mayer, but he wanted to meet his star couple. Better yet: he proposed to them an excursion to Tiffany's, the Fifth Avenue jeweler.

"Metro wants to offer you a wedding gift. Chose whatever you like…"

Being a young, well-educated woman, Judy pointed out a modest brooch in gold.

"Are you kidding?" retorted the austere Schenck. "Chose something that is livelier…"

In other words: more expensive. Judy complied and set her sights on a bracelet decorated with diamonds and emeralds. As for Vincente, he left with a gold-bracelet wristwatch.

★

Since starting shooting *Meet Me in St. Louis*, Vincente Minnelli had noticed Judy's mood swings. Moments of euphoria alternated with moments of dejection. She arrived late on a regular basis. In order to film the Christmas scene, which brought together one hundred fifty extras, she was called for eight in the morning. At nine, she hadn't shown up. At ten, eleven, twelve: still the same. Alerted, Arthur Freed came down to the set: ordinarily, she always gave advance warning. That day, she finally appeared at one. Rather than scold her, Arthur Freed just asked her, with a hand on her shoulder:

"What happened to my little girl?"

But he knew the reason better than anyone: the MGM doctor had continued to prescribe her pills. He also knew that by regularly taking them, Judy's body could no longer keep up. She, on her own initiative, talked about her addiction to Vincente:

"These pills invigorate me…"

"I know…"

"And allow me to be my best in front of the camera."

"I blame you for nothing, just don't take too many!"

Just once, in New York, Minnelli allowed himself to be tempted by these "magic pills." He had too much work. A friend gave him some Benzedrine pills. In no time at all, he was back in shape. But he hadn't forgotten the withdrawal symptoms…

Those three months in New York were for Judy like a weaning. *The Harvey Girls*, the movie she made just before getting married, was her twentieth feature film since *Broadway Melody of 1938*. A musical wasn't an ordinary movie. One had to act, sing, dance; but, before shooting, one also had to pre-record the songs, arrange the choreography, rehearse for days and days. All that requires considerable energy and, above all, stamina, which was a mix of endurance and strength.

In New York, Judy had no schedule, no pressure, no constraints. She was revitalized as never before.

One evening, when walking with Vincente next to the East River, she took his hand. With the other hand, she took out of her bag a bottle full of pills and threw it into the water. It was as if she had turned a page in her life. She was done with these medications which she knew were poisoning her life, in every sense of the word. At the very least, she wanted to believe those words.

★

A week before returning to Los Angeles, a Park Avenue doctor confirmed to Judy what she guessed: she was pregnant.

The spouses decided to keep the news to themselves in order to enjoy the last days of their honeymoon. But, barely back in California, Judy informed her mother. Icy silence.

"Is that okay with you?" she asked.

In reality, she couldn't care less about her mother's response. She was married. She didn't owe her anything. She was free.

On the other hand, she feared the reaction of MGM which had several projects lined up for her, most notably one of the leads in *Till the Clouds Roll By*, a musical biopic about composer Jerome Kern. The studio had never shown any patience regarding her. But Arthur Freed welcomed the news with warmth. He ordered that the shooting schedule be adjusted so that Judy's sequences be filmed before the others: the actress warned him that, in her family, pregnant women had a tendency to take on weight…

Although Richard Whorf was named director of *Till the Clouds Roll By*, Freed asked Minnelli to do the scenes with Judy, most notably the three dance numbers. Rehearsals began starting from mid–September and the shoot would last until November 7. She was in her fifth month, and it began to show. What's more, Minnelli showed great skill in concealing it. For the song "Who?" she comes down a staircase clothed in a yellow dress, hiding her figure under a shawl, at the same time that the dancers spun around her in the foreground. "If I had to continue, I think I would not have been able to," she confided to Dottie Ponedel. "The child in my belly would have come out of my belly button!"

MGM accepted to continue paying Judy's salary during her maternity leave. A favor. Thenceforth, she could devote herself to her new role: mother. Having chosen to live in Minnelli's house at 8850 Evanview Drive, the couple bought the neighboring lot for an expansion. Judy did her best to play the role of the perfect housewife. One day, Vincente discovered her on her knees, scrubbing the floor; on another day, she cooked a chicken fricassee by scrupulously following a recipe. The director was amused: "If I had wanted a super-housewife, I would have married Betty Crocker!" With the staff, Judy was more pal than boss, leaving the role of disciplinarian to Vincente, which usually finished in uncontrollable laughter.

8850 Evanview Drive in Hollywood Hills, where Minnelli and Garland lived.

★

Since her honeymoon in New York, Judy hadn't taken any more medication. It was important to her that her baby be born healthy. But the more the due date got closer, the more she seemed depressed. When the columnist Hedda Hopper suggested in late January that she organize a party where only the men with whom she had worked be invited — actors, directors, choreographers, etc. — she declined the offer:

"Forget me for now. At the end of March, I will be back in shape."

In agreement with her doctor, she chose to give birth by cesarean. On March 8, 1946, Vincente Minnelli accompanied her to Cedars-Sinai, and on the 12th, at 7:58 A.M., she gave birth to a seven-pound baby. If it had been a boy, they would have baptized him Vincente Jr. But it was a girl, and she would be named Liza, in tribute to the Gershwin song. When her pregnancy was announced, some snickered, implying that the child was the fruit of immaculate conception; but her black hair and long eyelashes left no doubt about the father's identity.

Judy's post–partum depression — or baby blues, a symptom well-known to doctors — was particularly severe. In the morning, she had difficulty getting up and didn't leave the house. At the end of April, she tried to go out, but felt faint on the Sunset Boulevard sidewalk. Her doctor advised her to stay in bed. In view of the growing concern in the Hollywood community, she consented to giving an interview to the *Los Angeles Times*: "I never felt better in my life," she declared. Pretend, always pretend…in the eyes of the press, stars didn't have the right to the least weakness.

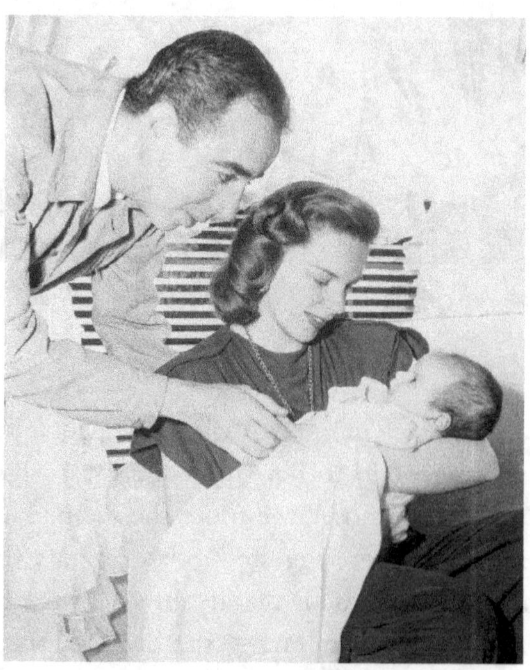

Vincente, Judy, and Liza May Minnelli.

But Judy Garland would not publicly reappear before July 20, 1946. That day, at the Hollywood Bowl, she interpreted three songs in tribute to Jerome Kern, who had died on November 11 the year before. A kind of live trailer for *Till the Clouds Roll By*, his biopic, whose release was scheduled for the holidays.

During the fall, she made do with recording records and participating in radio shows. MGM showed itself to be surprisingly patient towards her. It was true that she had begun renegotiating her contract. The Culver City firm was obsessed with the idea of losing her, but Judy, despite her dreaming of Broadway and her hard feelings towards a studio that had exploited her shamelessly since her childhood, was set on renewing her affiliation so as to stay close to her husband. MGM had — finally! — aligned her salary to that of the other house stars: $5,600 a week. And she obtained that Dottie Ponedel be her personal assistant. To announce the news, the columnist Louella Parsons wrote: "Judy has always said that she was at home at MGM and, in the end, where is one best off but at home, even when one is a movie star?" But was she really at home at MGM?

Judy Garland and The Merry Macs recording "On The Atchison, Topeka And The Santa Fe" for Decca. Judy's next film for MGM is "The Harvey Girls."

While in New York on her honeymoon, Judy Garland, on the far right, recorded four sides for Decca Records, including two on July 7, 1945 with The Merry Macs, "On the Atchison, Topeka and the Santa Fe" and "If I Had You."

13.

First Treatment

In early December, after thirteen months away, Judy returned to the Culver City studios for fittings for her next film. Once again, she was to be directed by Vincente Minnelli. He had had an idea of a new setting for her: adapting the play *The Pirate*, a farce by S.N. Behrmann first performed by Alfred Lunt and Lynn Fontanne on Broadway in 1943, into a musical. In the Caribbean, in the 19th century, a young woman, Manuela, who only dreams of adventure, is betrothed to the ultra-rich but potbellied village mayor. To seduce her, an entertainer on tour decides to pretend to be the famous pirate *Macoco*, nicknamed "Mack the Black"…

In this framework of a story, Minnelli imagined a phantasmagoria that would be flamboyant and tumultuous. Very involved in preparing the movie, he worked and reworked the script, persuaded Cole Porter to compose the music, and designed some of the costumes. The budget was big, and the director was convinced that the duo Judy Garland–Gene Kelly, for whom this would be their first musical together since *For Me and My Gal*, would cause sparks to fly.

Alas, nothing went as planned. Because of Judy. Despite her worthy resolutions, straight off she had the hardest time being on time. Sometimes, she went home in the middle of the day. The more the filming advanced, the more she was absent for one day, sometimes two, even three, while dozens of extras waited for her on the set.

Vincente even suggested that she return to consult with Dr. Simmel. "I have told him so many stories up to now that I am incapable of telling fact from fiction," she confided to Dottie.

Vincente did his best to adapt the shooting schedule to the star's absences. In addition to being accommodating, he tried to be the most reassuring possible. But his tender words were not enough. "Harsh words were exchanged. Our relationship became more and more hostile." Sometimes, in the evening, Vincente found it necessary to go away. He preferred to go sleep on the couch of their friends Ira and Lee Gershwin, who didn't live far away. When it wasn't Judy who went there, telling Vincente:

"After all, this is your house."

Judy Garland, Gene Kelly, Arthur Freed, and Vincente Minnelli on the set of the 1948 MGM musical, The Pirate.

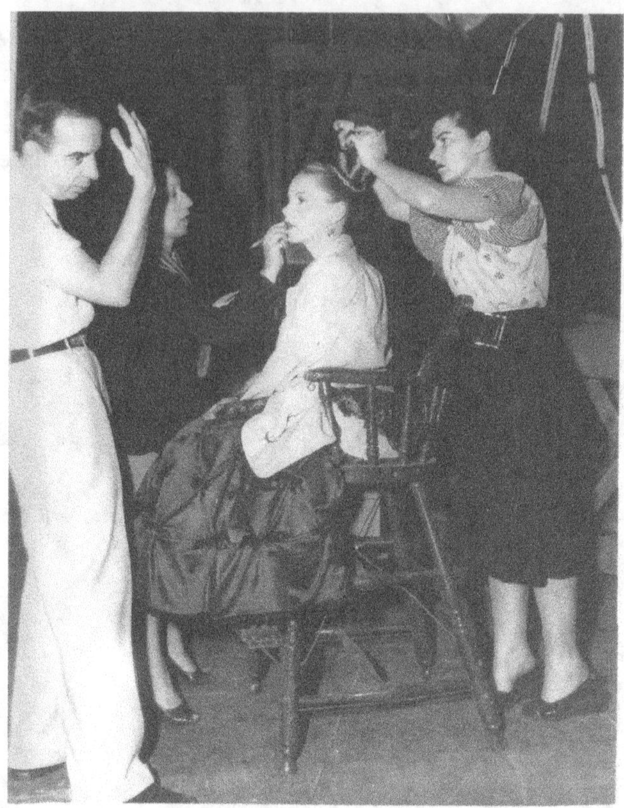

Vincente Minnelli gives directions to Judy Garland as Dottie Ponedel touches up Garland's make-up.

★

Judy had thus gone back to the medication. "I'm appalled by my naiveté at the time," Minnelli confessed in his memoirs. "I thought love would show us the way out of the quagmire. My most serious mistake was misinterpreting Judy's intense infatuations and violent swinging of moods as an exuberance for life. I was blind to the compulsiveness of her behavior for too long a time."

It was true that her pills never lasted long in the bathroom cabinet. "I was incapable of finding out who was supplying her," commented Vincente. In Hollywood, it wasn't complicated getting hold of them. Was it Benzedrine? Or something else? Whatever the case, her paranoiac crises were becoming more common: Judy constantly had the impression that everyone wanted to betray her. To Hedda Hopper, who was present for the shoot, she confided that everyone who ever loved her had now turned against her and that her mother had even bugged her phone: "She is doing everything she can to destroy me!" She needed to be removed from the set and accompanied home without taking off her makeup. Hedda Hopper had to wait to write her memoirs before ever recounting the incident, as the studio insisted.

Everything became a pretext to argue, starting with the privileged relation between Vincente and Gene Kelly. The two of them made a good pair: they were perfectly complementary.

"…my approach is less esoteric and more gutsy, while yours is evanescent and ethereal," Gene Kelly said to him one day.

His role in the film got thicker as Judy's absences continued.

"You and Vincente are having a lot of fun," she reproached to Gene Kelly one day. "You're both ignoring me. Well, how about doing something for me? Will you stage my numbers?"

"How about Vincente?"

"No, I want *you* to do it."

Completely losing it, she even insinuated that they were having an affair. Still, Gene Kelly did everything to help her, just as Judy had helped him with Busby Berkeley during filming on *For Me and My Gal*. To the point that one day, he pretended to be sick in order to delay filming scenes that Judy was incapable of doing…

One sign of fatigue in Judy's eyes, an inflection in her voice, and Vincente would be worried. Distraught, overwhelmed, devoured by his guilt at perhaps not being attentive enough to her, he became aware of a wall going up between them. "We continued working, Judy's cool behavior toward me a damning accusation. I was too much in turmoil, and too hurt, to talk it out," he wrote in his memoirs. Minnelli was a man of compromise: he detested conflicts.

At MGM, they gasped at the film's delays. It soon became apparent that Minnelli could not stick to schedule. Louis B. Mayer, now convinced of the usefulness of the psychiatrists, wound up hiring a second analyst, he too of Viennese origin, Frederick Hacker. Every time Judy went through the studio gate, he followed her step by step, making sure she was handled with kid gloves, ready to intervene should she totally collapse from some kind of crisis. It was a first in movie history, all the more incredible in that Louis B. Mayer was personally paying her salary.

But Dr. Hacker couldn't watch over Judy at home. Shortly before finishing filming *The Pirate*, she locked herself in the magnificent bathroom Vincente had designed for her and began to cut her wrists. Alarmed by her wailing, Vincente managed to open the door. Was it a call for help or real desire to end it all? The following days, Judy emerged with bandages on her wrists. To counterattack the rumors that had begun to spread, Louella Parsons wrote that Judy Garland was suffering from "moral fatigue," but denied any plans of a separation from Vincente.

On July 17, at the end of a marathon day, the film was finally in the can. If MGM's archives are to be believed, Judy Garland missed ninety-four days out of the one hundred thirty she was supposed to be present for.

★

Strange shift: Vincente Minnelli, whom Judy considered like a protector, had become her enemy. She no longer saw him as a husband, but the incarnation of MGM, this sprawling monster which had never stopped sucking the lifeblood out of her since she was thirteen. Wasn't it because of it that she was forced to sign this new contract which, however advantageous it may have been, kept her in this golden prison? She who only dreamt about having a go at a Broadway career…

There was no more talking possible between them. Once filming *The Pirate* was over, she never left her bedroom. She didn't sleep anymore, didn't get up anymore, didn't eat anymore. Nervous breakdown. Major depression. It was necessary to hospitalize her in Las Campanas, in the south of Los Angeles. A rehab clinic, as they say today: a detox center costing $300 a day, with pretty white bungalows surrounded by vast lawns.

Arriving there at night, she collapsed soon after getting out of the car. The nurses helped her up, but she fell again, stumbled again. They thought she was drunk: she discovered the next day that she had kept stumbling on the cricket wickets. A hundred times, a thousand times, she retold the anecdote to reminisce about her "first stay in the nuthouse," according to her expression: black humor, a polite form of despair. Concerning the "nuts," she soon discovered that the patients weren't crazy, but "desperately tired."

Every day, the staff went over her room with a fine-tooth comb. However much she protested that she had no drugs or alcohol, the search was systematic.

"Mama has gone away for a few days, she'll be back," said Vincente to their small Liza, then sixteen months old.

At Las Campanas, Judy insisted on seeing her. At first, they refused the visit, but then gave in. The joy of seeing her again was soon wiped out by the pain of seeing her go: As soon as Liza left, Judy threw herself on the bed and cried. "I had naturally known moments of sadness in my life, but never like this," she said.

After weaning her from the medication, Dr. Herbert Kupper suggested that she be transferred in early August to a clinic that was better equipped to treat her angst: the Riggs Foundation, in the small postcard village of Stockbridge, Massachusetts.

Formerly a student of Dr. Menninger, Dr. Robert P. Knight was a solid and friendly fellow, renowned for his contributions to scientific reviews on the difference between neurosis and psychosis. But treating depression, at that time, was still in its infancy. The first antidepressants had to wait until 1957 to come on the market. Furthermore, Judy, who had not appreciated being so shut off during her stay at Las Campanas, managed to convince Dr. Kupper to accompany her: he could stay in a hotel opposite the clinic. Despite his presence, the actress was bored stiff and, fifteen days after her arrival, asked to go home.

"It's too calm here," she explained to Dr. Knight.

"When you don't hear any noise around you, the noise inside you becomes deafening," he replied to her.

Fifteen days after arriving in Massachusetts, she returned home on Evanview Drive.

From left to right, Frances (Judy Garland), Suzanne, and Virginia, billed as The Gumm Sisters, in their first screen appearance, The Big Revue, *filmed on June 11, 12, and 13, 1929 for Mayfair Pictures at Tec-Art Studio, perform "That's The Good Old Sunny South." Filmed using an optical track, the short and soundtrack survive to this day.*

Judy Garland filmed "The Land of Let's Pretend" with her sisters, The Gumm Sisters, in the 1929 Technicolor Vitaphone short Bubbles. *The young Frances Gumm has a 2-line solo — "We'll weave a life of dreams, With threads from bright moonbeams" — and close-up in the film which was found in a black-and-white print at the Library of Congress in the early 1990s. The two other 1929 Vitaphone shorts,* A Holiday in Storyland *and* The Wedding of Jack and Jill, *The Gumm Sisters made are no longer extant, although the Vitaphone discs are.*

Judy Garland sings "It's Love I'm After" from the 1936 musical Pigskin Parade. *Already under contract since 1935 to MGM, which had no role to offer her at the time, the studio loaned her out to 20th Century-Fox for this movie, which was her first feature film in which she was last on the cast roster of stars. And it proved to be a big hit, with Stuart Erwin garnering an Oscar nomination as Best Actor in a Supporting Role. Never released as a Garland single and never again sung by her, the song was covered by the great jazz singer Mildred Bailey that same year on a Vocalion 78rpm.*

Judy Garland sang "Singin' in the Rain" in the 1940 MGM musical Little Nellie Kelly. *Although far less known than the classic 1952 Gene Kelly version from the MGM film of the same name, Garland's interpretation of the Nacio Herb Brown-Arthur Freed song is still one for the ages.*

Judy Garland sings "(Dear Mr. Gable) You Made Me Love You" to a photo of Clark Gable in MGM's Broadway Melody of 1938. *This was her first signature moment on screen.*

Recorded on October 7, 1938 and filmed by director King Vidor in late February-early March 1939, "Over the Rainbow," composed by Harold Arlen and E.Y. Harburg, was introduced by Judy Garland in MGM's The Wizard of Oz *and would forever be associated with her.*

Judy Garland sings "Minnie from Trinidad," composed by Garland mentor Roger Edens, from the 1941 MGM musical Ziegfeld Girl *in a sequence directed by Busby Berkeley.*

Judy Garland and Gene Kelly sing "Ballin' the Jack" in the 1942 MGM musical For Me and My Gal, *directed by Busby Berkeley. This was Kelly's first film, and it was the first of three times Garland and he worked together.*

Mickey Rooney, Judy Garland, and Tommy Dorsey and His Orchestra team up on "I Got Rhythm," the great George and Ira Gershwin number from the 1943 MGM musical Girl Crazy *in a sequence directed by Busby Berkeley.*

Judy Garland sings "Have Yourself a Merry Little Christmas," composed by Hugh Martin and Ralph Blane, from the 1944 MGM musical Meet Me in St. Louis, *directed by Vincente Minnelli.*

Robert Walker and Judy Garland in a publicity still for the 1945 MGM film The Clock, *directed by Vincente Minnelli. This was Garland's one and only non-singing role for the studio.*

Judy Garland with Ray Bolger in the famous sequence of "On the Atchison, Topeka, and the Santa Fe," composed by Harry Warren and Johnny Mercer, for the 1946 MGM musical The Harvey Girls. *The song went on to win an Oscar as Best Original Song of the year.*

Gene Kelly and Judy Garland perform Cole Porter's "Be a Clown" from the 1948 MGM musical The Pirate, *which was directed by Vincente Minnelli. A commercial failure upon its release, the film is today considered one of Garland's and Minnelli's best.*

Fred Astaire and Judy Garland perform "A Couple of Swells," an Irving Berlin song, in the 1948 MGM musical Easter Parade, *which was the highest-grossing musical film of 1948 and the second-highest grossing MGM musical of the 1940s, after* Meet Me in St. Louis. *This was their only pairing on screen.*

Mickey Rooney and Judy Garland sing "I Wish I Were in Love Again," a composition by Richard Rodgers and Lorenz Hart, from the 1948 MGM musical Words and Music. *Garland had previously recorded the song for Decca Records in 1947, this time alone. After all the MGM films they appeared in together, this was the last time they reunited in an MGM musical.*

Judy Garland performs "Get Happy," a song first composed by Harold Arlen and Ted Koehler in 1930, from the 1950 MGM musical, Summer Stock, *which was Garland's last film at MGM. Recorded on March 15, 1950 and filmed from mid- to late-March 1950, the song and sequence were also the last she ever did at the studio.*

Judy Garland sings "Swanee" from the "Born in a Trunk" sequence in the 1954 Warner Bros. musical drama, A Star Is Born. *Recorded on June 14, 1954 and filmed between June 30 and July 7, 1954, the song was written in 1919 by George Gershwin and Irving Caesar, and was most often associated with Al Jolson. Gershwin's first hit, it was first recorded by Garland in 1939 for Decca Records, and she performed it for the rest of her life, including at Carnegie Hall on April 23, 1961.*

Judy Garland, taking the stand in the 1961 Judgment at Nuremberg, *directed by Stanley Kramer, in the second non-musical role of her career after* The Clock, *plays Irene Hoffmann, who is accused of having a relationship with a Jewish man during World War II. The performance earned her an Oscar nomination for Best Supporting Actress.*

Judy Garland and Burt Lancaster in a scene from John Cassavetes' 1963 A Child Is Waiting, *which was Garland's third and last straight dramatic role in movies. The film, in which she plays a music teacher and Lancaster the headmaster at a school for mentally handicapped children, lost money upon its release. Cassavetes also disavowed it in that he did not have control over the final cut.*

Judy Garland belts "I Could Go on Singin'" in the last sequence from the 1963 musical drama, I Could Go On Singing, *directed by Ronald Neame. The title song was composed by Harold Arlen and E.Y. Harburg, who also wrote "Over the Rainbow" in 1938. The film, which co-starred Dirk Bogarde, bombed and Garland's screen career ended with this opus in which she gives a stunning performance better appreciated today than in 1963.*

147

14.

Salary Deduction

This hasty return home was madness. And what was even crazier was that barely a month later MGM called her in to make a new movie, *Easter Parade*: with seventeen songs – including eight new ones – composed by the brilliant Irving Berlin. Gene Kelly was to be her co-star, under the direction of Vincente Minnelli. A story of Pygmalion: in 1912, in belle époque New York, a vaudevillian dancer promises to make a star out of a woman he met in a bar. He buys her new clothes, teaches her how to dance. They are a triumph in a show that opens just before Easter.

"I think Gene and you are going to make something grandiose," she threw out to her husband.

According to Minnelli's memoirs, Judy returned from Massachusetts in splendid shape.

"Stay with me," she said to him in the morning, when he was leaving for MGM to prepare *Easter Parade*. "Don't work today."

It was as if nothing had happened. Everyone was in denial. Only Dr. Kupper showed any responsibility: by reconstituting the team from *The Pirate*, Judy risked a relapse. For her stability, it was essential that she be directed by another director rather than Minnelli.

Five days before the beginning of rehearsals, Arthur Freed called in his favorite director:

"Vincente, I don't know how to tell you this…"

"Please do."

"Judy's psychiatrist thinks it best that you not direct the movie."

"And why?"

"He thinks that Judy doesn't want you to make it. You symbolize in her eyes all her entanglements with the studio."

Freed's tone of voice was more than embarrassed. It was affectionate, but firm:

"It would be best that you withdraw."

Minnelli accepted, disconcerted by that fact that Judy had never said a word to him about it. They never brought up the subject again. Between them, from then on, the era of the unsaid had begun.

★

Judy Garland rehearses for Easter Parade *on May 31, 1948 with, from left to right, Louis B. Mayer, Irving Berlin on the piano, and Arthur Freed.*

Choreographer Charles Walters took over the movie at short notice: he had only directed a single film, but Freed trusted him completely and Judy, with whom he had worked on several numbers, did too. But rehearsals had just begun when Gene Kelly broke his ankle on a Saturday morning while playing volleyball. In that it was an emergency, Arthur Freed took a gamble: he contacted Fred Astaire.

Having starred in musicals in the 1930s at RKO, incarnation of the classical style, top hat and polished floors, he had trouble reinventing himself at the beginning of the 1940s and announced his retirement from

149

the movies. At forty-seven, he had the impression that his career was behind him. "I had read so many articles about my upcoming fiftieth birthday that thought I was a cripple," he said. But a musical produced by Arthur Freed with Judy Garland was an opportunity that couldn't be refused: Monday pronto, he showed up at Culver City to sign his contract and start rehearsing, despite Charles Walters' reluctance:

"Do you think the public will applaud when it sees a spring chicken like Judy get involved with a guy who could be her grandfather?"

At first, it was necessary to adapt the choreographies of Fred Astaire, whose dance style was radically different from that of Gene Kelly; but, right off, the king of tap dancing recaptured the ethereal elegance that had made him a legend. Alas, Cyd Charisse in turn had to pull out. Tendon rupture: she was replaced by Ann Miller. With the result that the film's only stitch of stability was none other than… the unstable Judy Garland. She knew Astaire and had participated in a 1943 war bond drive with him, but still, her first day with him was complicated: she stayed in her corner, not daring to speak to him, intimidated, frightened.

"Ah, if only people knew that she was a timid young girl!" he blurted that very evening.

But he knew how to make her feel comfortable and, galvanized by his presence, Judy gave her best, delivering some of her greatest numbers, such as "A Couple of Swells."

Fred Astaire and Judy Garland in the "A Couple of Swells" sequence.

Judy Garland and Fred Astaire in a publicity still for Easter Parade.

Rarely late, rarely absent, she was truly in great shape. And the shoot was completed on schedule, in February. During this period, she even worked again with Vincente Minnelli for retakes on *The Pirate*. There was no incident to report: they acted as if nothing had happened. On a personal level, they also acted "as if." They took care of their little Liza and dined regularly at friends'. Judy didn't hesitate to make fun of her difficulties. "She somehow made the difficult crises we had had funny," recalled Minnelli. "I even was able to laugh at them. I had to learn to adapt to this form of humor."

With her, Vincente, petrified at the idea of saying or doing something that would set off a crisis, had to watch his step. By becoming an outsider in her life, he had definitively lost the role she had assigned to him: that of a guide.

Released on May 20, 1948, *The Pirate* disappointed the critics and public: grossing $2.7 million for a cost of $3.7 million, it was the first time a movie starring Judy Garland lost money. *Easter Parade*, scheduled for release the following June 30, would erase this artistic, human and financial shipwreck: in a few weeks, it made $5.8 million for an investment of $2.6 million. It was her greatest success, outside of that of *Meet Me in St. Louis*. "A first-class movie," wrote Georges Barnes in *The New York Herald Tribune*. "Like fireworks. Fred Astaire is a hoofer more than ever. Miss Garland has truly come into her own."

Judy Garland was still bankable — a safe bet at the box office.

★

You don't change a winning team. Even before the release of *Easter Parade*, MGM already had new project lined up for Judy: another musical with Fred Astaire, *The Barkleys of Broadway*, under the direction of Charles Walters. They were forgetting that a depression not properly treated is a terrifying time bomb.

Judy soldiered on while shooting *Easter Parade*. Once finished, she collapsed. In a few weeks, her weight had dropped to ninety pounds. With Vincente, things weren't any better. Judy started to hate the house on Evanview Drive. Dr. Kupler — who had definitively replaced Dr. Simler, who had died that fall — advised her to live, for the time being, more independently. She therefore rented for $1,000 a month on Sunset Boulevard a large-chimneyed country-style house where she could regularly get away.

To make matters worse, MGM presented her with the bill for her absences during the filming of *The Pirate* and her stays at the clinic: $100,000! How times change: in 1948, MGM made a profit of $4.2 million, the weakest figure since 1933. "There are no bad films at MGM," Louis B. Mayer liked to say. Perhaps, but they weren't making as much as they used to. Too consensual, too family-oriented, they were no longer in phase with a post-war period where mentalities were evolving at full tilt.

In New York, Nicholas Schenck was growing impatient. Is Mayer still the right man for the job? He seemed to devote more time to his racehorses than to developing new projects for the studio. Ordered to find a new assistant, the equivalent of what had been Irving Thalberg for him in the 1930s, the mogul in the end chose Dore Schary, forty-two years old, former screenwriter and producer at MGM, who left to direct production at RKO.

When Carleton Alsop, a close friend of the Garland-Minnelli couple, learned that Judy's salary had been amputated of $100,000, he was disgusted. Formerly a member of the secret service who became a producer of radio shows after having married the actress Sylvia Sidney, he decided to take charge of Judy's affairs and asked Louis B. Mayer for an appointment.

"I don't think this deduction is legal. I'm afraid that only a court could decide the matter…"

In face of the threat, Louis B. Mayer compromised:

"If Judy accepts to film a sequence in *Words and Music*, we will give her a $50,000 bonus."

When Alsop told her about his negotiation, Judy was astonished: no one had ever stood up for her against the studio. In early June, she therefore devoted a week to filming her number: a remake, with her old buddy Mickey Rooney, of "I Wish I Were in Love Again," a song first sung by Grace McDonald in *Babes in Arms*. "She gave it her all, then came and collapsed at our place," Carleton Alsop later told. With his wife Sylvia, who prepared nice meals for her, he got into the habit of welcoming her in their Beverly Drive house whenever she gave out. Judy called him "Pa": he was her new substitute father. Her buttress. All the more so in that Vincente Minnelli was going through a difficult period: since he was let go of *Easter Parade*, the studio had continued to pay him, but only offered him low-level jobs: he filmed actors' screen tests and annotated scripts.

On June 14, rehearsals for *The Barkleys of Broadway* began. On the 21st and 22nd, Judy let it be known that she was sick. On the 30th, idem. Then again from July 7 to 12. Nine days absent in less than one month was too much: Arthur Freed called her doctor. "He told me that she could work four or five days in a row thanks to the medication, have a meltdown for a while, then return to film for a few days," he wrote in a memo. "He was convinced that if they let her rest, she would be able to feel better fairly quickly, but the act of shooting every morning could cause her mental disorders and put her in danger."

Should they delay the shoot? After a meeting on the Thalberg Building's third floor, the decision was made to take drastic action: Judy

Garland was removed from the film. When she learned of the news, she was distraught. She had gotten used to the studio's clemency. She had never imagined they could live without her. She felt all the more betrayed in that the missive confirming her suspension went hand in hand with a suspension of her salary, since she was no longer operational. "The anger turned inward," Minnelli wrote, "seething uncontrollably, threatening to destroy Judy herself… the sweetest and most perverse revenge of them all."

The announcement of Judy's firing made the headlines in the industry newspapers. The star's "fatigue" was euphemistically alluded to. Breaking the code of silence, Jimmy Tarantino wrote in *Hollywood Nightlife,* a scandal sheet, that Judy was a "pill head." To respond, Carleton Alsop suggested that she have dinner in town to show that she was fine. What better place than Romanoff's, the restaurant of the stars, 326 N. Rodeo Drive? That night, no one dared speak with her, except Mike Romanoff, the owner, who pretended not to have read the news.

Hollywood treated her like a pariah. What hypocrisy! For, Judy Garland was far from the only one overindulging in Benzedrine. But that had to remain secret…

15.

Out to Pasture

One step back, two steps forward. Barely a few weeks after having hit bottom, Judy was again ready to work. Carleton Alsop convinced Louis B. Mayer to entrust her with a second number in *Words and Music* for another $50,000, which was a way of wiping away her debt once and for all.

Judy Garland sings a second number, "Johnny One Note," in Words and Music.

Judy seemed to be in shape and… shapely. She had put on around twenty pounds between the two numbers. Making the most of a break in shooting, she ventured onto *The Barkleys of Broadway* set to say hello to the crew, who had been the privileged bystanders of her talent and frailties, and who had worked side by side with her for so many years. But Ginger Rogers, who had replaced her and was cast again with Fred

Astaire for the tenth time, ten years after their last pairing in *The Story of Vernon and Irene Castle*, locked herself in her dressing room and refused to come out as long as Judy was in the vicinity. She was therefore asked to leave the set, thrown out like an intruder. She was home at MGM, but she was no longer welcome. Another humiliation: but, in a certain way, it was this kind of affront that energized her.

Joe Pasternak, her producer on *Presenting Lily Mars*, was the man who was going to get her back on track: he proposed the lead in *In the Good Old Summertime*, a musical version of Ernst Lubitsch's *The Shop Around the Corner*. It was a low-budget movie, a regression by all appearances, but a good opportunity to bounce back and…get back on salary.

"Half dead, you will always be the best" he told her. "Arthur Freed might let you go, but me, I would do anything for you."

Judy Garland sings "I Don't Care" in the 1949 MGM musical In the Good Old Summertime.

Joe Pasternak was a man who cultivated happiness. His musicals were somewhat sugar-coated feel-good movies. And in Pasternak Land, as the office unit over which he officiated was called, an easygoing atmosphere was encouraged. Not only had Joe Pasternak expressly forbidden that the slightest reproach be made to her in case of late arrival or absence, but he

156

also asked that a red rose be placed every morning in her dressing room, accompanied by a note: "Have a good day, Judy." Intrigued, she asked Dottie Ponedel to identify the mysterious admirer, who only revealed his identity once shooting had been completed: Pasternak himself, of course. To establish a family atmosphere, he even suggested that Liza make her screen debut in a small role, that of Judy's own daughter in the last scene.

All this attention had a beneficial effect: shooting was completed five days in advance. "We made sure that she felt wanted and we joked a lot for her to remain in good humor," her co-star Van Johnson told Louis B. Mayer, who was surprised by this spectacular recovery, to say the least.

Reassured by the state of her health, MGM gave Judy the lead in *Annie Get Your Gun*, the film adaptation of Irving Berlin's musical, which had just triumphed on Broadway. This love story between two circus markspersons from Buffalo had a big budget: $3.7 million. But, unlike Pasternak who had done everything to reassure Judy, Arthur Freed chose to ask Busby Berkeley to direct. The man who, in olden days, had made Judy suffer immeasurably. Which reminded him of the times when she used and abused Benzedrine to hold up. And when it was necessary to exfiltrate her from filming *Girl Crazy* after he proved to be cruel with her.

How could a producer who was so aware of Judy's frailty commit such an error? It was a kind of perversity, or at the very least irresponsibility, all the more inexplicable in that Freed pertinently knew that Berkeley, who was more and more alcoholic, was he too not in the best shape. Though Judy tried to express her concerns, he didn't want to hear of it.

In March 1949, the actress thus got started on preparing *Annie Get Your Gun*. During the prerecordings of the songs, her voice was firm, powerful, incomparable. But from the start of shooting, she clashed with a Busby Berkeley, who sorely needed to recognize her limitations.

"This monster treated me like when I was fifteen," she bitterly complained.

Judy Garland in a 1949 rush of "I'm an Indian Too" from Annie Get Your Gun.

When she saw the rushes, she was crushed. Now used to making films with directors who knew how to make her beautiful, give her a touch of glamor, she had the impression of going backwards. Thrown off, she began again to arrive late, to cancel. She had a migraine, she gave as justification. Actually, she was back on medication. She was losing weight and her hair. "I can hear the hair fall on the floor," she joked. Unable to get to sleep, she spent her nights on the phone. A new doctor, Dr. Fred Pobirs, convinced her to undergo six electroshocks, which rather than making things better, made them worse.

Costume test photos of Judy Garland for Annie Get Your Gun *taken in 1949.*

In the end, Freed replaced Busby Berkeley — not because he didn't know how to handle Judy, but because his directing left a lot to be desired. Charles Walters, called in to replace him, was devastated by the rushes already filmed: "It was horrible! Judy had never been worse." But his arrival came too late: Judy was completely exhausted, morally and physically. Even when the camera was running, she was haggard, a ghost, as if lost.

On May 10, after several phone calls to warn that she would be late, Judy arrived on the set at 11:18 A.M. to film the song "I'm an Indian Too." After the lunch break, an official message on MGM letterhead stationery was handed to her in person:

DEAR MISS GARLAND:

You must be aware of the fact that your contract with us requires you to be prompt in complying with out instructions and to perform your services conscientiously and to the full extent of your ability and as instructed by us.

We desire to call your attention to the fact that on a great many occasions since the commencement of your services in "ANNIE GET YOUR GUN," you were either late in arriving on the set in the morning, late in arriving on the

159

set after lunch, or were otherwise responsible for substantial delays or curtailed production, all without our consent. The damage to us due to these infractions of your obligations under your contract with us is very substantial…

In view of the accumulated delays, Dore Schary took things in hand. He was a cold man, without misgivings, whose only goal was to replace Louis B. Mayer as head of the studio. Champion of movies that were based on the real world, he abhorred musicals, except when he read the balance sheets of the Freed Unit. In favor of cutting costs before it was too late, he called Nicholas Schenck in New York to get the nod on the option of replacing Judy. Schenck's laconic response was: "Do what you have to."

This message was thus more than a warning: it was a trap. In which Judy, needless to say, was going to walk right into. In full fit of hysteria, she refused to continue shooting, "not now, not ever." Which were exactly the words Dore Schary's emissaries wanted to hear.

Dottie Ponedel managed to calm her down. The time was ill-chosen to put herself at fault. Judy agreed to leave her dressing room. She had barely gone through the studio gate before she saw actors, dancers, and other technicians going the other way.

"Where are they going?" she asked Al Jennings, the first assistant.

"They're leaving. We're finished…"

"Tell them to come back."

"Too late."

MGM had taken Judy at her word and interrupted filming. She never filmed "now or ever" the rest of *Annie Get Your Gun*: a new message awaited her saying that she had been removed from the film and that her salary was thenceforth suspended. Two days later, MGM replaced her with Betty Hutton.

★

At heart, Louis B. Mayer was a softy. Known to burst into tears watching the melodramas he produced, he was devastated by the fate of his "little hunchback." Of course, he had put her through hell: but, from his point of view, it was always for her good. Judy Garland never stopped being his protégée. His creature. By ejecting her from *Annie Get Your Gun,* Dore Schary gave her no choice. Mayer experienced it as a crushing personal defeat: was he still the boss in Culver City?

"What can I do to help Judy?" he asked Carleton Alsop.

Judy Garland and Carleton Alsop at The Mocambo, 1949

Alsop suggested that Judy distance herself from Hollywood and the doctors who were drowning her with pills. Louis B. Mayer acquiesced and suggested an establishment in Boston. To sort out the financial aspect — for, Judy had no savings, Carleton organized a meeting between the mogul and the downfallen star.

"The least we can do is to pay her hospital bill," declared Mayer.

Picking up the phone, he called Nicolas Schenck to ratify the proposition. As the conversation went on, his face sunk. After hanging up, he let out:

"Mr. Schenck suggests that you go to a hospital for charity cases because 'we aren't a loan office'."

Silence, a look at Judy, and he added:

"You know, if they can do this to you, they can do the same to me."

From that moment on, the king was naked.

Having threatened to pay the bill himself, Louis B. Mayer ended up getting MGM to cover the $40,000 hospital bill. And on May 27, Judy Garland took the train for Boston, accompanied by the faithful Carleton Alsop, for a new medical leave. At Peter Bent Brigham Hospital, she wasn't treated by a shrink — she had known a good dozen and not one had ever reconciled her with herself, but by a neurologist, Dr. Rose. His verdict: she needed to re-learn how to live normally. To eat, sleep. "It will come back," he assured. No pills, but three good meals at regular mealtimes and, each evening at nine o'clock the lights went out, whether she wanted to sleep or not.

Judy, who then weighed barely eighty pounds, lent herself to this rhythm willingly. She truly wanted to get better. A week after her arrival, she gave a press conference in the form of an outing.

"Without a doubt, I have taken too many sleeping pills," she declared, "but who in Hollywood didn't? Working on a set is so exhausting that at night one can't even get to sleep. But, not sleeping means that, the next day, you are incapable of picking up where you left off because your face will show the traces of this sleepless night. So, what to do…?"

In passing, she announced her separation from Vincente Minnelli, who was then filming *Madame Bovary* — MGM had finally given him a new film.

★

On June 6, 1949, Garland entered Peter Brent Brigham Hospital in Boston to "cure her dependency on prescribed medication," in the words of biographer Scott Schechter.

Liza Minnelli and Judy Garland on the beach on Cape Cod, Massachusetts, for the Independence Day holiday, 1949.

For the July 4th weekend, Judy, with actress Sylvia Sidney, the wife of Carleton Alsop, spent three days on Cape Cod with Liza, who had been brought to the East Coast by her nanny. Frank Sinatra, with whom Judy had had an affair the last few weeks, had flowers delivered to her every day. Once, he even visited her, bringing flowers, perfumes, records, and a record player. Insofar as Ethel and Judy's sisters, they were conspicuous by their absence: not a single phone call.

At the end of July, *In the Good Old Summertime* was released on screens. The reviews were glowing: the picture grossed $3.5 million, whereas it cost $1.6 million. America couldn't care less about the actress' problems: she was still one of its favorite stars. Which warmed the heart of Judy, whose health was improving quickly. Free during the day, she and Carleton attended a local baseball team's training and visited the sick children's pavilion. Their suffering touched her deeply. She spent a lot of time talking about her life to a small girl, who was a victim of parental mistreatment and hadn't said a word in two years. "If I got better," she said, "it was solely because of these children." One always learns from the suffering of others.

In early September, the doctors thought she could go home to Los Angeles. Judy's recoveries were as spectacular as her falls.

Sister Jimmie's nightclub debut at Slapsy Maxies in Los Angeles in 1949.

Dorothy Virginia "Jimmie" Gumm Thompson (1917-1977), Garland's middle sister, made minor appearances in Garland's movies Babes on Broadway, Presenting Lily Mars, *and* The Harvey Girls, *and changed her name to "Miss Dorothy" sometime in the 1940s, as seen in the above publicity still. In 1956, she released a single on Lin Records of "Beyond a Shadow of a Doubt" and "Crying in the Night," which she composed and her husband Johnny Thompson arranged.*

Judy Garland as seen in the November 1949 Photoplay *magazine.*

16.

That's a Wrap

Back from Boston, Judy reconnected with Vincente. "We had reconciled and were ready to start over again together," he wrote. Liza was happy to see her two parents, who had been so often separated since her birth, back together again. And Louis B. Mayer, who rarely left his third-floor office in the Thalberg Building, took the time to visit them at their Evanview Drive villa.

"She only needs one thing, he said to Minnelli: "to be loved and to feel wanted."

Then, turning to the star:

"I love you like a father, Judy. You know that I am and will always pay special attention to your problems."

Judy Garland smiles at her MGM boss, Louis B. Mayer, in glamorous Ciro's. That's her director-husband, Vincente Minnelli, on the left.

Vincente Minnelli, Judy Garland, and Louis B. Mayer at Ciro's, 1950.

Louis B. Mayer wanted above all to see for himself that Judy was once again in good shape. MGM indeed had a new project for her: *Summer Stock*. She was to play the role of a rural Connecticut farmer who reluctantly allows a troupe of actors who were looking for a place to stage their musical to use her barn in exchange for doing chores on the farm. Joe Pasternak, in charge of the production, had chosen Charles Walters as director and Gene Kelly as her co-star. Judy would be in her element: with them, there would be no risk of conflict. Mayer even brought the crew together and declared:

"We're organizing Judy's big comeback. I want everyone to support her and make her happy."

Judy Garland relaxing on the set of Summer Stock, *1950.*

There was one problem: with her three meals a day, Judy had put on twenty pounds. She had never been this heavy. The studio asked her to diet. Which, of course, was the last thing to do. "The less I eat, the more I am nervous," she would later say. "The migraines came back, as did the insomnia. I had the impression of again being in a nightmare that I thought was over. I found myself caught in a trap."

Judy relapsed, slowly but surely. The diet's effects were compounded by fear. She feared more than anything to be fired from the film. There are fears that jolt you, and those that paralyze you. She was absent for six of the first twenty rehearsals, which earned her a letter of warning from MGM. Even when she showed up, she wasn't really there.

"What am I doing here?" she cried out one fine day in the middle of a scene.

Another time, she lost her temper:

"Everyone is against me!"

Even Joe Pasternak was fed up and threatened to abandon the movie, despite his promise to support her to the end.

Willy-nilly, shooting came to an end in early February. The movie had cost $2 million, that is $43,000 more than initially budgeted. At the party celebrating the end of filming, Judy, at the end of her rope, blurted out:

"I'm a fat slob. Ugly and untalented."

Understanding she had to again get away, she left to get some rest in Carmel, a small seaside resort south of San Francisco. Back at MGM, the first viewings confirmed that there lacked a good final number. Charles Walters himself called Judy to tell her that she had to come back to Culver City. To his great surprise, she welcomed the news with a smile and suggested a song first performed on Broadway that she had always wanted to perform: "Get Happy": what a great way to thumb her nose at life, which had not treated her kindly all that often!

Everything was done to simplify her life: accordingly, rehearsals with the dancers took place without her. Judy had no equal in memorizing a choreography. But, during the first day of shooting, she was way off the mark. She knew it and, at the end of the day, she hurled imperiously to the director:

"I'll be here tomorrow at nine in the morning. I advise you to be ready to shoot!"

She kept her word, and then some. Her legs sheathed in black stockings, dressed in a simple tuxedo jacket, and wearing a black fedora, the star wrapped up shooting in a single day. Vertiginous, radiant. Illuminated by grace. Once again, the reviews were enthusiastic. "No one can bring as much to a musical," wrote *The Los Angeles Times*. The movie brought in $3 million, that is a million in profits. The $40,000 Boston stay had largely been recuperated.

With Vincente Minnelli, the relationship had again gone downhill. Indisputably, the filmmaker — who was then filming *Father of the Bride with Spencer Tracy* — was not the right man for her.

Judy Garland sings "Get Happy," a song composed by Harold Arlen and Ted Koehler in 1930, in Summer Stock, *1950.*

In spite of his goodwill, he was in over his head. Too kind, too conciliatory, too diplomatic — in short, too soft. It was surprising to see the degree to which this man who had directed her so well on the screen was incapable of guiding her in real life. In his memoirs, he wrote: "I was still saying to Judy that I loved her, after that love had given way to the empathy that one concerned person can have for the troubles of another. My feelings could never turn to hate or indifference, but my affection for Judy was now colored by a harsh realistic view. As for her, I don't know what she felt. Perhaps I never did... I could only analyze my own feelings and failings. I'd been too sympathetic, too ready to see it her way, when I should have been more assertive. Rather than lose my

169

temper in front of her, I'd leave the house to cool off. I suppose it was just as obvious to her that I was bottling up the explosion. 'You think Vincente's a doll,' she told Dottie Ponedel, 'but you should see him when that dago temper of his gets going.' She took this strength for weakness, and she was right, for that's what it had become. Our relationship was drastically damaged."

They nonetheless continued to live together in the Evanview house. Judy understood that she needed time to recover her balance and, for once, she had lots of time: in effect, the studio had no project for her in the immediate. On the other hand, she refused to be hospitalized again in a psychiatric institution: "I am not crazy!" When she learned that her mother had traveled to Topeka to get Dr. Menninger's opinion, she saw red and broke off all relations with her. Ethel no longer had the right to see her granddaughter. Disappointed, she left Los Angeles and moved to Texas, where Jimmie and Ethel's new son-in-law, along with Judalein, a daughter from Jimmie's first marriage, now lived. This time, the split was unequivocal. There would be no turning back.

Judy, who liked Carmel's tranquility, decided to rent a house there for six months. In early April 1950, she moved into this small beach resort, to the south of Monterey. She wanted to lead a life of a normal woman, far from Hollywood, with Liza. Hardly three weeks had passed when she received a call from MGM: a few days after beginning rehearsals for Arthur Freed's latest production, *Royal Wedding*, June Allyson discovered she was pregnant. She needed to be replaced…

What a strange paradox: MGM had under contract an actress who ensured the studio comfortable profits and whose fragility they were aware of, but they did nothing to go easy on her, at the risk of killing the goose that lays the golden egg. In terms of human resources management, as they say today, it was pure blindness. And what would have happened had Judy Garland refused? No doubt nothing. At worst, they would have suspended her salary. But her relationship with MGM at this point resembled Stockholm syndrome: repulsion and irrepressible attraction. She knew that the studio was her torturer, but she couldn't live without it. So, instead of continuing to take long walks along the cliffs of Carmel, she returned unhesitatingly to Los Angeles to get to work under the direction of Gene Kelly's former assistant, Stanley Donen, who had been signed to make his first feature film on his own.

Costume test photo taken on June 16, 1950 of Judy Garland and Fred Astaire for the song "How Could You Believe Me When I Said I Love You When You Know I've Been a Liar All My Life?" for the film Royal Wedding.

During the first week of rehearsals, Judy was punctual. But, very quickly, it seems that she had overestimated her forces. She didn't miss any of the eighteen days of rehearsal, but arrived late nine times, anywhere from a quarter of an hour to three and a quarter hours.

Since filming was to begin the following Monday, Stanley Donen asked her to come in and rehearse for an hour on Saturday. Judy didn't come. And received the same evening a telegram from MGM informing her that she was once again suspended. Carleton Alsop might well have tried: the studio would not go back on its decision.

★

In baseball, three strikes and you're out. In less than two years, Judy Garland had purely and simply been fired from three movies. It was clear to everyone that there would not be a fourth.

Ten days after leaving *Royal Wedding*, Judy, Vincente Minnelli, Carleton Alsop and her secretary Myrtle Tully met to take stock of the situation. They brought up the way in which she could make a comeback. The offers were already plentiful: not from the other studios, but from Broadway and London. The television network NBC had also shown interest: Carleton then left: he continued to negotiate with MGM.

As for Judy, she was elsewhere. She only thought about forgetting it all. Suddenly, she told anyone who would listen:

"Don't worry, I have something in mind."

Then she went to the bathroom. All hell broke loose. There were strident screams. Vincente and Myrtle They rushed to her. But the door was locked from inside.

"Leave me alone, I want to die!"

Vincente forced the door open with a chair. The mirror was broken. Judy, her neck covered in blood, held a piece of glass — like in a movie when the director wants to show the broken identity of a character. Fortunately, the wound was superficial: she wouldn't even require stitches, a band-aid would do.

Nothing should have filtered of this episode. Yet, the press, no doubt informed by MGM's publicity department, which saw in the incident a good occasion to justify Judy's recent firing, didn't take long to know everything about it. All the tabloids picked up the story and vied with each other with articles about stars destroyed by the studios.

Judy Garland confided to Dottie Ponedel that she hadn't acted out of despair, but "to get the sympathy of public opinion." Had she taken the effect for the cause? What is certain is that MGM did not come out of the episode any stronger. Her triple eviction from *The Barkleys of Broadway, Annie Get Your Gun and Royal Wedding* had been reported on as a professional meltdown; now, she was looked upon as a victim. Florabel Muir, in the *Los Angeles Mirror*, reminded readers that after the injury of Busher, one of the best racehorses in Louis B. Mayer's stable, he took him out to pasture for more than a year. "The same consideration should have been shown little Garland, whose golden voice and acting talent are no doubt worth as much as Busher." Even Hedda Hopper was on her side: "So much talent, so much pressure, so much bad advice."

MGM, which hated scandals, in the end published a press release: "Accepting its responsibilities, the studio has only one option: to let her go, cover the costs caused by her delays, recast the film, and pick up filming [with Jane Powell]. Replacing an actor is never a sure bet and there is no doubt that an actress as talented as Judy Garland cannot be easily replaced. Replacing her was therefore not decided as a result of a fit of bad humor. It was a last resort."

She had to wait for the Korean War to be declared on June 25, 1950 for the papers to move on. But by bringing up Judy's addictions, the media campaign had had an unexpected result: getting the attention of Harry J. Anslinger, the first commissioner of the Federal Bureau of Narcotics in Washington. In a memo, he concluded that Judy was a "good woman" who found herself "in a situation that could only destroy her." Then he went to New York to meet Nicholas Schenck. Well-informed of the case and of studio practices, Anslinger recommended that MGM's Chief Financial Officer pay for a one-year stay in a sanitarium for her.

"I can't afford to," replied Schenck.

Anslinger then pointed out to him that the death of Judy Garland from an overdose or by suicide would cost him far more, at the least in terms of image. Schenck ended the conversation pithily:

"That's a risk I'll have to take."

★

In late July, Judy Garland left to relax on the banks of Lake Tahoe, then in Sun Valley in Idaho, and finally in New York. One evening, she decided to go see *Summer Stock* at the Capitol Theatre. At the end of the movie, the audience recognized her. Shouts of praise streamed in from every which way.

"We love you, Judy!"

Her popularity was intact. She was receiving four times more fan mail than before. She also had solid support at MGM: that of Louis B. Mayer, who had come to see her after her suicide attempt. He told Louella Parsons: "Judy can live another fifty years if she follows the doctors' orders." He was negotiating with Nicholas Schenck the possibility of continuing to pay her at least a part of her salary. Without success: in Culver City, Dore Schary was fed up hearing about her.

Judy Garland's fishing trip while on vacation in Sun Valley, Idaho, on August 5, 1950.

From her point of view, Judy understood that MGM was toxic for her. She was almost relieved by the turn of events — some would say she had done everything to bring them on. Carleton Alsop was negotiating on her behalf an honorable way out. On September 29, the studio officially freed her of her obligations, one year before the end of her contract — "with reticence and regret," read the press release signed by Louis B. Mayer.

She was barely thirteen when she signed her first contract with the Culver City studio. She now was twenty-eight. In fifteen years, that is more than half her life, her films had made $80 million for MGM.

A page was turning. For her, but also for the studio, of which she had been the most popular face for a good ten years. Already sidelined, Louis B. Mayer went for broke a few weeks later: he asked Nicholas Schenck to choose between Dore Schary and him. A form of professional suicide because the answer was obvious.

17.

Rebirth

Judy Garland and Vincente Minnelli were still married, but for how long? Hadn't he fully backed her to defend her at the studio? The year he spent without work, after the disaster of *The Pirate*, was an ordeal he had no desire to go through again. Since the success of *Madame Bovary* and *Father of the Bride*, he was once again in good standing at MGM. Now, in the autumn of 1950, he was preparing to film *An American in Paris*, which would mark his return to musicals. In the dispute opposing Judy and MGM, he had no choice other than to apply the saying by Jules Renard: "Listening only to his courage which told him nothing, he kept from intervening."

Judy expected more brio. She didn't take kindly to the fact that Vincente hadn't gone to bat for her and couldn't stand his leaving for Culver City each morning, whereas she was again unemployed. Her husband was indissociably linked to MGM, and everything that was associated with the studio, directly or indirectly, was for her a source of rejection.

From his point of view, Minnelli was not dejected at her taking her distances. For months, she had caused him more problems than joy. He seemed to let things fall apart. He didn't want to be responsible for leaving her. What's more, the tenderness he had for her was intact. Such a decision, he foresaw, would be fatal to his self-esteem. But he realized that their marriage was satisfying for neither one of them.

As for Judy, she didn't want to hear about moviemaking anymore. She dreamt of a comeback in New York onstage. At the end of 1950, she thus left for Manhattan in the company of Myrtle Tully and Dottie Ponedel. The three women checked into a suite at the Hotel Carlyle on the Upper East Side. Carleton Alsop had also made the trip, but their paths were moving apart: in the process of separating from his wife Sylvia, he had decided to go back to the CIA. His first mission was to negotiate the rights to *1984* with the widow of George Orwell in order to make an anti-totalitarian cartoon, financed by the American spy agency. From then on, Judy was represented by Abe Lastfogel, from the William Morris agency.

In New York, far from the Hollywood microcosm, Judy was able to observe that her popularity was intact. Whenever she entered a night club, invariably, the orchestra began to play "Over the Rainbow." In this town, she felt loved.

In Manhattan, she met up again with Fred Finklehoffe, the screenwriter of some of her biggest hits, such as *Strike Up the Band*, *For Me and My Gal* and *Meet Me in St. Louis*. Divorced from the singer Ella Logan, he was a joyful and optimistic man, more amorous of Judy's talent than Judy the person. But they enjoyed life one day at a time, carefree and light-hearted.

One Saturday night, at the Little Club, one of the fashionable nightclubs in Manhattan on 55th Street, a man approached her: Sidney Luft, one of Fred's best friends.

"Can I sit down?"

Knowing his predatory side, Fred replied:

"Don't give us a hard time, Sid. Didn't I tell you to beware of this sad sire, Judy?"

"They told me at great length", smiled Judy, who nevertheless allowed the intruder to take a seat.

Sid couldn't stay: he had an appointment with another woman. But the next day, Judy called Fred to ask him to invite Sid Luft to the Riviera, in New Jersey, where they were to attend a concert by Billy Daniels. Making the best of a bad job, Fred carried out the mission: he now knew Judy was going to slip away from him. "I just met a guy, I like him and I'll have him," she confided to Dottie before meeting with him again…

If one had to imagine the opposite of Vincente Minnelli, Sid Luft was most certainly it. Around thirty, with black eyes, always dressed to the nines, and with the physique of a quarterback: six feet tall, massively built, headstrong. He was virility incarnate.

The young Sid Luft.

Quite a rascal was this Sid Luft. Son of a jeweler and a shopkeeper, he grew up north of New York, in the Waspy suburb of Westchester County where it was best not to be Jewish. At twelve, to defend himself, he bought a .22 revolver that was later confiscated by the police. One year later, the captain of the hockey team rejected his candidacy, saying: "No Jews here." And to drive it home, he beat him with a baseball bat, which got him several stitches. Understanding that there was no place in this world for weakness, Sid took boxing lessons and developed his body, to the point of climbing the stairs on his palms. Three years later, he was good and ready to get back at his old assailant: he held grudges as well!

In early 1941, nearly a year before the United States went to war, Sid Luft enlisted in the Royal Canadian Air Force. Upon returning home, he became a test pilot of the aircraft manufacturer Douglas. Seriously burnt in a bomber crash, he took another look at his priorities: survive, yes, but first enjoy life. Having become the actress Eleanor Powell's secretary, he divorced his first wife, married Lynn Bari, an actress in B movies at Paramount, produced two films that went nowhere, and bought three thoroughbreds. Passionate about horse racing, over many years he developed a film project devoted to Man o' War, considered one of the best American horses of all time. Consistently a badass, willingly a profiteer, occasionally a racketeer, preferring racetracks and nightclubs to life in an office, more braggart than dependable, a swaggerer, as the kings of con were called, he was nicknamed "Mr. Wrong" in Hollywood.

After "eight years of slavery," Lynn Bari ended up asking for a divorce. "I was the breadwinner in the family," she said. She expected more from a husband who allowed himself to be taken care of financially. Was Sid the man Judy needed? In any case, it was this kind of guy she needed at this moment in time. A bulldozer. A guy who wouldn't hesitate to lay down the law and get into a fight for her. A guy she could be passionate over and dream about, instead of considering her like a little delicate thing.

After the sparks of their first meetings in New York, Sid distanced himself. Newly separated, he wasn't sure he wanted a serious relation. He instead wanted to enjoy a bachelor's life. But Judy contacted him again several times. Even before he decided to give up on her, she announced to Vincente her intention to divorce him. He sincerely recognized his failings. "He was too indulgent, too kind with her," commented Louella Parsons. With her usual bitchiness, Judy nicknamed him "the man with perfect taste."

She moved to and settled into West Hollywood, in an apartment on Sweetzer Avenue occupied a few years earlier by Marlene Dietrich. The divorce was officially granted on March 23, 1951. Judy got custody of Liza, but the judge decreed that she would spend six months a year with each of her two parents.

Judy Garland appears in court for her divorce from Vincente Minnelli.

★

When she was married to Vincente Minnelli, Judy Garland lived the high life. Two houses most of the time. Servants, cooks, chauffeurs, gardeners. Liza's nurse. Her secretary Myrtle Tully, her personal makeup artist Dottie Ponedel. Her doctors, her shrinks. Her meds. Her hairstylists, her dressmakers, her limousines rented by the hour which waited for her and she forgot to take. Not to forget her salary suspensions at MGM.

A star since she was seventeen, Judy had no notion of money. Poorly managed, that is until Carleton Alsop brought some order to her affairs, she had yet to reimburse $60,000 in back taxes. In other words, the end of her contract with the Culver City studio represented an important loss of income. Since 1951, she could only count on the fees for her radio shows — most notably, she guested on *The Bing Crosby Show* on CBS several times. Lucrative, for sure, but altogether insufficient.

Of all the offers gathered by the William Morris agency, the most lucrative one came from overseas: $70,000 for four weeks of concerts at the Palladium in London. Since way back, Londoners adored her. At the time of the Blitz, she repainted their life with colors of the rainbow. Unlike the

French, the British were able to continue to see American films during the war. For Judy, to sing in London was also a good occasion to have a go onstage, far from Hollywood's sharp tongues. A way of reassuring herself.

"The history of my life is in my song": thus did she conceive her program of her concert. From "You Made Me Love You" (that she sang in 1938 in *Broadway Melody of 1938*) to "Get Happy," by way of songs from *The Wizard of Oz* and *Meet Me in St. Louis*, Judy chose to revisit the soundtrack of her filmography. A collection she prepared with her two most faithful supporters at MGM: Roger Edens for the arrangements and Charles Walters for the choreography. Buddy Pepper accompanied her on the piano. Vincente and Judy remained good friends — but were they ever anything other? — and he attended rehearsals. He came away relieved: "Her voice was better than ever, as if she had found a new maturity."

On the SS Île de France.

On March 30, 1951, Judy Garland embarked on the liner Île-de-France to take her to England. She asked Vincente to take care of Liza. "I have found my rhythm again," she declared before leaving. "Things have been hard the last few years, but I have come out of my depression and have recovered my energy. The future is bright." The ten-day crossing in the company of Myrtle Tully, Dottie Ponedel and Buddy Pepper was like a vacation with friends, a timeless moment, without any pressure.

As on any cruise, there wasn't much to do but eat. And Judy went for it. When she landed in Plymouth, the journalists who greeted her on the dock were struck by her corpulence. "I am horribly fat, but I feel horribly well!" she told them. At the train station in London, hundreds of fans awaited her. It was a riot: the police had to get her out.

As for Sid Luft, he stayed in the United States to work on his project "Man o'War." In fact, as he later recounted, he didn't want to be taken as the star's boyfriend, the prince consort. Before leaving New York, he had offered her a Cartier watch engraved with the sentence he never stopped repeating to her: "I am with you, baby."

Since her departure, Judy longed for him. During the crossing, under Judy's urging, Dottie called him and suggested he join her. Having just arrived, she called him again. This time, he gave in, took the plane for London and joined her at the Dorchester Hotel, where she had taken up residence, the day before the opening.

"I knew you would never abandon me! I'm so afraid, darling."

At the Dorchester Hotel in London, April 6, 1951.

She just discovered stage fright, something she had never known before. In movies, one can always do retakes. Onstage, that was impossible.

"It's as if I were going to my own execution," she admitted a few hours before opening.

Instead of an execution, it was a coronation: in her organdy dress flecked with gold, she sang from the guts. Her voice was sumptuous, her presence exceptional. It wasn't a simple concert, but a true communion with an audience in full delirium. "I just lived the most beautiful night of my life," she cried out to the public. In recognition, she received "the most extraordinary standing ovation the Palladium had ever seen," the papers wrote the next day.

At two shows a day, one at 6 P.M., the other at 8 P.M., all of her London concerts were sold out. Maurice Chevalier crossed the Channel to see her. Laurence Olivier and Vivien Leigh came to applaud her, as did Katharine Hepburn and Humphrey Bogart, back from Africa where they made *The African Queen.*

For two months, Judy didn't have a single meltdown.

She was born anew.

Onstage at the London Palladium, 1951.

Sid had bought a round-trip ticket: he planned on spending only a week in London. But Judy could no longer live without him. Sid gave her a sense of security. He was her anchor. He decided to extend his stay.

Judy Garland and Sid Luft dancing in London, April 12, 1951.

Up until then, nothing had filtered out about their relationship. Upon his arrival, she presented him to British journalists as her new impresario. In that they didn't hesitate to go out together to restaurants and nightclubs, no one was fooled. It's true that Judy hadn't lied, she just anticipated. Between two shows, she indeed asked Sid to be her manager, in place of Carleton Alsop. He at first refused:

"I am not a manager; I am just trying to produce a film… I don't have the experience to take care of you."

Fiercely independent, Sid was reluctant to put all his eggs in one basket. Taking charge of Judy's career was like tying a rope around his neck. It meant negotiating contracts, but also accompanying her everywhere, attending endless meetings on her behalf, managing her daily schedule, being attentive twenty-four hours a day… In short, he would have to give up everything else. Say goodbye to his own life. More than a professional choice, it was a life choice.

She insisted, he hesitated, and yet he caved in. Since they first met, he always caved in. This paper tiger. He was deeply moved by this ill-fated Judy. Thenceforth, she paid him $500 a week to take care of her.

When she told him that Bing Crosby had sent her the script for *Just for You,* he advised her to turn it down. First of all, because the script was mediocre — and the movie would therefore be a flop. But above all, he was convinced that she had to continue to reinvent herself far from Hollywood and its pill pushers who pushed pills of all sorts: since they met, she hadn't relapsed. She just took a sip of wine before going onstage.

On the other hand, he encouraged her to agree to a proposal made by the William Morris agency: a tour in the United Kingdom and in Ireland. A week in all the big cities: Manchester, Dublin, Glasgow, Birmingham, etc. At the end of the tour, Sid and Judy would take a few days' vacation in Paris, the City of Love. They would then take the Train Bleu to Monaco, Antibes and Cannes on the French Riviera, the Côte d'Azur in French. Liza would come join them, accompanied by her nanny Cozy. "Judy's relationship with her daughter was full of tenderness," said Sid, who was discovering them together for the first time. "I was amazed by her maternal gifts. Their bond was so great that I was almost jealous."

Free from MGM, Judy blossomed.

18.

New York, New York

Sid Luft returned to the United States by plane, Judy Garland by boat on the Queen Elizabeth, with Liza. In their room at the St. Regis, where they took refuge from the torrid heat of a New York summer, Sid couldn't calm down. Not a single journalist to welcome them coming off the liner on August 12!

"The press is like the police: where are they when you need 'em," she replied while smoking one of those menthol cigarettes she was fond of.

More worrisome in her eyes was that the William Morris agency had proposed nothing to her. Outside of a few radio shows, there was no serious project on the horizon. As if the triumph at the Palladium in London had never taken place. Out of sight, out of mind: had America forgotten her?

It was while walking on Broadway that Sid Luft got the idea that would mark Judy Garland's big comeback in the United States. On 47th Street, his eyes noticed the Palace Theatre, the mecca of vaudeville in the 1920s. Since then, it had lost its luster. Transformed into a movie theater, it now only showed B movies. The façade was decrepit, and the theater closed for repairs. He had met Sol Schwartz, the president of RKO Theatres, which owned the Palace Theatre, and decided to phone him:

"I know what you've got in mind, Sid," said Schwartz. "I'll clean this fuckin' place. We'll reopen the Palace."

"That's just what I had in mind, Sol."

"We'll bring in the chandeliers, I'll change the seats, I'll paint the joint, and we'll open with Judy."

Wasn't she a child of vaudeville? It would be as if the theater and she reconnected with their own past: they would mutually forge a new identity.

It was soon a done deal. Four weeks were booked, with two concerts a day, six days a week. A real marathon! Sid was worried: Judy would need to rest. But it was she who had insisted, sure of being in shape again. She wanted to prove to herself that she could do it.

To prepare this new show, Judy and Sid returned to Los Angeles. Roger Edens was writing a new intro for her entrance onstage and new arrangements. Charles Walters was working on new choreographies in that Judy would be accompanied by eight dancers; it would be he who would perform with her the duo "A Couple of Swells," the number first introduced with Fred Astaire in *Easter Parade*. Hugh Martin, who had written the songs for *Meet Me in St. Louis*, would replace Buddy Pepper on piano. Irene Sharaff would design a new wardrobe. All were members of the Freed Unit, all had worked with Judy at MGM. It was like a major-league reunion.

Officially, Judy lived in West Hollywood, Sid on Wilshire, but they were inseparable. Fusional lovers, they were also inextricably connected in their professional life. But one evening, while dining at Cock 'n Bull on Sunset Boulevard, Judy dropped a bomb:

"Darling, didn't you notice that I didn't have my period? I did the test, and it's positive…"

"You are…?"

"Pregnant, yes, and I want to have this child with you."

Sid was stunned. First of all, there was the show in New York. Second, he still wasn't divorced from Lynn, who, for months now, had been giving him a hard time through her lawyers. He also imagined the headlines in the papers: "Judy Garland cancels the Palace to give birth to an illegitimate child of a married man." From Sid's point of view, he was stupefied and angry.

"Clearly, you don't want a child," Judy let out.

"Of course, I want one," he replied, "but we have a show to prepare."

"Because of my negative reaction," he wrote in his memoirs, "Judy never told me where or when she got an abortion." They didn't argue, but the next day, at the La Cienega Boulevard studio where Judy was rehearsing, she avoided him and left without going to the dressing room where they always met. On the following days, Sid, sick with a bad infection, was bedbound. Judy didn't call him. When he tried to reach her, it was Dottie or Tully who picked up the phone: no, Judy wasn't there. A strategy of avoidance…

Feeling better, Sid went to the studio. He had drunk a few bourbons to give him courage, and mixing bourbon and antibiotics didn't do him any good. Judy's attitude was detached, distant, cold, absent. When leaving the parking lot at the angle of La Cienega and Beverly Boulevard, he failed to stop at the stop sign and crashed into the car of a young student who collided into that of a dentist. The conversation became heated, and Sid punched the latter, broke his nose, and shattered his glasses. At the same time, Judy, rushing over, slapped the student. "She had just given me the cold shoulder and now was in a hurry to stand up for me." The police intervened and Sid was taken to the police station, where Judy had to pick him up that same evening once she had paid the $150 fine for drunken driving. It was a scene that was both touching and comic, made for the movies, and which sealed their reconciliation…

Obviously, the papers relished the incident and Lynn Bari, Sid's first wife, couldn't help making the most of the scandal. It was unthinkable, she argued, that a drunk could take care of John, their three-year-old son. His visitation rights had to be restricted. What's more, Lynn was furious that Sid had spent twice as much for his three racehorses than for his son, and double her alimony demands. Wasn't he cashing in on his relationship with his new companion? Summoned to go before the court, Judy went white when Lynn's lawyer asked her how much Sid was being paid to handle her:

"He takes what he needs," she mumbled.

Sid got off with paying $400 a month to his ex-wife.

★

The Palace marquee in New York, 1951-1952.

New York, October 16, 1951. Judy took a taxi with Charles Walters to go to the Palace. Nearing the theater, the car was blocked in a gigantic traffic jam.

"What's going on?" she asked the chauffeur.

"It's because of Judy Garland's opening."

Onstage at the Palace, 1951-1952.

Judy Garland sings "Over the Rainbow" at The Palace, 1951-1952.

Even those who weren't able to get a ticket wanted to be witness to the event: the Broadway debut of a national idol.

After a first act that mixed acrobats, dancers, and comics, in the vaudeville tradition, Judy came onstage. In addition to her own hits, she had added a few of the great standards as sung by others, "Shine On, Harvest Moon" by Nora Bayes, "My Man" by Fanny Brice, and "Rock-a-Bye Your Baby with a Dixie Melody" by Al Jolson. Between jokes ("I'm a few pounds overweight…"), she gave of herself more than ever, before launching into, without microphone, almost whispering, "Over the Rainbow." There wasn't a noise in the theater, which was fascinated, mesmerized by this voice which seemed to come from another planet. A voice which couldn't be compared to her records, which paled by comparison. A clear, pure voice, with an incredible vibrato, and unequaled power. Forty-five minutes of singing which earned her a standing ovation. A reporter timed it: three minutes and eighteen seconds. The Duke and Duchess of Windsor, Elizabeth Taylor, Montgomery Clift, Marlene Dietrich came to congratulate her in her dressing room, covered with congratulatory telegrams. Rather than rushing into her car parked in front of the stage door, Judy decided to exit by the lobby that evening to greet the thousands of fans who had waited for her outside, behind the police barricades.

Judy Garland backstage at The Palace after her opening on October 16, 1951.

The next day, the newspapers were rapturous. *The Hollywood Reporter* compared her to "an atomic bomb." Every evening, the Palace was full to the brim. Every evening was like opening night, the audience ecstatic. Soon enough, more performances were added, then more, then still more.

One night, Judy fainted and was taken to hospital. She explained to Sid that a doctor, recommended by Marlene Dietrich, had prescribed pills for her to lose weight. After a three-day break, Judy returned to performing. When the quack doctor showed up a few days later to give her a new prescription, Sid led him out firmly. Considering Sid's build, the doctor didn't insist… There were no other incidents.

By the time she closed on February 24, 1952, Judy had sung for nineteen weeks in a row. A record for a solo concert. One hundred eighty-four concerts, nearly a million attendees. Financially, the run had been lucrative: $800,000 in receipts, of which $285,000 for her alone. Enough to keep her afloat. As for MGM, it capitalized on her brilliant comeback by re-releasing several of her films, including *Babes in Arms*.

"There are no second acts in American lives," wrote Francis Scott Fitzgerald in *The Last Tycoon*. Fired from MGM like a servant two years earlier, Judy had just proven the opposite.

★

Joan Crawford and Judy Garland at Romanoff's after her Philharmonic Auditorium opening in Los Angeles.

After New York, Los Angeles. On April 24, 1952, Judy was on the bill at the Philharmonic Auditorium. The house was delirious. After the show, Sid had organized an evening at Romanoff's, where the Hollywood "crème de la crème" flocked to congratulate her "resurrection," as the headlines in the papers put it in a town that had seen her blossom, but also self-destruct. Even Louis B. Mayer insisted on honoring Judy by his presence. He hugged her warmly and confided to Sid:

"I think you're her best remedy."

Judy played four weeks at the Philharmonic Auditorium, which was two times as big as the Palace in New York, thereby allowing Sid to negotiate a record fee of $25,000 a week. Another engagement already awaited her: four weeks at the Curran Theatre in San Francisco.

One evening, in an Italian restaurant they liked, Judy announced to Sid that she was pregnant.

"Darling, do you want to marry me?" he replied out of the blue.

On June 8, taking advantage of a day off, the two lovebirds headed for the small town of Hollister, south of San Francisco. Their marriage was celebrated in a strictly private ceremony on a ranch of a friend of Sid's, but the Hollywood gossip columnists soon found out. And had a field day. For them, Sid was a bum, a loser, one of these parasites who live off the stars. "If Judy had a dollar from all the friends who had whispered in her ear that Sid wasn't the best man for her, she would have a loaded bank account." And another nail in the coffin: "Sid Luft is what a woman finds over the rainbow."

The house at 144 S. Mapleton Drive, Holmby Hills, California where Judy Garland,
Sid Luft and their children lived between 1952 and 1960.

What could have been a huge tour throughout the United States stopped there. Judy and Sid moved into a five-bedroom house in gray and yellow stone between Bel-Air and Beverly Hills at 144 S. Mapleton Drive, where Liza joined them regularly. In this miniature Tudor-style palace, purchased for $120,000, Judy and Sid each had their own suite, with bathroom and dressing room. Liza and Lorna each had their own room, as did Johnny, Sid's son. "Our house was a castle for a princess and her courtiers," said Sid, who had a Steinway, which none other than Vladimir Horowitz played at a concert in Los Angeles, placed in the living room.

Now married, they no longer hesitated to be seen together at fashionable restaurants and night clubs. At Ciro's, they went to hear the Will Mastin Trio, and were fascinated by the voice and talents of the dancer and youngest member, who would come to be known as Sammy Davis Jr. Sid even tried to put him under contract.

But the more Judy's pregnancy advanced, the more she suffered from insomnia. Sid had the worst time getting used to it. The migraines came back, and she became grumpy. She asked to see a doctor and let Sid know unambiguously that he mustn't meddle.

On November 21, 1952, Judy gave birth by cesarean at Saint John's Hospital in Santa Monica to a little blond girl with blue eyes, a six-pound sweetie whom they named Lorna. Judy stayed in the hospital for a week, but Sid wasn't waiting for her at the exit: he was attending a horse race in San Francisco where Florence House, a thoroughbred they had bought together in Dublin, won.

As was the case for Liza's birth, the following weeks were marked by severe baby blues. "She was irritable with the help and angry at me," Sid told. "It was clear that she was taking something. But what? And how? There was no communicating between us on the subject." Sid decided to talk about it with Marc Rabwin, her family doctor, who explained to him Judy's addiction to amphetamines and retraced the history of her psychiatric troubles since her start at MGM. Having discovered the extent of the damage, Sid, who had taken an office a stone's throw away from the house, asked the help to watch her at all times.

A few days later, one of them called him:

"I'm scared, Mr. Luft. She's in the bathroom, not answering. I can't get in."

Sid rushed over and broke the door down with his shoulder. "Blood, bright red in sharp contrast to the whiteness of her skin, was pouring out of her neck. I thought, she's dying, I'm losing her. Judy had cut her throat with a razor blade… What demons inhabited her soul just when life seemed so rich and productive? It was a gigantic puzzlement that she would poison herself with pills, and that the toxic reaction to whatever she swallowed would create an impulse for self-mutilation"

Sid was all the more confused in that the next day, barely awake, Judy, more cheerful than ever, asked for a gargantuan breakfast of eggs, sausages, pancakes, and jam. Her first real meal in several days. Not a word about what happened the day before, as if nothing had happened.

"You have to see someone to get over this inexplicable depression," Sid told her.

"Don't worry, it's over," she replied with vigor.

"I chose to believe her," Sid recounted. Of course, he was burying his head in the sand. But without this naiveté, would he have had enough confidence to carry off the major project he had been hammering away at for several months: Judy Garland's return to the screen?

Portrait of Judy Garland by Cecil Beaton, 1953.

19.

No Tears

At the beginning of the 1940s, Judy Garland and Walter Pidgeon were invited to interpret on the radio an adaptation of *A Star Is Born*, the film by William A. Wellman released in 1937, with Janet Gaynor and Fredric March. Fascinated by this love story between an alcoholic actor on the decline and a young star on the rise, she had even suggested to Louis B. Mayer that he produce a musical remake in which she would play the lead. The MGM boss didn't take her up on it, judging Judy too young for such a character. He preferred to limit her to young, innocent roles.

Impatient to return to movies, Judy Garland brought up this idea with Sid Luft. He in turn contacted the new owner of the rights, Edward Alperson, who was utterly thrilled. They now just had to conclude the deal.

Hollywood was in full upheaval at the time. After a long judicial procedure, the Supreme Court had just issued a ruling: in order to comply with the antitrust law, the studios had to part with their movie houses which guaranteed an outlet for all their films, however minor. The entire studio system was in danger of collapsing. A new economy was falling into place, especially as the film industry was more and more in competition with television.

It was now out of the question for stars to be on salary at a studio. Long-term contracts which bound them body and soul were over. Make way for the law of supply and demand, which opened the door to partnership relations. As a good opportunist, Sid Luft stepped into the breach: he wouldn't propose that a studio produce *A Star Is Born*, he would co-produce it thanks to a company he created with Judy, baptized Transcona.

But with what major should he associate? Not MGM: too many bad memories for Judy. Bitter at not having been contacted, Arthur Freed called Sid and Judy "alley cats incapable of producing a movie." Sid preferred to solicit Jack Warner, who had just signed a co-producing agreement of the same kind with John Wayne's company. The youngest of the Warner brothers, who founded the studio of the same name in 1923, Jack was a jovial man, smiling, seductive, brilliant, and who stayed in the shadow of his older brothers until Sam's death. From then on, he took charge of production and developed the Warner style, based on exciting detective movies with realistic tendencies. Nicknamed "the Colonel," he was known for his authoritarianism. At permanent war with his brother Harry, the president of the studio, who wound up plotting one of these ploys he had the secret for in order to evict him.

The head of Warner Bros. attended Judy's opening at the Philharmonic and openly admired her. "Your talent goes beyond what words can express," he wrote her. "I sincerely think you are one of the greatest entertainers the world has ever known. What more can I say?" In view of such enthusiasm, Sid wagged his tail: he knew he was in a position of force. Not only had he obtained excellent conditions — shared profits and a guarantee that losses would be absorbed by Warner Bros. in case of commercial failure, but he also negotiated a package: a three-movie deal. *A Star Is Born*, but also *Man o' War*, this project he had been dragging around for years, as well as a third one devoted to the Donner expedition, a story about eighty pioneers on their way to California in the 1840s, blocked by snow in the Sierra Nevada, and forced to practice cannibalism to survive.

He who no one took seriously had just succeeded in realizing one hell of an exploit. Mr. Wrong had become Mr. Right.

★

Judy had gotten over her post-partum depression. Sid and she decided to spend the end-of-year holidays at the Waldorf Astoria in New York, where she was to participate in a charity benefit. But they had to precipitously return to Los Angeles: Ethel had just died at age fifty-nine.

Between Judy and her mother, a reconciliation had never happened. Since she had kicked her out of her life, they never again saw each other. After her daughter's first suicide attempt, Ethel, who was living in Texas, came back to Los Angeles. At the time, Judy quickly sent her away, which hadn't stopped Ethel from telling the papers that she had "the situation under control."

The end of the MGM contract was a hard blow for Ethel. Up until then, she continued to be paid $150 a week, directly deducted from her daughter's paycheck. Now without income, she found work at Douglas Aircraft for a salary of $61 a week. During rehearsals at the Philharmonic in Los Angeles, Ethel tried to reconcile with her daughter. One afternoon, she showed up at the auditorium.

"Do you think I could see Judy?" she asked Sid Luft.

Aware of their falling out, he didn't think it was the right time. But how could he resist a mother's plea? During a break, he asked Judy if she would agree to give her mother a few minutes.

"Please, darling, don't bother me, I'm rehearsing," she replied with an icy look which clearly meant mind your own business.

Humiliated, Ethel asked for an allowance. But she preferred to refuse the handout proposed by Sid — $25 a week — and told the whole story to the *Los Angeles Mirror*, which detailed how Judy Garland's mother had been reduced to working in a factory, whereas her daughter was raking in several thousand dollars a week. When the news of Judy's remarrying got out, Ethel went as far as to declare to the same paper: "Sid is a good for nothing. I am not surprised by this marriage, but I would have preferred that it not take place. He's a creep. When will Judy ever grow up?"

From then on, insofar as the two of them, it was war. Arriving at the clinic to give birth, Judy forbade her mother from entering when she showed up to see her granddaughter.

"What did I do wrong?" she asked her friends. "Why does she hate me?"

But when Ethel, victim of a heart attack, collapsed in the parking lot of the Douglas Aircraft factory in Santa Monica in the early morning of January 5, 1953, Judy took the first plane from New York, where she was at the time, to organize the funeral in the small Forest Lawn chapel where, seventeen years earlier, that of her father had taken place. She did her duty, without emotion.

In interviews, Judy never spoke kindly of her mother: In 1967, on television, when asked if she had had a stage mother, she remembered: "One who wouldn't quit. My mother was truly a stage mother. A mean one. She was very jealous because she had absolutely no talent. Now she's going to knock my earring off. You know, my mother died and whenever I talk about her — and I should because she was so wicked — but whenever I start talking about her, she inevitably knocks one earring off. So, she's still around. So now mother, you behave yourself. She would sort of stand in the wings when I was a little girl, and if I didn't feel good, if I was sick to my tummy, she'd say you get out and sing, or I'll wrap you around the bedpost and break you off short. So, I'd go out and sing."

At the funeral, behind the dark glasses, she shed no tears.

January 7, 1953, Judy Garland (right) is accompanied by her husband, Sid Luft, and her sister, Mrs. Sue Cathcart, at the private funeral services for Garland's mother, Mrs. Ethel Gilmore.

20.

From Victory to Rout

Who should play opposite Judy Garland in *A Star Is Born*? Hardly had he gotten wind of the project before Frank Sinatra showed interest. Since their affair, "the voice" and Judy remained close. The only thing was that Jack Warner vetoed the idea:

"Sinatra? He's through."

To get the role, Sinatra put the pressure on. He offered Judy a painting, a Cartier billfold in gold for Sid. But Jack Warner remained inflexible. Furious at having been given the brush-off, Sinatra in the end made use of his friends in the mafia to be hired for *From Here to Eternity*…

Humphrey Bogart? An actor 100% Warner Bros., but Jack found him to be too old. Sid then contacted Cary Grant. They had tequilas and bet at the races together, but Sid didn't know if he was interested in the role. Cary Grant, one of the rare actors who built his career without the help of a studio, finally specified his conditions: $300,000 and 10% of the box-office. Jack Warner proposed increasing the fee to $100,000 but refused to give him a percentage. Negotiations stopped there.

Marlon Brando and Laurence Olivier refused. Tyrone Power and Richard Burton were interested, but not available. Finally, the choice came down to James Mason, a brilliant British actor, who, although not a star, had made a strong impression in *East Side, West Side*, *Pandora and the Flying Dutchman*, and above all *The Desert Fox*, in which he played field marshal Rommel.

To put together this musical drama, which was strictly speaking more than a remake of *A Star Is Born*, Sid Luft and Judy Garland enlisted the biggest names: the playwright Moss Hart would write the script, George Cukor — whose participation had played a key role in the success of *The Wizard of Oz* — the direction. Refined and subtle, Cukor was an exceptional director of actors: under his direction, twenty-one actors had been nominated for an Oscar, and five had won.

★

Two doors away from their Mapleton house lived Humphrey Bogart and Lauren Bacall. Judy knew them well: at the first hearings of the House Un-American Activities Committee in 1946, which was the starting point of what was to become the McCarthyite witch hunt, she had participated with them in the creation of the Committee for the First Amendment in favor of freedom of speech. This was the beginning of a group of entertainers who were revelers but were also attached to democratic values. Frank Sinatra and David Niven were in the habit of meeting them at the restaurant Romanoff's and finishing off the night at the Bogarts' at an hour when all L.A. was fast asleep. A lit light in front of the Bogarts' meant that they could come in at any hour of the night. One morning when she found Bogart and Sinatra haggard after a night of boozing, Lauren Bacall remarked:

"You look like a goddamn rat pack!"

Between two plastered evenings, the Rat Pack was born, at least in its initial version. It didn't take long to establish the "board": Sinatra was the master, Bogart in charge of public relations, and Lauren Bacall, the youngest, was…the doyenne. Judy, who was vice-president, wasn't the last to bend an elbow, with a preference for vodka or Blue Nun, which was a sweet white wine.

A few streets away from S. Mapleton Drive also lived Dr. Fred Pobirs, who had prescribed electroshocks for Judy just before *Annie Get Your Gun*. She reconnected with him. When she was suffering from migraines in the middle of the night, she called him and he came hurtling over in bathrobe and slippers, with his doctor's bag full of pills.

As shooting on *A Star Is Born* got closer, Judy was worried about her weight.

"Darling, I don't want to be fat in front of the camera."

Sid understood the danger: he knew the degree to which these weight problems had devastated her at MGM. As he was unable to stop her from resorting to amphetamines, he offered Dr. Pobirs 2% of profits if he took care of her all the time and if he gave Sid a daily report on the state of her health. She would at least not be tempted to see any old sorcerer's apprentice who came her way. Likewise, having noticed that she got along well with Harry Rubin, a handyman who could fix anything and who contributed to the Mapleton house's maintenance, Sid hired him as Judy's personal assistant: it would be he who would drive her every day to Burbank, Warner Bros.' headquarters.

Playing safe, Sid had a clause added to Judy's contract stipulating that she would never be called to the studio before ten in the morning. Knowing how difficult it was for her to get up, he didn't want anyone to reproach her for being late, as she could be at MGM. The stakes in *A Star Is Born* were double: to prove that Judy was still a movie star, but also that she had become a reliable actress, on whose name a movie could be made without risk.

October 12, 1953, director George Cukor and Judy Garland on the set on the first day of shooting A Star Is Born.

On December 12, shooting finally began at the Burbank studios. Jack Warner had assigned Judy one of the most prestigious dressing rooms:

Bette Davis's when she was under contract to Warner Bros. It had been three years since she last made a movie, and the first few days went by without problem. On the other hand, George Cukor had to deal with a difficulty that was soon insurmountable: WarnerScope. To counter television and its small screens, the studios had developed a procedure that allowed one to obtain an image 2.35 wider than high. To replace CinemaScope, which allowed one to obtain an anamorphic image at the time of filming and restore it at projection, Warner Bros. had developed its own technology. After a week, it turned out however that it was far from being as efficient: the image was deformed. Jack Warner had to face the facts: they would have to use CinemaScope and reshoot everything. They had spent $100,000…for nothing.

As for George Cukor, Judy and he got along perfectly. She gave of herself with great intensity. After shooting an emotional scene for which he asked her for two takes, the director was worried he might have pushed her too hard.

"Oh, that's nothing," she responded with humor. "Come over to my house. I do it every afternoon — but I only do it *once* at home!"

James Mason, Judy Garland, Sid Luft, and George Cukor on the set of A Star Is Born, *1953.*

In the final weeks, Judy proved to be more difficult. She sometimes called in to say she was ill, whereas she had been seen in the afternoon at the horse races and in the evening in a nightclub. It was true that filming went on and on. There would even be an overtime: a few weeks after the end of shooting, a musical number, "Born in a Trunk," in the form of a summary of her career, was added. But severe insomnia forced her to use sleeping pills. Sid was careful to organize the shooting schedule accordingly, even if it meant exploding production costs: shooting would not begin before the beginning of the afternoon and would continue late into the night, sometimes until four in the morning.

On July 29, the film was a wrap, at long last. Filming had stretched out to nine and a half months… When the first test screening took place in early August Judy's fans were in heaven; but most people admitted that the movie was too long: three and a half hours. "Neither the human mind, nor the human ass can stand three hours of concentration," Cukor recognized.

The director then went back to editing it. Sid and Judy preferred to join Jack Warner on the French Riviera for a three-week vacation. However, the director had all the more difficulty making cuts given that it was his first musical. Upon their return, *A Star Is Born* had most certainly been shortened, but it still lasted three hours and two minutes, that is one hour and eleven minutes longer than William A. Wellman's original version — which admittedly didn't have any singing or dancing in it.

It was thus a work that was unusually long — the longest since *Gone with the Wind* — which previewed at the Pantages in Los Angeles on September 29, 1954. "Probably the most remarkable premiere that ever took place in the tinsel town," wrote the *Los Angeles Times*. More than twenty thousand fans crowded Hollywood Boulevard to pay tribute to Judy's return to the screen. Jack Warner saw things big: having negotiated with the television network NBC to ensure that the red carpet be for the first time broadcast live on television, he had personally sent invitation telegrams to the biggest stars in town. Joan Crawford, Elizabeth Taylor, Dean Martin, Lucille Ball, Humphrey Bogart, Frank Sinatra… All of them rushed to the preview, followed by a dinner at the Ambassador

Hotel, then an evening at the Cocoanut Grove above whose entrance had been hoisted a gigantic banner: "Welcome Judy."

The print media couldn't praise her enough. According to *Time* magazine, "Judy Garland offers us the greatest performance by an actress in the history of the movies." *The Saturday Review of Literature* considered that she "has the true quality of stars, that little something extra which adds charm and emotion to everything she does. In all her gestures, there is an ease and grace, an originality and intensity that surpasses the skill of the most experienced actresses." *Films in Review* concluded that *A Star Is Born* was "the perfect example of what Hollywood can do when money is well spent." In a word, Judy Garland had just succeeded in making a sensational comeback to movies. The producer Sam Goldwyn was sure that "the movie should make at least $25 million."

As soon as the movie was released everywhere in America, movie theaters were full. For each showing, people had to be turned away. Jack Warner had invested $5 million in the production, and he was well on his way to recouping his investment, even if he had to share the profits with Sid.

Judy Garland and Jack Warner at a party at Romanoff's on October 28, 1953.

205

That said, things were about to go downhill. Until then, no one had complained about the film's length, but exhibitors jumped in. Ever since theaters no longer belonged to the majors, exhibitors' power had grown; for, they could only project *A Star Is Born* three or four times a day, whereas ordinarily they programmed five or six shows for a movie lasting less than two hours. A solution could have consisted of increasing the ticket price, but the film fell victim to the rivalry between Jack Warner and his brother Harry who, as president, had the upper hand on distribution. Without consulting anyone, Harry brutally ordered new cuts. Patrons who were not able to see *A Star Is Born* in the first fifteen days of theatrical exhibition would now only have access to a version amputated of twenty-eight minutes.

In that George Cukor was now in India to prepare his new film, it was the editor Folmar Blangsted who was in charge of the butchery. The resulting movie was unbalanced and wobbly. "Wholesale massacre," stated Cukor. "Judy Garland's best sequences were arbitrarily and stupidly mutilated," he went on. But the worst was yet to come: a movie chain on the East Coast proposed programming the film in its five thousand five hundred theaters in exchange for 90% of the receipts for Warner Bros. and 10% for the chain, on the condition that the film not exceed … two hours! Harry Warner accepted. In this version, *A Star Is Born* was no longer a movie, but a piece of Emmental. Bosley Crowther, *The New York Times* critic, in a review entitled "A Star Is Shorn" wrote: "Every cut leaves a giant hole. The original dramatic narrative and very sense of the work have been lost." As the press made the most of the affair, the amputated movie suffered a veritable counter-publicity campaign and, after an excellent opening that foreshadowed a triumph, receipts collapsed, and some patrons went as far as to write Warner Bros. that they were not willing to pay a hefty price to see an abridged movie!

Sid and Judy decided to terminate their association with Warner Bros., which gave Jack free rein to spread the idea that the couple was mainly responsible for the fiasco. Demoralized by the studio's betrayal, disgusted by the movies, Judy refused two new projects, *Butterfield 8* and *The Three Faces of Eve*, which she passed on in favor of Elizabeth Taylor for the first and Joanne Woodward for the second. Both went on to win an Oscar…

★

Since she began making movies, Judy Garland had dreamt of winning the Oscar as best actress. The only award she had received to date was the Academy Juvenile Award for *The Wizard of Oz*. Musicals had always been underrepresented in the quest to win the statuette, but on March 30, 1955, at the Pantages, when the awards show opened, Judy Garland was seen as the overriding frontrunner, even though *A Star Is Born* hadn't been nominated in the best film category or that of best director — who would vote for a movie that had been tampered with in such a short-sighted way?

That evening, Judy wasn't in the theater, but in a room on the third floor of Cedars of Lebanon Hospital. She had just given birth to her third child, a premature five-and-a-half-pound boy, Joseph Wiley Luft. In that all the bookmakers in town had bet on her winning, Judy had asked Lauren Bacall to accept the statuette on her behalf. NBC, which was broadcasting the ceremony live, had placed cameras in her room to get her reaction. Alas, someone else's name was in the envelope: that of Grace Kelly. At twenty-six — which made her the youngest winner in history, she had just edged Judy out thanks to her interpretation of the wife of an alcoholic actor, played by Bing Crosby, in *The Country Girl*.

To console her, Groucho Marx, never short of witticisms, sent her a telegram: "Dear Judy, this is the biggest robbery since Brink's." Even Grace Kelly's father was surprised that the Oscar had been awarded to his daughter: "They should have given out two Oscars," he said. But Warner Bros.' butchery, in addition to the acrimony of part of the industry which viewed Judy's erring ways as mere caprices by a star, got the better of a victory which seemed to be hers.

For Judy, the defeat was all the more bitter in that the film hadn't recovered costs in its first run. Counting promotional costs, it only earned $6 million. However, Judy hadn't gotten paid: she and Sid, via Transcona, were co-producers along with Warner Bros. Whereas they thought they would share in the profits, they got nothing at all. Judy had worked her fingers to the bone in vain. To make matters worse, during the year taken up preparing the filming and editing of *A Star Is Born*, they had spent lavishly. At the end of this adventure, they were so broke that not only was Sid taken to court by his ex-wife for non-payment of alimony for their son, but a sheriff had issued a summons for not having paid a $600 loan on a piano…

Judy had no choice but to return to touring in order to financially support Sid, her three children, and the half-dozen cooks, servants, and nannies they employed full time.

Garland sings "Swanee" from the "Born in a Trunk" sequence in A Star Is Born.

21.

On the Road

In early April 1955, Sid Luft announced Judy Garland's return to the stage. A long tour across America. The star would travel onboard a special train, surrounded by her family. Thirty-three stops would be on the program, before closing in New York.

The MCA agency, which thereon in replaced William Morris to manage her career, first got the idea of this plan which thrilled Judy, who was happy to return to the stage and was a mother blessed with little Joe. After his birth, Judy hadn't gone through any baby blues: she was crazy about her son Joe. She had dreamed of a boy and only had eyes for him.

On the other hand, her insomnia had resumed with greater intensity. Judy never went to bed before daybreak. Set on treating her alcohol addiction, she even accepted to participate in Alcoholics Anonymous meetings — but she only went once.

In June, Judy got to work rehearsing before giving her first concerts in early July in San Diego, and then Long Beach, where many of her friends would join her. Frank Sinatra rented a Greyhound bus in which he installed a bar. The merry flock, Sammy Davis Jr. and Dean Martin included, would join her onstage for a memorable jam.

But the tour came to an end there: logistic difficulties were a pretext to prematurely cancel it; for, reservations were down in the big northern cities, something which didn't bode well for the rest of the tour.

To all appearances, this news was a catastrophe for the Lufts' finances. But MCA got them out of a tight spot by making them aware of the juicy proposition from the CBS television network: $100,000 to participate in her first program in color, to be broadcast on September 24, 1955. In the United States, the explosion of this new medium was fulgurant: 0.4% of homes were equipped with a TV in 1948, 34% in 1952, and by 1956 64.5% would be and by 1959 the figure would be 95%.

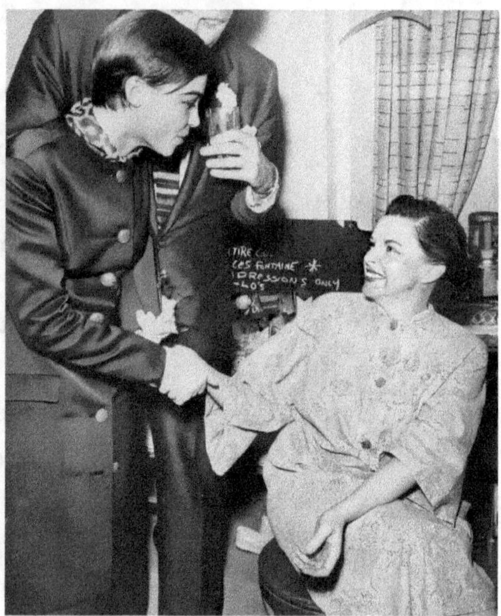

(Left) Judy Garland and Humphrey Bogart get off the rented bus in Long Beach on July 11, 1955. (Right) Leslie Caron and Judy Garland in her dressing room the same night.

It was impossible to refuse such an astronomical paycheck, all the more so in that the show would be a formidable launching pad for her new album, *Miss Show Business*, the fruit of her new contract with Capitol Records. But Judy, nervous as ever, was terrorized: according to the norm for broadcasts at the time, she was going to have to sing live, without a safety net, with a camera as her only partner. A veritable leap in the dark for this actress known for her fragility. Paul Harrison, in charge of the show, warned his crew from the start of rehearsals:

"Judy is like a child. The least remark that she had a shiny nose could cause her to exit the set with no hope of coming back. But don't forget that she is one of the most talented entertainers you will ever work with. Keep that in mind and love her."

The broadcast was a phenomenal success: forty million viewers, an unprecedented audience. That said, it nearly didn't take place. Worried about sleeping well so as to be able to get up at six for the final rehearsals, Judy took sleeping pills the night before. When Sid came to wake her, she groaned as if she were in a state of semi-unconsciousness. He managed to get her back on her feet, got her under a cold shower, but her voice was slurred. Dr. Pobirs, whom they called for help, prescribed Benzedrine and a Chinese meal with rice to absorb the pills. Sid wondered how she was going to sing. At the beginning of rehearsals, in the middle of thirty-eight musicians, she snapped:

"I'm not singing this afternoon; I'm keeping my voice for tonight."

She was brilliant, vibrant, radiant. Not the least hesitation, not the least slump, whereas the program lasted ninety minutes.

Singing was her best therapy.

An early publicity still for Judy Garland's first CBS television special, The Ford Star Jubilee, *in 1955.*

Judy Garland sings "Over the Rainbow" on her CBS special aired live on September 24, 1955.

★

Thanks to the success of her first television show, Judy became the small screen's best ambassador. CBS didn't take much time to offer her a five-show contract, the second of which would be programmed on April 8, 1956. Presented by Ronald Reagan, it was aired at the same time that her second Capitol album, *Judy*, came out.

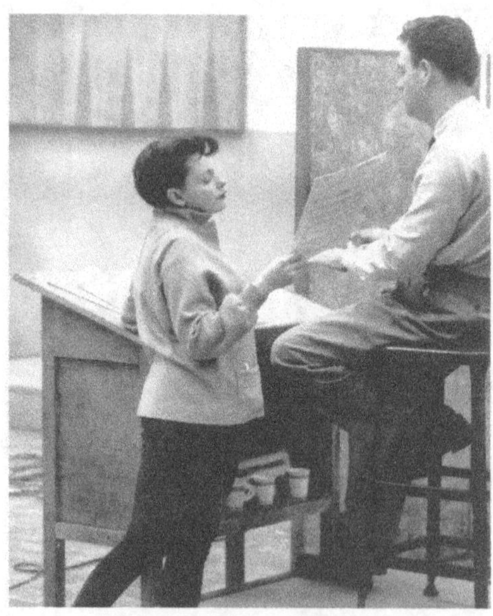

Judy Garland and Nelson Riddle, arranger and conductor, during a Capitol Records session for the 1956 LP Judy.

Immediately after, she announced her debut in Las Vegas. Ever since Bugsy Siegel saw in the place an opportunity for the mafia to launder dirty money, the small Nevada town was in full expansion. On the sidelines of the small casinos in the historic center, the big complexes were multiplying on the Strip. To attract a clientele of gamblers, they organized concerts and rolled out the red carpet for popular stars. Judy was hired for five weeks at the New Frontier for a record fee of $55,000 a week — $5,000 more than any entertainer had ever received in Sin City. And once when she had to cancel one night, because of laryngitis, Sid organized at short notice a show where Jerry Lewis sang her songs while Judy mimed the words, in the vaudeville tradition.

Opening night at the New Frontier Hotel in Las Vegas on July 16, 1956.

The owners of the New Frontier fervently wanted her to stay longer, but Judy had another commitment: her return to the Palace in New York. She signed to sing for eight weeks, but prolonged the engagement for nine weeks more, which was almost as long as her first appearance there years earlier. "New York is a city that stimulated Judy," Sid later said.

Far from the Hollywood studios which weren't offering her much, except for *Funny Girl*, which she refused, Judy Garland had thus known a profitable 1956. The next years looked good, too, with a third television show on CBS on February 25. Alas, it was cancelled a few days earlier.

Artistic differences: Judy and Sid hadn't been able to come to an agreement with the station on the program's artistic approach.

The incident might have stopped there, had an article by Marie Torre in the *New York Herald Tribune* not stirred up a hornet's nest. An anonymous source who worked at CBS declared to her that: "We think that she quite simply didn't want to work," blaming it on her weight. Outraged at being attacked about her figure, a sensitive subject, Judy decided to take the journalist to court. At the trial, a few months later, Marie Torre refused to divulge her source. Not surprised, the judge qualified her as the "Joan of Arc of her profession" and decided to throw her in prison for ten days! To be the cause of imprisoning a mother of two children was definitely not what was best for Judy: she had just made the newspapers her enemy.

★

In May of 1957, Judy returned to Las Vegas, this time to the Flamingo, the first hotel built on the Strip. For these three and a half weeks of performances, she was accompanied by her family in full. Judy adored being surrounded by her children. The divorce decree stipulated that Liza was to divide her time between her father and her mother, but Vincente was always accommodating, and Liza almost never left her mother's sight. She too was a born singer. On May 18, at eleven years old, she came onstage to sing "In-Between" and "Swanee" with her mother whereas Lorna, four and a half years old, interpreted "Jingle Bells," a song with which Judy had taken her first steps onstage in Grand Rapids when she was two and a half. A wink to the public — but a strange decision, when one knew the degree to which Judy suffered from being pushed onto the stage by her own mother…

The singer undertook her first American tour: after two weeks in Los Angeles at the Greek Theater, an open amphitheater capable of seating six thousand spectators at the foot of Griffith Park, she went on to Dallas, Detroit, then Washington, D.C., where she arrived with a bad sore throat to perform for five days. In that a doctor had stuffed her with pills, everything went well for the first four shows. But on the fifth day, after breakfast, she rushed to the bathroom and came out dressed in a short lace negligee, her arms outstretched.

"Look, darling, what I just did!" she cried out to Sid.

She had cut her wrists and was bleeding abundantly. Sid made a tourniquet of a tie and called the hotel doctor, who gave her tranquilizers. They had to cancel the evening show. During the concerts in Philadelphia, she performed with bracelets on her wrists to hide the bandages.

Immediately after, she left for London with the whole family. Just arrived, she recorded "It's So Lovely to Be Back Again in London" by Roger Edens: the record was given out at her opening at the Dominion Theatre. She remained there for four and a half weeks. She hadn't sung in the British capital in more than six and a half years but hadn't forgotten what she owed this city which had made her resurrection possible after her being fired from MGM.

Judy Garland, with her "Ten Boyfriends," onstage at The Dominion Theatre in London for a four-and-a-half-week engagement starting October 16, 1957.

Back in the United States, she dashed off to Las Vegas for the end-of-year holidays: $40,000 a week at the Flamingo was an offer she couldn't refuse! But she was reluctant to go: she was exhausted. Sid tried to negotiate a postponement, but without success. Vocal problems forced her to cancel four shows.

Everything changed dramatically Christmas evening. The audience was all the more unruly because the casino had chosen to continue serving drinks during the show, contrary to the terms of her contract. The atmosphere was more tipsy than festive. It was no longer a show, but a shindig. For lack of adequate security, a woman came onstage to dance with her. Furious, she left the stage, went to her room, and turned on the television without saying a word. The next morning, she settled the score with Sid: if the evening turned into a catastrophe, it was entirely his fault. It was out of the question that she continue to sing at the Flamingo. He tried to reason with her when she replied:

"Whose side are you on? Are you protecting us or are you with these bastards? You know perfectly that they didn't keep their word."

Judy cancelled the two weeks remaining in the contract she was supposed to honor, and the matter finished in the courts. She also wanted to cancel her next engagement: three weeks at the Town & Country Club in Brooklyn. Extenuated, she really didn't have the energy to cross the United States once again. The last few months had exhausted her. But she had no choice: she had already been paid an advance of $15,000…

★

Since her marriage with Sid, Judy Garland took pleasure in the image of an inseparable couple. In Los Angeles, people didn't say "Judy and her husband," but "the Lufts." In a 1955 interview, she declared: "He's a good husband. He's a good father. He is intelligent. He's good at everything he does. He knows what's good for me. He's the man I need."

In addition to negotiating juicy contracts, Sid had to manage her highs and lows as well as he could. They slept in separate bedrooms: he slept at night, she during the day. As for Dr. Pobirs, he was continuing to play Dr. Feelgood. Seeing him come and go, Sid had the impression that he had the situation under control to some extent. It was true that Pobirs reported to him all the treatments he was administering to Judy. But was he telling the whole truth? One day when Sid pointed out to the doctor that his married life was hell, the doctor replied:

"Did you ever ask yourself why you married such a woman?"

For Judy, the pills were a subject that was taboo: she categorically refused to talk about it. As soon as Dr. Pobirs came into her room, she shut the door. It was out of the question that Sid venture into the dark side of her life. One night, Sid nonetheless decided to search his wife's room. He found pills hidden in the curtains, under the rug, in the hem of her bathrobe, behind books, in cigarette packages, as well as empty bottles of vodka in the laundry hamper. He would have to undertake some major housecleaning.

The next day at breakfast, Judy snapped at him:

"So, did you find what you were looking for?"

"Yes, I cleaned it all up. For your good, baby."

"You missed your calling in life: you should have been a cop."

Suspecting she had sources of supply other than Dr. Pobirs, Sid looked into her inner circle and discovered that the culprit was Harry Rubin, the handyman. He decided to get rid of him, which did not stop Judy from continuing to restock on the sly: she wasn't short on parallel circuits. One day opening a package sent by a friend of Judy's and coming from Saks Fifth Avenue, Sid found tubes of Tuinal, a powerful sedative, hidden in a white dress…

Asked what she expected from a man, Judy Garland answered in the magazine *Coronet:* "Good fights." Was it a provocation? That was not so sure: the married life of the Lufts was far from a bed of roses. Doors slammed regularly at 144 S. Mapleton Drive.

Confronted with Judy's more-and-more uncontrollable addiction to medication and alcohol, Sid decided one day to go for broke: he threatened to move out of the house. After having filled a suitcase with clothes, he went to see her in her room:

"Why don't you put a stop to the medication and alcohol?"

"Mind your own business."

"In that case, I'm going."

"You want to leave your children? Well, go, you son-of-a-bitch!"

"Very good, darling. If that's what you want…"

"I don't care. Get out of here…"

Trapped in his own trap, Sid took a room at a hotel on Wilshire Boulevard, while remaining in contact with the Mapleton staff. Two days later, reading the newspaper, he learned that Judy had started legal proceedings to divorce. She told her lawyer, Jerry Giesler, that Sid had "threatened" and "hit" her and had even "poisoned the dog!"

Judy's addictions were not the only source of conflict. Since *A Star Is Born*, Sid had run after cash and juggled with advances. Both of them were against the wall. In October 1957, just before the trip to England, he signed bad checks for $15,000. A situation which could have caused him serious trouble had not life's hard knocks gotten him out of this tight spot. At a horse race in New York, Rover the Second, a horse he owned half of, broke his leg. He was insured for $30,000: with his share, Sid managed to wipe away his debt.

For the moment, Judy alone thus went to New York to give her concerts at the Town & Country Club. Hardly had she arrived in Manhattan before she was summoned by the Treasury, which was asking for $8,000 in back taxes since her first series of concerts at the Palace. Without a settlement, she couldn't leave the state of New York. They settled: $3,000 would be deducted each week from her salary. The news soon enough got out. She conceded to a reporter from the *New York Journal-American*:

"Yes, I'm broke, but I'm well. There's nothing to worry about."

How could she be broke when she had never stopped working to exhaustion? Between her concerts, sales of her records, and her television shows, her estimated income for the year of 1956 alone was estimated to be $600,000. In that Sid admitted that she had earned a million dollars over the past three years, the *Los Angeles Examiner* opened the can of worms: "What happened to the millions of dollars?"

Of course, there was the mortgage on the S. Mapleton Drive house. Of course, there was their incredible lifestyle: seven salaried workers full time, a butler, a cook, a housekeeper for the ground floor, a housekeeper for the first floor, a nanny for the older children, a babysitter for Joe, a gardener — not including Harry Rubin, who had just been let go. Of course, there were the expenses brought about by Judy's concerts far from

Los Angeles, the suites in the luxury hotels, the best restaurants, taxis, the tailor-made suits and silk shirts for Sid.

For all that, they were way off the mark, for one mustn't forget that Sid frequented the horse races. Not just because he owned several horses, but because he had his own addiction: a die-hard gambler, he could lose $10,000 in one afternoon at the Santa Anna racetrack.

"No one ever won by playing the races!" Judy one day blurted out.

In Las Vegas, Sid also frequented the gambling tables. They said that during her dates at the New Frontier, Judy had to give a free show to erase his debts. In a town controlled by the mafia, one didn't joke about this kind of arrears. In a word, Sid had an obnoxious tendency to consider money Judy earned as his own.

★

Judy's first shows at the Town & Country took place without incident, but the Brooklyn of the 1950s was nothing like the fashionable middle-class Brooklyn today. Relegated to this sordid suburb, she had never had such an impression of chasing after any sort of work.

At the same time, Sid was also in New York. They were still estranged, but he had taken a room at the Warwick. Just in case…

After a week, Judy's health got worse. On the eleventh evening, Ben Maksik, the club's owner, advised her to cancel the show. He was convinced she wouldn't hold up. After singing a few songs, Judy stopped:

"Ladies and gentlemen, please forgive me. I have laryngitis and have to stop the show. Anyway, I was just shown the door."

And so, she called Sid for help. He was expecting it. Reconciled, they took up residence at the Drake Hotel. Because of the IRS, they were stuck in New York. Sid did his best to borrow money anywhere he could so as to reimburse their debts and return to Los Angeles.

From Chicago to Miami, by way of Las Vegas, Judy went back on the road. Her earnings only allowed her to reimburse the loans and other credits. In early 1959, she was worn out more than ever. Depressed, she trudged about the house, incapable of going out, with no desire other than to rest in bed. She had never been fatter.

"Look at me," she shot at Sid. "I am miserable and the phone never rings."

Sid understood that she needed a new challenge.

"You'll sing at the Metropolitan Opera House in New York. I swear to you, I'll get it."

No entertainer had ever sung at the Met. That was enough to replenish her ego and re-motivate her. Capable of moving mountains, Sid managed to arrange the concert by involving several charities. It was thus that on May 11, 1959, accompanied by thirty-five musicians and back from the brink, Judy performed before New York's high society decked in tuxes and evening gowns in a show devised by Roger Edens.

Judy Garland onstage at The Metropolitan Opera House in New York for a run which went from May 11 to 17, 1959.

It had been a long time since Judy had had such glowing reviews. "Her voice, powerful, moving, and vibrant, rose in the great cathedral of vocal culture, filling the entire stage above the orchestra. Even

Maria Callas hadn't had a better welcome," wrote the *New York Journal-American*.

Exhilarated by this success — she had always loved challenges, Judy went out on tour again. Other cities, other concert halls, and always the same obsession: earn money, reimburse the creditors, make enough for her family. More than ever, she was the breadwinner of the Lufts. Except for the Met interlude, it had been ages since her shows reflected any kind of career strategy: it was all about lining up the most dates possible, despite the wariness of organizers who doubted her reliability.

As long as she was onstage, she had the impression of being alive. The public's applause had always been the best ointment. But the more the weeks passed, the more she got bigger. Her body and her face were puffed up. At thirty-seven, she moved with difficulty. Her eyes were glazed, her memory more and more faulty. "As if I were in a fog," she said.

Sid regularly suggested she see a doctor. In her self-destructive spiral, Judy refused all help. Back in Los Angeles, he used a trick and asked two doctors, who would pretend to be musicians, to see her. Their diagnosis was definitive: she was full of water and had to be hospitalized urgently. Knowing that she would only accept to be treated at Doctors Hospital in New York, Sid pretexted a party organized at the Drake Hotel by Elsa Maxell in honor of their friend Ali Kahn to get her to New York. For once, she agreed to take a plane, but her feet were so swollen that she had to travel in slippers.

The day after the reception, upon waking, she announced to Sid:

"I am very sick. Take me to the hospital."

The examinations revealed acute hepatitis. Her liver, four times larger than normal, was no longer filtering anything. The alcohol and pills she had absorbed since the age of sixteen had attacked and destroyed her organism like acid. She was slowly poisoning herself and risked falling into a coma at any moment. A few days later, a doctor revealed to Sid:

"I won't hide the truth from you: she is through."

Judy Garland on her opening night at the Cocoanut Grove on July 23, 1958.

22.

Like a Sphinx

Seven weeks after arriving at Doctors Hospital in Manhattan, the doctors authorized her to leave the establishment on January 5, 1960, despite her weakened state. They warned Sid:

"She has at best five years to live. If she lives longer, she will be a semi-invalid."

Upon her return to Los Angeles, Judy remained bedridden almost the whole day. Nurses watched over her night and day. She got around in a wheelchair and was a shadow of her former self. "The truth is that she will no longer be the superstar she once was. She was simply my wife and that was perfect as such," said Sid. He no longer had a choice: it was he who from thereon in would take care of their needs and those of their children.

When Judy was hospitalized, a friend showed Luft a kind of miniature tape player made by a small firm in Minneapolis, Viking. At the time, audio cassettes didn't exist yet. To listen to music, one had to have a record player. Sid's idea was different: he wanted to develop an audio system for airplanes. Hadn't Howard Hughes' TWA just broken new ground by projecting movies onboard his planes? With Edward Alperson, he therefore created a company baptized Aerophonics Electronics Corporation to develop his project.

While Sid devoted his time to advancing his new business, Judy got back on her feet, slowly but surely. Weaned from alcohol and medications, with the exception of one or two pills of Ritalin, a new tranquilizer on the market, "she seemed in better health than she ever had been since we first met," said Sid. "Her behavior was balanced, completely normal, but I remained prudent: I didn't think that her recovery would last." At thirty-eight, despite illness, her voice had lost nothing of its power. So, there she was, recording a new album, *That's Entertainment!*

Studio recording sessions had never been a problem for her. On the first take, she gave everything. Most of the time, a second take wasn't even necessary. The LP was well received: "A tour de force," commented the *New Musical Express*.

On July 10, 1960, she made her first public appearance in more than six months at a banquet meant to raise funds for the Democratic Party in the presence of the candidate John Fitzgerald Kennedy. As always, Judy was a fervent Democrat. She had met the future President by way of Peter Lawford, his brother-in-law, at the New York opening of *A Star Is Born*. And she was convinced that he was the man America needed.

Adlai Stevenson, Judy Garland, and John F. Kennedy on July 10, 1960 at a Democratic National Convention breakfast fundraiser at the Hilton Hotel in Beverly Hills, California a few days before Kennedy won the Democratic nomination.

★

Los Angeles is a metropolis that looks to the future: one only exists if one has projects. But Judy had none. In her Mapleton Drive house, she was now like a foreigner to the movie industry, the nuclear core of the city. She belonged to the past. "I was someone who had been a star," she said. Rather than being a relic of the past in a city in full mutation since the fall of the studios, she chose to continue her recovery on the other side of the Atlantic, in England. To lose her blues, she needed fresh air and new faces.

Sid Luft didn't need an accountant to know that Judy didn't have the means to pay for a long stay in London, but he understood that it was a question of survival: he thus didn't hesitate to sell the Vlaminck that adorned their living room to finance the trip, and in early August, Judy flew off, alone, for the British capital. "The tempo is slower than in the United States," she explained to British journalists. "It stimulates me and puts me in excellent spirits."

Checked in the Westbury Hotel, she spent weekends at Noel Coward's place or in Dirk Bogarde's country house, but Sid's absence weighed on her. She had never lived alone on a day-to-day basis. "I miss you," she wrote him. "London isn't the same without you."

In late August, Sid decided to join her. Aerophonics Electronics Corporation had been started up, and he could work out of London, as he could Los Angeles or New York. In that Judy had expressed her wish that Lorna and Joe join them — Liza was continuing her studies near Annecy so as to perfect her French, he rented a house belonging to the filmmaker Carol Reed on King's Road, in the Chelsea neighborhood. Lorna and Joe went to a private school and Liza came to see them regularly.

Judy spent time with her children. They had become her priority. She also made recordings at Abbey Road for EMI/Capitol in early August. But she was an entertainer at heart: without an audience, she died. Sid organized two concerts at the Palladium and a few dates in Europe. On October 5, she sang in Paris, at the Palais de Chaillot. Two hundred tickets were handed out free to fill the theater. For, the French public didn't really know about Judy Garland. Her masterpieces of the MGM era, including *The Wizard of Oz*, never came out until after the war: during the Occupation, American films were forbidden in France. Released non-chronologically, and rushedly, they hadn't made an impact. Furthermore, American records were poorly distributed: they could only be found as imports in specialized shops. Following the concert, the press was enthusiastic: "Now we know why she is called 'Miss Show Business' in America," wrote a critic. Two days later, for the second performance, the show was sold out: and there were eight curtain calls. As a result, she gave two additional shows at the Olympia on October 28 and 29, the first of which was recorded by the radio station Europe 1.

Maurice Chevalier and Judy Garland having breakfast at Chevalier's home in Marnes-la-Coquette, France, September 28, 1960.

Judy Garland at the Palais de Chaillot in Paris on October 5, 1960.
Photo by Jack Garofalo.

At the request of Peter Lawford, she also participated in late October in Wiesbaden in a concert to support John F. Kennedy in front of American troops stationed in Germany. The election was going to be tight, and every vote counted. Kennedy won on November 8, 1960 with 112,827 more votes than Richard Nixon, that is 0.17% of registered voters. That night, she attended an election celebration organized by the United States ambassador at the Dorchester, wearing a badge with Kennedy on it.

"I hope you voted for him," she shouted to all the guests.

★

Judy was like a phoenix which endlessly rises from its ashes. In London, she rediscovered what she missed the most: desire.

But Sid kept the doctors' diagnosis it in his head: Judy would soon be an invalid. He didn't believe her better health would last. Entirely devoted to his projects, which seemed like the only way to support his family in the long run, he preferred to abandon his role as manager. At the end of 1960, he therefore contacted Freddie Fields to ask him to manage Judy's career. An appointment was organized in London in early December. For this former MCA man who had just created his own agency, it was out of the question that he be satisfied with chasing after fees, as Sid had done since *A Star Is Born*. For him, she was a formidable calling card. And for her, who was considered a has-been in the United States, this new blood was a great opportunity. At first glance, this was the perfect win–win arrangement: everyone benefited.

On December 31, 1960, it was time for the Lufts to go home to the United States, if only to honor a contract signed a long time ago for a date in Miami. While waiting for it, they settled into the Carlyle in New York, where Freddie Fields laid out his plans: a tour, her debut on Broadway in a musical, the lead in *The Unsinkable Molly Brown*, an upcoming musical in London, a television show on CBS, and a return to the screen in *Judgment at Nuremberg*. Was it he who had sought out Stanley Kramer, or the opposite? Each claimed the paternity of the idea, but in the meantime, Judy Garland was invited in March to join one of the biggest productions of the year, an evocation of the Nuremberg trial during which, from November 20, 1945 to October 1, 1946, twenty-four dignitaries from the Third Reich were judged for crimes against humanity by a jurisdiction put in place by the Allied Powers. From Burt Lancaster to Spencer Tracy, from Richard Widmark to Montgomery Clift, the greatest Hollywood stars had been mobilized for this work, which was supposed to bear witness before history. Judy would only have a small role: only eleven days of filming. But the $50,000 fee was royal and her character of Irene Hoffman, a German housewife whose Jewish friend had been executed for "illegal" relations with her, offered her, who had always been confined to musicals, a chance in gold to show her full dramatic potential.

In March 1961, six years after *A Star Is Born*, Judy therefore went before the cameras again at Universal Studios in Studio City, on the other side of Beverly Hills. The first day was difficult: she tried six times but couldn't manage to cry.

"I am too happy to shed tears," she told Stanley Kramer.

Judy Garland on the set of Judgment at Nuremburg, *1961.*

The seventh take was good, and the shoot took place without a problem. Judy had reconciled with the movies and the movies with her. Her performance of rare intensity earned her a nomination for Best Supporting Actress. An award which was won by a narrow margin by Rita Moreno in *West Side Story*, the great victor that year.

Obviously, Judy was unlucky at the Academy Awards. But studio doors were no longer closed to her. "1961 was one of the best years of my life," she said.

★

A photomontage of pictures taken at Judy Garland's second show at Carnegie Hall on May 21, 1961 by Joe Covello that can be found in the inner gatefold of the double-LP Judy at Carnegie Hall.

Even before filming *Judgment at Nuremberg*, Judy played Dallas on a new tour whose greatest moment was on April 23, 1961 at Carnegie Hall, the most beautiful concert hall in Manhattan, with its exceptional acoustics and its two thousand eight hundred seats on five levels. From the Palace to the Met, Judy always had a magic link with the New York public. But this concert would forever leave a deep impression on the public. It lasted two-and-a-quarter hours and had a brief intermission. Twenty-six songs, and a new simplicity: no dancers, no show business glitziness, just a little lady who kept her audience spellbound by the magic of her voice. Judy Garland had already given excellent concerts; this one was just perfect. Sixteen months following a hospitalization after which she was given up as dead, she had a resurrection that evening that became the stuff of myth, amplified by that fact the show had been recorded. The double-album, *Judy at Carnegie Hall*, left its mark on the record industry by charting for ninety-five weeks in *Billboard*, including thirteen at number one. An achievement that would earn *Judy at Carnegie Hall* five Grammy Awards, including album of the year, which for the first time went to a woman. That year, she received all the awards a singer could receive. The record industry showed itself to be infinitely more appreciative of her than the movie world…

Meeting Freddie Fields had been a pick-me-up for her. "With him, something started," she declared to *Life*. "He knew how to do what I had no idea how to do: to guide my work." Very quickly, Fields presented his new associate to her, David Begelman, whom he had hired to take care of her full time. She liked their youth, their enthusiasm, their cool. America had just entered into the effervescence of the 1960s and their way of doing things was in phase with the era.

"You're the best thing that ever happened to me," she told them.

She nicknamed them "Leopold and Loeb," after the two students, sentenced to life in prison in 1924, who thought they could commit the perfect crime. But were they the real killers? At the very least, they would have one victim: Sid Luft.

By choosing Freddie to take charge of his wife's career, Sid thought he could keep an eye on it at a distance. Set solid on getting his share, he even negotiated behind Judy's back a $1,000 kickback for every new contract. In reality, he put the cat among the pigeons. From the day Freddie became her manager, Judy never ceased to keep her husband away. She loved Sid, believing he was indispensable. She had just discovered that she could live without him very well: "I don't give a damn about Sid," she remarked.

Starting in January 1961, Judy created with her two young wolves who now were in charge of her affairs a company baptized Kingsrow Enterprises. Their first order of business was to clear up her financial situation: Freddie and David discovered that she was $375,000 in debt. Sid never stopped accumulating bills and the six months in London only worsened the deficit. At the time of her Dallas concert, he was presented with an unpaid hotel bill dating from… 1957. "I hate owing money," she said. "It's humiliating, especially when you have every reason in the world not to be in hock."

When Judy informed Sid that he wouldn't have the least share in Kingsrow Enterprises, tempers flared. They no longer agreed about anything. She wound up storming out of the Stanhope Hotel and moved into an apartment at the Dakota with her daughter and son. Throughout the first semester of 1961, they went from quarrel to reconciliation. When they met up, as they did for the Carnegie Hall concert, Sid made sure that she didn't succumb to the temptation of starting to take pills again. In this period, their relationship was less conflictual: Judy even decided to put him on salary as an associate producer at a rate of $400 a week. To celebrate the agreement, they went out to dinner. But the evening came to a sudden end.

"What do you think about what I just did for you," she asked him.

"Why, that's a two-bit tip compared to what I've given and done for you," he replied. "You don't know a fucking thing about finances. If you think that $400 a week is anything, when you're making $100,000 a week, you're misinformed."

Judy's response was scathing: she slapped his face.

During the summer, the star decided to rent a house in Hyannis Port, in Massachusetts, two steps away from the summer home of the Kennedys. Sid, who hadn't been invited there, returned to Los Angeles. But when she was hospitalized with a kidney problem, he called her regular doctor right away.

"How could you contact him behind my back?" she reproached him roundly.

He nevertheless decided to join her on Cape Cod. She welcomed him so coldly that he went to a motel. When they finally saw each other, she spoke her mind:

"You know, I'm going to get a divorce."

That night, he drank to the point of passing out in his room, but nevertheless called Judy for help. She found him dead drunk. In a certain way, the roles were now inversed. But the spectacle of seeing Sid on the verge of an ethylic coma was not going to help her revive the love she once had for him… All the more so because she had a serious crush on David Begelman.

Sid and David had many points in common. Both were Jewish and came from the New York suburbs. They weren't quite good-looking, but they had the same taste for luxury clothes. Both were wheeler-dealers and knew how to make deals that were next to impossible in appearance. David nonetheless had something extra: a true artistic sense. It was he, for example, who had gotten Mort Lindsey to lead Judy's orchestra on her 1961 tour and at Carnegie Hall, which allowed him to move up a notch. Very quickly, she became his mistress, even though he was married. "Judy was in thrall with him. Obsessively…," remembered Stevie Phillips, then Begelman's and Judy's assistant. "Judy was sure that David was in love with her. And I was happy to leave it right there. I knew the truth, and it was ugly. David was ugly… The truth would have hurt. The truth might have cured some other person, but not Judy who lived in a make-believe world."

Contrary to what he made people believe, David never intended to divorce, but refrained from interrupting their relationship: he intended to keep her under his thumb.

One day, he joined her in Boston, where she was to give a concert. He was in the corridor leading to the dressing rooms when she cut her wrist. "It hurt me to see Judy taken in by David's outrageousness, but I could not or would not attempt to convince her that David loved no one but himself. She believed what she wanted to believe, and in spite of their fights about his prolonged absences, regardless of his limp ad-libbing about his failure to get a divorce, Judy remained a believer. And now

David had come to Boston to attend her concert and was dressing in a room almost next door when she slit her wrist. Judy Garland would show him. Judy Garland would die for him. Who was Judy Garland really punishing? It wasn't David Begelman."

Judy Garland at The Hollywood Bowl on September 16, 1961.

Judy Garland, as photographed by Douglas Kirkland in 1961.

23.

This Can't Be Love

Once back in Los Angeles, Sid Luft had no other choice but to sell the Mapleton Drive house. In any case, Judy no longer wanted to go anywhere near it: too many bad memories. He got a good price for it, $225,000, but once the mortgage was paid there would only remain $10,000.

On her side, after having recorded the voice and songs for an animated feature, *Gay Purr-ee*, Judy moved into a house in the suburbs of New York, where Sid joined her in December 1962. "One doesn't throw away ten years of marriage easily," Judy said when invoking their numerous separations and reconciliations.

Although he didn't accompany her to Germany for the world premiere of *Judgment at Nuremberg*, he was there when she was sick. At the least crisis, he ran to her: it was his way of turning things around. They spent the end–of–year holidays together and took a house that Sid had rented in Bel–Air. Judy appeared on a CBS special, then filmed *A Child Is Waiting* for United Artists. Originally, Stanley Kramer was to direct the film which takes place in a clinic for developmentally-challenged children. Judy was set to play a former aspiring concert pianist who had been hired as the school's music teacher, who opposes some of the policies of the director of the establishment, played by Burt Lancaster. For Kramer, who had given Judy the desire to make movies again, Judy was ready to do anything. But he was occupied with other projects and gave the project over to an actor who had just begun directing, a certain John Cassavetes. After the feverish *Shadows*, a prototype of independent filmmaking that was ahead of its time, Cassavetes was trying to fit into the studio system. But whereas Kramer knew how to reassure actors, Cassavetes only liked chaos. On the set, the atmosphere was electric.

"I'm going to kill him!" one day shouted Judy, who above all didn't need to be destabilized to give the best of herself.

On edge, she got into another fight with Sid and, for the last days of shooting, moved into a room at the Beverly Hills Hotel. When her lawyer phoned Sid to tell him that she once again wanted a divorce, Sid replied:

Judy Garland, 39, Liza Minnelli, 15, Lorna Luft, 9, and Joe Luft, 6, leaving New York International Airport for Los Angeles on January 1, 1962 after holidaying in the east. Garland began rehearsing her CBS special with Frank Sinatra and Dean Martin on January 2, 1962.

"This is nothing but a mishap that should not be taken seriously. For Judy, this was just a trial balloon. She takes her inhibitions and anxiety out on me."

Back in New York, Judy fell ill, which required her to be hospitalized for a week at Manhattan's Columbia Presbyterian Medical Center. She was exhausted. After fifteen months of non-stop activity, including her 1961 concert tour, making the films *Judgment at Nuremburg, Gay Purr-ee*, and *A Child Is Waiting*, a television special with Frank Sinatra and Dean Martin in early 1962, and recording a new Capitol single in late 1961 and a live album in early 1962, she should have taken a break, but she had signed to make *I Could Go On Singing* in England. A few days before leaving, Sid reappeared: he had taken a suite with Lorna and Joe at the Stanhope Hotel, whereas Liza had preferred to spend her nights at a friend's. Judy agreed to join them, but in another room. When she suggested that the children accompany her to Great Britain, Sid was firmly opposed.

Judy Garland performs solo (left) and with Frank Sinatra and Dean Martin (right) on The Judy Garland Show, *taped on January 5, 8, and 9, 1962.*

Seeing herself dispossessed of her children had always been Judy's greatest fear. She contacted her lawyer, who showed up at the Stanhope with two private detectives. The lawyer had concocted a scenario: Judy would enter alone into Sid's room, she would provoke him, tensions would rise and, as soon as they raised their voices, the detectives would force the door down.

The plan took place as planned: Lorna and Joe were removed from the hotel by the two detectives, while Liza, already in the car, waited for them. Judy had every intention of leaving for England with her three children.

★

Judy Garland had won the first set, but Sid wasn't calling it quits. Five days after the arrival in London of the woman who was still his wife, he landed in the British capital with the goal of recuperating his children. Judy once again put a spoke in his wheel by obtaining from the London High Court a status quo authorizing her to keep the children while awaiting a definitive decision, which would take several months to be made. That left her free to make *I Could Go On Singing*, albeit in deplorable psychological conditions.

Directed by Ronald Neame, the movie marked her return to musicals. The storyline was melodramatic: a successful American singer takes advantage of a show at the London Palladium to try to re-contact her son, now fourteen years old, whom she gave up at birth and whom his father had raised. Her friend Dirk Bogarde was her costar: that was her reason for accepting the film, on the condition that she be able to contribute some modifications to the script.

At her arrival at the Shepperton studios, which were about twenty miles from London, the producers spared no expense: flowers in her dressing room, boxes of chocolates and bottles of Blue Nun. The music director was Mort Lindsey and the title song by Harold Arlen and Yip Harburg, the composers of "Over the Rainbow." But when she discovered the new script, she hit the roof:

"I can't play this crap! I'm not going to do this fucking script."

"She was in despair," said Dirk Bogarde. "In despair for her children, in despair because she didn't have anywhere to live — Sid had made her frightened of going back to America — and in despair because of a script she loathed. Everything was on top of her. She felt trapped." When the actor showed her the corrections he had already made to the dialogues, she began to smile again. But a few hours after the first day of shooting, Judy was back in the hospital: she had tried to commit suicide. Too much medication. Worn out by her personal situation, involved in a film she didn't believe in, in conflict with a director she tried to have fired, she was overcome by her old demons. After missing five days, she made a second suicide attempt. Another hospital stay. On the set, British humor oblige, members of the crew called out to each other:

"How's it going today?"

"Fairly well: Judy hasn't committed suicide."

Recording session at Abbey Road for I Could Go On Singing.

At the end of July 1962, filming came to an end. After a new court hearing, Judy returned to the United States where, after a few days' vacation on the banks of Lake Tahoe, she got back to what she did best: sing onstage at the Sahara Hotel in Las Vegas. Four weeks, which was extended to six which earned her the tidy sum of $240,000…

On their end, Freddie Fields and David Begelman cold-called the TV networks with an idea: a weekly show by Judy Garland. The three major ones competed with financial offers, and on December 28, Judy signed an astronomical contract with CBS: $20 million over five years for twenty-six show a season.

Knowing Judy's chronic instability, some wondered how long she would hold up. On television, live, there was no security net.

A glamor shot by John Engstead from 1962.

Obviously, her ongoing soap-opera hard-luck story with Sid Luft was never ending. Like a remix of the play *Who's Afraid of Virginia Wolf?* interspliced with the song "This Can't Be Love."

At the end of November 1962, at the Slate Brothers Club, one of the fashionable nightclubs in Los Angeles, Sid was taken to task by a movie producer who accused him of living off Judy. Sid demanded he apologize, and he refused. Not willing to be humiliated, Sid knocked him down. The Hollywood tabloids had a field day. They never had had much respect for Sid. But Judy liked men who had panache. In her eyes, this episode signaled the return of "one-punch Luft," the man she fell in love with at the beginning of the 1950s. A tough guy not easily taken in. She needed to admire a man in order to love him and, though her relationship with Sid was degraded, it was first and foremost because she no longer admired him.

Judy Garland and Dirk Bogarde at the London opening of I Could Go On Singing *on March 6, 1963.*

That was all they needed to reconnect. On February 14, 1963, the headline in the *Los Angeles Times* read: "Judy and Sid reconciled." Immediately thereafter, the tear-away lovers took a few days' vacation in Las Vegas then in San Francisco. Then, Judy flew to London for the opening of *I Could Go On Singing*. The reviews were glowing ("Her acting has never been better," wrote *Time*), but the movie was a flop, both in England and in the United States. In late March, Judy and Sid took two weeks' vacation in the Caribbean before going to New York to attend the off-Broadway opening of *Best Foot Forward*, a musical which marked the official debut, at sixteen, of Liza Minnelli. In fact, they missed the evening: officially, because of a missed plane, but in reality, because Judy didn't want to steal the limelight from her daughter. But she attended the second evening with the pride of a mother who knew that the future was assured: Liza was dazzling in this show which launched her career.

Upon returning to Los Angeles, they moved into a house at 129 S. Rockingham Avenue in Brentwood. Sid, who had never digested being excluded from Kingsrow Enterprises and even less so for having allowed David Begelman to court his wife, was dead set on eliminating him from the picture. Convinced that Begelman had financially profited from Judy, Sid managed to convince her to order an audit of Kingsrow by an outside observer. The verdict was categorical: "It was worse than I had imagined," said Sid. Between $200,000 and $300,000 had purely and simply been embezzled, not to count the suspicious withdrawals. To justify a check for $50,000, Begelman explained that he had paid a paparazzi who threatened to publish a photo of Judy in a hospital, but the amount was far greater than transactions practiced in this kind of blackmail, that is if it ever took place. It also appeared that Begelman had kept for himself a Cadillac offered to Judy, who was planning on buying a car, for her appearance on a Jack Paar television show.

David Begelman was indeed the profiteer Sid suspected. In the 1970s, when he became president of Columbia, he was dismissed for having embezzled $65,000. But instead of agreeing wholeheartedly with Sid, Judy minimalized the disloyalty.

"Let's say he stole $200,000 or $300,000 from me, what's that in comparison to the $20 million CBS is going to pay me?"

Furious, Sid left the Brentwood house. Returning a few days later, he discovered that Judy had had his things moved to a storage unit.

This time, there would be no reconciliation.

*

Between two quarrels with Sid, Judy devoted most of her time to preparing her series for CBS. Before confronting the television cameras, she had gone on a diet which allowed her to slim down to a weight she had not been at for years: 100 pounds. The shows were to be taped in the Los Angeles studios. George Schlatter, who was the producer, cajoled Judy. The network pulled out all the stops and gave her a thousand-square-foot dressing room that had in it a pool table, a piano, and a bar full of Blue Nun.

Judy Garland performs at the SHARE Benefit in Los Angeles on May 27, 1963 at which she auctioned off her performances. Gene Kelly and Sammy Davis Jr. joined her onstage. The charity was close to Garland's heart in that it benefited developmentally disabled children.

Leigh Wiener, in a photo entitled "Judy in White," captured Judy Garland on June 23, 1963 on the set of the dress rehearsal for the first episode of The Judy Garland Show.

On June 24, for the premiere of *The Judy Garland Show*, she welcomed her partner of olden days, Mickey Rooney. It had been years since they shared the same bill, they who for so many years and films had been inseparable. The first six shows went well, but on August 2, George Schlatter was curtly fired. They reproached him for having made each show a special occasion, whereas the heads of the network thought that the viewing public wanted nothing more than to tune into a show with weekly segments they liked. "It's not up to television to adapt to Judy Garland, but for Judy Garland to adapt to television," declared James Aubrey Jr., the CBS president, nicknamed "the smiling cobra." A new producer was hired: Norman Jewison, the future director of *The Cincinnati Kid* and *The Thomas Crown Affair*, but he was having a hard time producing a show that was going every which way depending on more-or-less-funny jokes. In November, a third producer, Bill Colleran, who put the spotlight on the musical aspects of the show, was named.

Photographed by Leigh Wiener at a dress rehearsal on June 23, 1963 for the first show of her 1963/1964 television series, Judy Garland interprets "Keep Your Sunny Side Up," intended as the opening number but deleted from the air tape.

(Left) Judy Garland sings "Ol' Man River" on June 24, 1963. (Right) "Come Rain or Come Shine" on July 16, 1963 on the CBS-TV weekly series The Judy Garland Show.

In an atmosphere that was more and more tense, Judy became uncontrollable. After John F. Kennedy's assassination in Dallas, she insisted on interpreting "The Battle Hymn of the Republic" to pay tribute to this president she so admired. The network refused. "The country's mourned Kennedy, it wants to go on to other things," James Aubrey insisted. She disregarded him and delivered an astonishing interpretation.

By programming *The Judy Garland Show* on Sunday evening opposite *Bonanza*, CBS had made a bet. Since 1959, the western had never left the top of the ratings. Judy's show was never going to unseat it. How about changing the day of the week it was on? James Aubrey preferred to put an end to the experience: there would be no second season and the final show was broadcast on March 29, 1964.

That night, neither Freddie Fields nor David Begelman was with her: they were attending the Broadway opening of *Funny Girl* with their new client, the promising Barbra Streisand. For several months, they no longer answered her calls. They were convinced that her career was behind her.

Because of her CBS contract, Judy Garland thought she was free from want until the end of her life. She had to begin at zero again.

(Left) Count Basie and Judy Garland on The Judy Garland Show, *taped July 7, 1963. (Right) Barbra Streisand and Judy Garland on* The Judy Garland Show, *taped October 4, 1963.*

(Left) Judy Garland and Mickey Rooney on The Judy Garland Show, *taped June 24, 1963. (Right) Lena Horne and Judy Garland on* The Judy Garland Show, *taped July 23, 1963.*

(Left) Peggy Lee and Judy Garland on The Judy Garland Show, *taped November 8, 1963. (Right) Tony Bennett and Judy Garland on* The Judy Garland Show, *taped July 30, 1963.*

24.

Black Hole in Australia

For Judy Garland, solitude was more than a fear: it was an abyss. Vertigo. She needed the attention of a man to exist. "I need to be needed."

Separated from Sid, she piled on the affairs. Bobby Cole, a pianist whom she had worked with on *The Judy Garland Show*, was one. André Philip, a French actor passing through Hollywood, was another. Glenn Ford, a star of films noirs (*The Big Heat*) and westerns (*3:10 to Yuma*), yet another. "My heart belongs to you and I adore you," she wrote him. He introduced her to his doctor, Dr. Lee Siegel, who had treated many celebrities. In these early years of the 1960s, psychotropic drugs were in the midst of a major revolution with the arrival of antidepressants. But Judy swore by her blood-red capsules of Seconal, this powerful sedative whose intake required her to take uppers. A sly fox, Dr. Siegel had a trick up his sleeve: he asked his pharmacist to grind up the Valium pills and fill the Seconal capsules with them.

Unknowingly off the barbiturates, Judy found new vigor. But Glenn Ford couldn't be at her beck and call all the time, as she would have liked. He didn't always answer her middle-of-the night calls because he had to be in shape the next day and on set. Despite their complicity, they grew apart.

During the end-of-year holidays, at a party organized by the costume designer from the TV series, she met Mark Herron. Tall, slim, elegant, educated, with a catlike gaze, he had a dry humor she couldn't get enough of. When he was still a student, he had been a promising actor — the best in his theater arts class at the Los Angeles City College in 1952, but his career never took off. Once a young hopeful and now a has-been, he left for Italy where he was able to get a small role in Fellini's *8 ½*. He had just returned to the United States but had no projects. On the other hand, he had plenty of time. He found a new role for himself: that of devoted admirer.

In the papers, people were asking questions: who was this Mark Herron who was accompanying Judy everywhere and living at her place almost permanently? She wanted to do a play with him. He was flattered and hung on. Who knows: perhaps this was the opportunity of a lifetime?

*

In May of 1964, a new tour awaited Judy: a series of three concerts in Australia for $52,000. In order to forestall the fatigue engendered by such a long trip, Mark and Judy decided to first take a week's vacation in Hawaii. They stopped in Honolulu to enjoy the beaches of fine sand in Waikiki. They then arrived in Sydney, where customs confiscated her medication case filled with pills. It was "only through the offices of a Chinese abortionist who had black-market connections was she able to replenish her stock," according to author Gerold Frank, "but they were European drugs with dosages unfamiliar to her, and they were to play a role in some of her catastrophic moments in Australia."

Despite all, she thrilled the ten thousand audience members at Sydney Stadium. "Miss Garland earned the greatest ovation in show-business history in Australia," wrote *Variety*. "As soon as she appeared onstage, she held the audience in the palm of her hands." Three days later, same stadium, same triumph.

After a twelve-hour train trip, Judy arrived in Melbourne for her third and last concert. Exhausted, she retreated into her room, and refused to answer journalists' questions. They had to pretty much drag her onto the stage at the Festival Hall, one and a quarter hours late. A discourtesy the audience was ready to forgive had it not been for the fact that that night she was in bad shape. She tripped over the microphone cable, couldn't stay in tune, and forgot the lyrics before calling it quits: a black hole. The Sydney doctor's prescriptions had plunged her into a trance. The audience began to heckle her. From all over the concert hall one could hear "boo!" and "another drink?", just as she collapsed onto her stool. The first row of people heard her murmur to the orchestra: "Why don't we play cards?" When she managed to get up, she began to sing "Over the Rainbow," unable to finish her signature song. In the end, she left the stage after fifteen minutes.

The next day, when she was leaving to take the plane with Mark to Sydney, a hysterical almost-hateful crowd was waiting for her at the airport. They were pushed to the boiling point by a local press which had always taken a dim view of tours by American entertainers in Australia: in their eyes, they only came there to replenish their bank accounts. The American papers would have evoked just another meltdown, but the aborted Melbourne concert was described in the local press as an insult to the Australian public.

*

Ashamed of this disaster, Judy was devastated by the audience's violent reaction to her, who, in her worst moments, had always been able to count on the public's unconditional love.

"I will never sing again," she said to Mark.

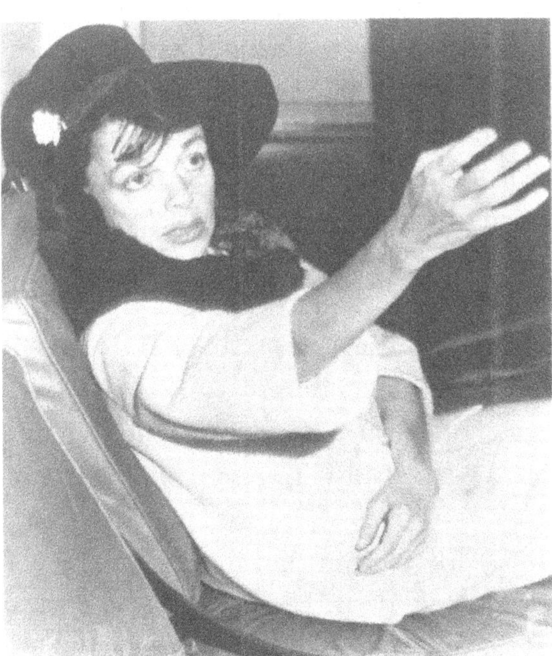

Judy Garland at the Sydney airport on her way to Hong Kong, May 23, 1964.

Should she return to Los Angeles? She didn't have the energy. She preferred to take short-hop flights. Mark therefore reserved a ticket for Hong Kong, where they took a suite on the twenty-second floor of the Mandarin Hotel. But after the Australian maelstrom, there was another storm that awaited them: typhoon Viola. Confined to their room, Judy and Mark, to kill time, had fun dubbing Chinese programs, of which they couldn't understand a single word, into English. At least, she was smiling again. But Mark made the mistake of buying the international papers in the hotel lobby. The weather outside consisted of downfalls and gusty winds, but Judy began to skim through Time magazine and her eyes fell on an article devoted to her. "At forty-one," she read, "Judy Garland just went over the rainbow for the last time in her career." She had already had bad reviews, but this one was a premature death notice.

"I can't go on this way," she said to Mark. "Give me some pills and let me finish it all."

Mark managed to calm her down and fell asleep next to her. But in the morning, he looked for her hand, but only found the empty sheets. He hurried to the bathroom: Judy was lying there, lifeless, on the tiled floor. He immediately phoned the hotel's front desk to have her transported to the emergency room. It was impossible because of the typhoon, the city was paralyzed, no ambulance could get to her. With the help of the staff, Mark managed to get her onto a wheelchair and transport her to a small hospital three blocks away. She was intubated, then her stomach was pumped, but the overdose had gotten into her bloodstream. The doctors' prognosis was pessimistic. A nurse went so far as to declare her dead. Judy remained in a coma for fifteen hours.

Up until then, all of her suicide attempts had been cries for help. This time, she had really wanted to kill herself. She had never taken such a dose.

Contacted by Mark Herron, Dr. Siegel and Kart Bent, her road manager, flew to her bedside in Hong Kong. She just left the hospital when Lee Siegel diagnosed her with an early-stage pleurisy. Her body was in pieces. In that the intubation had damaged her vocal cords, the

Hong Kong doctors warned her that she would never again sing. It was a kind of reflex with her, but the more she was at the bottom of the barrel, the more she found the energy to be reborn. Ten days after having narrowly escaped death, she attended a concert by the Allen Brothers and made the rounds of nightclubs in the city…

★

During her convalescence in Hong Kong, an English-speaking nurse took care of her: Snowda Wu. A certain complicity developed between the star and the young woman. Judy proposed that she take care of her full time. It was thus with Snowda that Judy and Mark took the boat for Tokyo. Onboard, they took time to enjoy life. Although Judy was not officially divorced from Sid, they claimed to have been married by a Buddhist priest — which they were careful not to deny.

From Japan, they went to London, where they rented a house in the Chelsea area. The British capital had remained a place of renaissance for Judy. On June 23, she participated in the "Night of 100 Stars" gala at the Palladium. Originally, she was slated to make a simple appearance, but the audience was so enthusiastic that she sang two songs followed by thunderous applause. The next day, the press wrote that she had stolen the show from the Beatles, also on the bill…

Back from the dead, Judy chose to make her big comeback in London at the Palladium, her lucky stage. She phoned her daughter, who had just sent Judy her first record:

"My God, you must have worked hard to make such a wonderful record! What do you think about singing with me at the Palladium?"

"Why don't you sing on your own?" replied Liza.

Regardless of her daughter's reluctance, Judy had hardly put the phone down before she called a press conference to announce that she was going to give a concert with Liza! By the afternoon, it was sold out and a second date had to be added a week later.

Publicity shots of Judy Garland (left) taken at The Boltons, Kensington, London on September 25, 1964 and of Liza Minnelli and Judy Garland (right) on October 27, 1964.

On November 8, mother and daughter were onstage together. They sang about twenty duets, and Judy sang about fifteen songs alone. Four hours of rehearsals in the afternoon had made her voice somewhat hoarse, but the emotion was exceptional. She put her guts, her suffering, her breakups, all her heart on the line. The audience was rapturous, the reviews were raves. "Judy received the ovation of her life," commented the *Daily Mail.* "To speak about her rationally is as difficult as explaining her magic."

Once again, she had won her bet.

Liza Minnelli and Judy Garland duet at The London Palladium in 1964.

★

On December 19, 1964, Judy flew to New York where she returned for the first time since her departure for Australia six months earlier. She had hoped to spend Christmas with her children, but it was full-out war between her and Sid who, to gain guardianship, brought up Judy's addictions. When she wanted her children to cross the Atlantic to attend her concert at the Palladium with their half-sister, a California judge curtly vetoed the request. Another judge authorized Lorna and Joe to join their mother in New York for the year-end holidays, but Sid refused to comply. A warrant was issued against him, he was arrested, then released after bail was deposited. Finally, on December 28, Judy was reunited with Lorna and Joe, over whom she would officially obtain guardianship on May 19, 1965, when the divorce was finalized. All of Sid's schemes had been for nothing, except to poison his life.

Professionally, the new year wasn't anything to write home about: no major projects, but a series of concerts in Toronto, Miami, Chicago,

Cincinnati, Las Vegas, as well as TV appearances, most notably on *The Andy Williams Show* and *The Ed Sullivan Show.*

Mark Herron was still with her. On November 14, 1965, at 1:30 in the morning, he became her fourth husband at the Little Church of the West in Las Vegas. Clearly, the ceremony was improvised: Judy had made an appointment with the jeweler Marvin Hime for him to come to her Brentwood house at 3 P.M. in order to adjust the wedding rings. Her witnesses were Guy McElwaine, her publicist, and Snowda Wu, her nurse.

"How do you feel?" asked a journalist.

"Like Mrs. Mark Herron," she replied.

Their relationship took no time to go south. For Judy Garland, marriage was always the beginning of the end.

Judy Garland and Mark Herron at their wedding ceremony in 1965.

Morally and physically in ruin, she continued to live on the razor's edge. The presence of Snowda Wu, whom the children called "Snowy" — and who would soon return to Hong Kong, turned out to be disastrous. "She gave them every day all kinds of injections of who knows what," wrote Sid Luft. "I hold her responsible for Judy's condition, characterized by explosions of hysteria and violence, at this time. The children were often terrified by their mother's behavior."

Moneywise, the situation was only getting worse. In March, Judy received a court order enjoining her to sell the Brentwood house if she couldn't pay her debts. Her finances were at a low point: she owed $122,000 to one hundred twenty lenders, not to speak of back taxes which amounted to $400,000.

More irascible than ever, she was mad at everyone, especially Mark, who got it into his head to become an actor again. He for that matter was able to get the lead in a new version of *Private Lives*, Noel Coward's play, which was running in Los Angeles. Judy had the impression that he had used her fame and the publicity their marriage had furnished him. She feared to see him go off on his own and to no longer be the center of his attentions. Every time he tried to be alone to memorize his text, she managed to disturb him, to the point where he had to go elsewhere far away from her to work. When he returned home, he discovered that she had thrown all his clothes in the swimming pool! On April 12, 1966, she nonetheless attended the opening of *Private Lives* at the Ivar Theatre in Hollywood with George Cukor. But, three days later, Mark left the Brentwood house forever. It took another fifteen days for Judy's lawyer to announce their separation, which was definitive.

Judy Garland and George Cukor attend the opening of Noel Coward's Private Lives, *in which Mark Herron starred, at the Ivar Theatre in Hollywood on April 12, 1966.*

255

Judy subsequently cited Mark's lack of appetite for sex, even affirming that their marriage was never consummated because Mark was homosexual. Rather than a divorce, on December 3 she demanded the annulment pure and simple of their marriage. In her memoirs, Lorna Luft affirmed point blank: "Mark was gay, but I hadn't realized it when he married my mother. I'm equally certain my mother didn't realize it, either, not until after she married him. Mark was handsome in a traditional masculine sense; there was nothing to mark him as homosexual. He was not effeminate, and he didn't flaunt his sexual orientation." It is difficult to imagine that Judy hadn't discovered it before her marriage, since they had lived together for two years… What's more, everyone in Hollywood knew that Mark Herron, before he met Judy, lived with an actor of German origin who was sixteen years older than he, a certain Henry Brandon, known for his role as a scarred Indian Chief in *The Searchers*. They reconnected, for that matter, after the divorce and lived as a couple until Brandon's death. It is perhaps that which hurt Judy the most: this return to the man he had loved and perhaps never stopped loving.

As if she had only been a parenthesis which allowed him to become what he had always dreamt of being: a celebrity.

Judy Garland sings "Comes Once in a Lifetime" on the ABC-TV The Hollywood Palace *on April 1, 1966.*

25.

Down and Out

Newly arrived from the East Coast to try his hand at public relations, Tom Green, twenty-six years old, wondered why Guy McElwaine, Judy's press secretary, had asked him to take care of a star who was as prestigious as Judy Garland when he had so little experience. The answer was simple: because she demanded too much time for a more experienced better-paid employee.

Judy Garland and Tom Green in San Francisco, September 1966.

Tom, who was discovering the world of show business, was both awestruck over Judy and stupefied by her loneliness. No one took her calls anymore and no one came to visit her out of fear she might ask for money. In Hollywood, it is best not to be broke.

Extremely devoted to her, Tom took good care of Judy.

"You'll wind up leaving me like the others," she told him one day.

After the separation from Mark Herron, Tom effectively became the one who ran her daily life and accompanied her wherever she went. With the naiveté of youth, he thought he would be able to get her life back on track. "I was really stupid to think I could help her," he later admitted.

In August of 1966, they went together to Mexico, where Judy was to sing at the El Patio Night Club. Over twelve days, she was to give fourteen concerts, with a fee of $17,500 a week, plus a copious amount of cash paid under the table, thus out of sight from the IRS. Accompanied by an orchestra with fifty musicians, the first evening she gave a ninety-minute show, even though her contract only required thirty; galvanized by the audience's welcome, she hadn't hesitated to prolong the show. But, whereas the second concert went well, Judy decided to cancel the rest of the engagement, officially citing laryngitis. The irony of the story is that she was replaced by Betty Hutton, who had replaced her years earlier after her departure from *Annie Get Your Gun*. With Judy, history repeated itself endlessly. She was therefore not paid the hefty sum she had hoped for, and in that the bills were mounting up, she decided to let go of Mrs. Chapman, the private tutor for Lorna and Joe, then fourteen and eleven respectively.

Despite the eighteen years that separated them, Judy and Tom became lovers. In December, they took the Super Chief for the East Coast. They talked about getting married. In his hometown of Lowell, which was twenty-five miles from Boston, Tom presented her to his family.

"I'm tired of being Judy Garland," she told his parents.

In January, she and Tom even visited his old alma mater, Dartmouth College, in Hanover, New Hampshire.

Judy was Episcopalian, Tom Green's family Catholic: did she have the right to attend the Christmas mass with them? It was she who phoned the archbishop.

"God loves everyone," replied Cardinal Cushing.

★

Judy Garland playing pool at Dartmouth College in Hanover, New Hampshire on January 9, 1967.

Once back in Los Angeles, reality caught up with Judy. No grocer would give her credit anymore. Sometimes, Alma and Lionel, her servants, called Sid in secret to ask him to bring over milk and cereal. She was flat broke.

Since their divorce, Judy had avoided Sid. When he came to fetch the children, she made sure she wasn't there. But in that everyone was now giving her the cold shoulder, she had no other choice but to swallow her pride and turn to he who had previously pulled her out of so many tight spots.

When Sid showed up in Brentwood, he was taken aback by her figure: Judy was a skeleton. She weighed ninety pounds.

"I don't know where to begin. I'm broke, I have no more money, no income. I need you. The children need you. We need you. I am too sick to work. We're going to wind up in the street…"

"I'm going to try to start over," promised Sid.

Not only did Sid break off all relations with Fields and Begelman's CMA agency, which was continuing to manage her career, but he demanded $3 million for having "deliberately and systematically abused her trust in order to two-time her, cheat her and despoil her." A gamble to make her creditors know that she just needed more time…

★

Was the novelist Jacqueline Susann thinking of Judy Garland when she wrote her second book, *Valley of the Dolls*? One of the three women who gets burned upon contact with Hollywood is indeed an actress who, after a lightening start, allowed herself to be prescribed too much medication, thus ruining her career and her two marriages.

The book became a bestseller, Fox bought the rights and went on the hunt to find someone to play the lead. Judy Garland, who was contacted, asked the impresario John F. Dugan to handle negotiations: she would be paid $75,000 plus $25,000 a week more if the filming was extended. To announce her return to the screen, a press conference was organized at the St. Regis Hotel in New York, in presence of the novelist. Inevitably, journalists questioned her about the points in common she had with the character, but Judy Garland had them under her thumb.

Author Jacqueline Susann and Judy Garland at a press conference at the Versailles Room of the St. Regis Hotel in New York on March 2, 1967 to announce Garland's signing to play Helen Lawson in the film Valley of the Dolls.

"The book deals with pills, to some extent. Have you found that prevalent around show business people?"

"Well, I find it prevalent around newspaper people, too."

The next day, still in New York, Judy had to attend her daughter Liza's marriage to the Australian musician Peter Allen, whom Judy had introduced to her. Before the ceremony, she phoned Vincente Minnelli, who had come to New York to attend the wedding.

"If you had any class, you'd escort me to your daughter's wedding."

Vincent agreed. It was thus together that they attended the marriage of Liza and Peter, which took place at the apartment of Stevie Philips, Judy's former assistant, who had become Liza's manager. It was a pretty picture, that of a legendary movie couple reunited for the last time. They would never see each other again…

Judy Garland, Liza Minnelli, Peter Allen, and Vincente Minnelli at Liza Minnelli and Peter Allen's wedding on March 3, 1967 in New York.

Judy Garland and Vincente Minnelli share a tender moment together at Liza Minnelli and Peter Allen's wedding.

★

Judy Garland poses for wardrobe tests for Valley of the Dolls *on April 14, 1967.*

Having returned to Los Angeles, Judy began preparing for *Valley of the Dolls* in late March. She recorded the song "I'll Plant My Own Tree" for the movie but was not thrilled with it. She even asked Fox to contact her former MGM cohort Roger Edens to write another or allow her to record "Get Off Looking Good" by her former musical arranger, Bobby Cole, on her ill-fated 1963/1964 CBS television series. But nothing ever came of the propositions.

On the first day of shooting, she arrived at 7:30 A.M., as planned, and had her makeup and hair done. But by 11 A.M., she still hadn't stepped foot onto the set.

"We'll shoot this afternoon," declared the conciliatory director, Mark Robson.

But the afternoon came and went, and everyone was still waiting for her. Cloistered in her dressing room like some shellfish, she seemed to panic at the idea of playing a character that hit too close to home. Having taken too many tranquilizers, she no longer saw the difference between what she once was and what she had become. It was a strange optical illusion where reality and fiction had become bedfellows.

The second day brought no improvement. The third, it was impossible to locate the caps she had used since her early years at MGM to hide the imperfections of her incisors: they would have to go to a dentist for him to make another set. She would not be back before 3 P.M.: barely enough time to shoot a smattering of a scene…

One evening, Judy began to grow delirious. Lorna decided to call Dr. Marc, who was now taking care of her.

"Come over, please! Mama is crying, she has no more medication, she needs something to sleep. And we have nothing left to eat."

Dr. Marc came over with hamburgers and gave Judy a tranquilizer. At this period of time, Judy was taking twenty Ritalin tabs a day, an upper whose secondary effects were aggressivity, hallucinations and paranoia. The usual dose prescribed was three a day. The next day, Dr. Marc phoned Fox: they mustn't leave Judy alone. The studio complied and hired a nurse.

Ten days after filming began, Judy still hadn't shot a full scene. The decision was taken to dismiss her. Judy implored Sid to speak with Darryl Zanuck, the head of the studio, to take her back in the movie.

"We have given her every break possible," he decided. "We can't go on with her."

Fox showed itself to be rather lenient, considering that she had been fired for professional misconduct: they paid Judy half her salary, that is $37,500 — of which $23,500 went to the IRS, $3,500 to her agent, and $10,000 to her. Fox also offered her the beaded pants suit she was to have worn in the movie. She wore it onstage for her final concerts...

★

Sid was able to postpone the foreclosure on the Brentwood house by several months. In May of 1967, it sold for $130,000. Judy only got $15,000, the rest went to the IRS and her creditors. Having placed her furniture in a storage unit, she was now homeless. The papers had a field day. Judy made the best of it, with a grain of humor:

"In a way I'm glad they're taking the house. It's too big, too impractical. Besides, the man who lived there before didn't love his wife. That sort of put a pall on it from the beginning! There are acres of gardens, and a swimming pool, and the place needs at least four servants and four gardeners to keep it in shape. I never really liked it. It looks like a Gloria Swanson reject. I say good riddance!"

The new owners, who were flexible, accepted that she could stay until June 8, the date on which she had to leave for the East Coast, where Sid Luft booked her for a series of concerts. From June 13 to 18, she would headline the Westbury Music Fair on Long Island, near New York. Ten months after her last appearances onstage, her shows delighted audiences. The critics, persuaded that she would blow up in mid-flight, were surprised by her vitality. *The Hollywood Reporter* wrote: "Her appearance at Westbury confounded all those who thought she was no longer capable of such performances. She has never sung as well and has never been in such good shape." After two other concerts in New Jersey, she returned for the third and last time in her career to the Palace Theatre in New York between July 31 and August 31. The show was entitled "Judy Garland at Home at the Palace": she was like at home in this theater that had witnessed her greatest comebacks.

Judy Garland onstage at The Palace in New York in 1967 in the Valley of the Dolls *beaded pants suit designed by Travilla that was gifted to her after she left the film.*

Since the end of the 1950s, Judy Garland's audience included many admirers in the gay community. This latest run at the Palace turned her into a gay icon. *Time* magazine couldn't help reporting that "a disproportionate part of her nightly claque seems to be homosexual. The boys in the tight trousers roll their eyes, tear at their hair and practically levitate from their seats" during Garland's performances. "Homosexuals tend to identify with suffering. They are a persecuted minority group, and they understand suffering. And so does Garland," analyzed in *Esquire* the future screenwriter of *All the President's Men*, William Goldman. Better yet, Judy Garland was one of the muses of the camp style popular in the gay community and defined by Susan Sontag as "fundamentally the enemy of what is natural, inclined to artifice and exaggeration."

The marquee at the Palace for Judy Garland's third and last run at the famed theater between July 31 and August 26, 1967.

Judy Garland arriving at the opening-night after-show party at El Morocco on July 31, 1967.

Sid Luft and Judy Garland at the after-show party.

Judy Garland in her dressing room at the Palace on opening night, July 31, 1967.

In four weeks at the Palace, Judy earned $227,602. To avoid that her paychecks be seized by the IRS and her creditors, Sid intended to have them deposited onto the account of the Group Five company run by one of his friends, Raymond Filiberti. Officially, Judy only earned $1,000 a concert; on the other hand, all of her expenses, including food for the children, were entirely picked up by Group Five, which also covered her lodging. It was thus she who, under her own name, rented a house on 63rd Street East, where she lived in a typical New York brownstone, with its walls in red sandstone and its staircase leading to an elevated ground floor.

The year 1967 should have ended in fireworks: seven concerts from December 25 to 31 at Madison Square Garden. But there would be no rebirth without relapse: after three shows, Judy cancelled the rest because of laryngitis — the usual excuse.

In early January, she had her eyes on starring in *Mame*, the Jerry Herman musical that was a big hit on Broadway. Angela Lansbury, who was playing the title role, was to leave the show in the spring. But the producers politely gave her the cold shoulder, deeming that she was not reliable enough to give a daily performance several months in a row. Her ego was hurt: it was the first time she had been turned down.

Her unreliability was on full display on February 19 at a concert at the Baltimore Civic Center. Tony Bennett, who was the opening act on the double-header bill, had to lead her onstage holding her by her waist. Tottering, holding on to a stool not to fall, Judy on that night muddled through and sang out of tune, delivering one of the worst shows in her career. Furious, the audience started to boo, whistle, and walk out. The next day, it was necessary to issue a press release: "Miss Garland was victim of food poisoning." No one was fooled.

Judy was then staying at the St. Moritz hotel with Tom, Lorna and Joe. On the morning of March 18, she fell in the bathtub and broke her collar bone. At the hospital, they prescribed Demerol, a powerful opioid painkiller, but Tom couldn't pay the bill. Judy explained to him how, in their most difficult periods, Sid put her jewels in hock while waiting to get some money. He decided to do the same and "borrow" two rings, which he exchanged for $1,000 at a pawnshop on 23rd Street, even though they were worth a hundred times more.

Had he told Judy? Had she forgotten, in the no-man's-land she was living in because of the opioids, what he had said to her? Noticing a few days later that her rings were missing, she brought charges for theft against Tom, who was arrested and thrown in prison. His lawyer reminded people that, since meeting the entertainer, his client had been of great service to her, "emotionally as well as financially."

The men who used Judy were numerous. But, of all her latest lovers, in addition to being the only one who had truly been able to get a handle on her drug intake, Tom Green was most assuredly the most honest. He calculated that he had spent $48,756 of his own money for her. "I was only trying to help her," he wrote Sid after the imprisonment. "Perhaps it is hell, but good God, I love her more than anything."

In truth, he was too kind for her. For weeks, she incessantly threw him out and took him back in. He had become her toy. Despite prison, they were still seen together. But the wedding that had been announced months earlier never took place.

★

Sid Luft and Judy Garland disembark from a train on May 23, 1968 at the Back Bay station in Boston, where Garland gave a concert at the Back Bay Theatre on May 24, 1968. She was the last artist to ever play there.

Over the course of weeks, her relationship with Sid had deteriorated. Judy had a fight with the wife of Raymond Filiberti, complicating their relations with the principal stockholder of Group Five. Furthermore, by using a front company run by a figurehead, Sid thought he was doing the right thing, but he had omitted the most important: making sure of Filliberti's moral fiber. He had found himself in trouble with the law many times. He had even spent a year in a federal prison. How much was he siphoning in exchange for his services? That was a mystery, but it was clear that Sid was imprudent in associating with this dubious character. Soon enough, many bills went unpaid, all the more so because Judy's income barely covered her expenses. Filiberti pressured Sid to borrow $18,750 from two businessmen of whom one had been condemned for armed threats. It's called fraud…

Financially strapped, Sid didn't see how Judy could once again dig her way out, except to pull herself together. He threatened her with throwing in the towel. "She answered: 'Get out!' So, I left." Not without a guilty conscience: he knew she was an easy prey for the vultures. Who were not far off, beginning with Fields and Begelman who, knowing she was broke, offered her $8,000 to get her back on contract, on condition that she withdraw her complaint against them. Which infuriated Sid who was not about to give up on a trial.

Completely adrift, oscillating between moments of lethargy and nervous breakdowns, Judy sometimes threw her children out — they took refuge at their sister Liza's place. At the end of their tether, Joey was the first to go back to his father in California. Lorna followed.

Judy was alone, abandoned, and rejected more than ever.

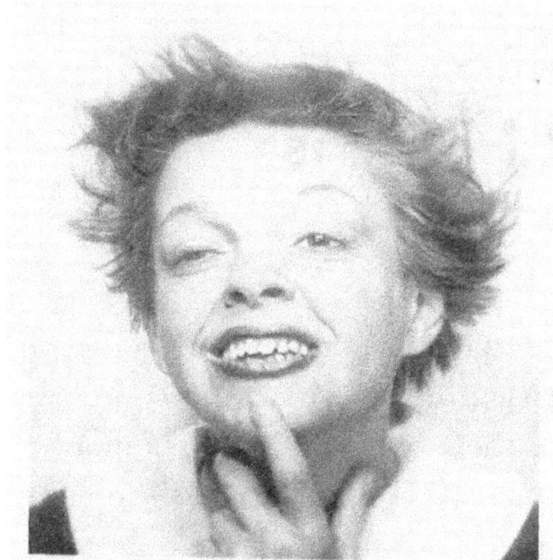 

These two snapshots were taken in a photo booth in Asbury Park, New Jersey on June 16, 1968.

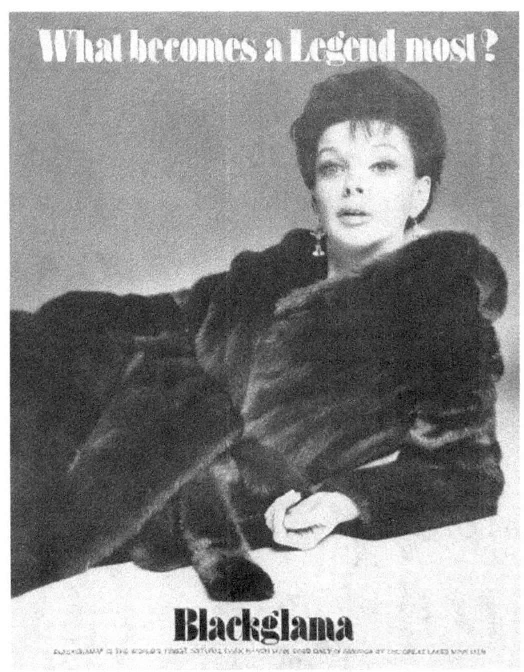

Judy Garland in a Blackglama "What Becomes a Legend Most?" ad, as photographed by Richard Avedon in October 1968.

26.

The Last Months

During the autumn of 1968, Judy Garland met a young composer, pianist and singer named John Meyer (born May 21, 1937) in New York. They had the same musical tastes; he loved her ravishing humor and let himself be seduced by her desperate need for love. Hadn't she one day said: "I can live without money, but not without love"?

Like Tom Green, John was fascinated by this extraordinary entertainer who lived, in her own words, "in a fourth dimension." He too strove to do everything to get her head above water. But did Judy really want to be saved? Her financial situation was so catastrophic that they had to live with John's parents, Herbert and Marjorie Meyer, in their apartment at 993 Park Avenue, Apartment 7E, from October 25 to November 19. In the end, John's father, disturbed by the disorder, asked them to leave… In 2022, John recalled that "Judy *was* the world's messiest houseguest."

John Meyer and Judy Garland in late 1968 when they were living with John's parents, where this photo was taken by Marjorie Meyer, John's mother. Courtesy of John Meyer. From the collection of Kim Lundgreen.

John accompanied her when she was summoned by the IRS and asked the boss of a gay and lesbian bar he played in to hire her. The man at first refused his request, not understanding how an entertainer who had filled the Palace Theatre a year earlier could wind up in his establishment. Seeing how Judy's situation was desperate, he finally gave in. Two or three weekends in a row, she came in and sang a few songs, leaving with a hundred dollars cash in her purse. John negotiated for her a few TV appearances, a new record contract with Blue Records — she would only sign the document once she had deposited the $2,500 advance, and a month of concerts in London at the Talk of the Town, where she was to be paid $6,000 a week. Nothing glorious: John didn't have the network of a David Begelman or Sid Luft. But it was better than nothing.

Judy Garland sings John Meyer's "It's All for You" on The Tonight Show *on December 17, 1968 in her last American television appearance. The videotape of the performance has been preserved because a staff member on the show marked the tape container "Nominated for an Emmy," even though it was not, so it wouldn't get erased.*

For months, Judy Garland, an American icon *par excellence* was living one day at a time. Like a junkie from the ghetto, she was willing to do anything to buy her damn pills. "I fed her self-destructive compulsions by providing her with pills," recognized John Meyer. "But if I hadn't done it, she would have left and found someone else to get them, as Mickey Deans did after me."

★

Flashback. The scene took place in New York a few days before the wedding of Liza Minnelli and Peter Allen in March 1967. Judy, on the verge of a nervous breakdown, called one of her friends, the pianist and singer Charlie Cochran, who tried to find some Ritalin. He approached Mickey Deans, who managed the fashionable nightclub Arthur, which was owned by Sybil Burton, Richard's first wife. Before the sun came up, they made it to her place with a bottle of pills.

"There's the doctor!" shouted Lorna to her brother Joey, frightened by the sight of these two guys showing up in the middle of the night.

With the naiveté of adolescence, Lorna had just summarized Judy's world: doctors were dealers, and her dealers were doctors.

Fifteen months later, one evening when Judy was singing at the Palace, her friend Bobby Cole proposed that they have dinner at a posh Manhattan restaurant. Once arrived, they were refused entry under the pretext that she was still wearing her stage outfit, which was the Travilla pants suit she had been gifted after the *Valley of the Dolls* debacle. At the time, women had to still wear a skirt or gown in so-called "select" places. Bobby suggested they go to Arthur, where Judy discovered the other face of Mickey Deans. Born Michael DeVinko, with blue eyes and a deep voice, he came from a Greek family. A pianist, he played in jazz groups before trying his hand at the night-clubbing business. Both seductive and charming, he burst into great cascades of laughter at the slightest joke. He was thirty-four, which was twelve years younger than she, but had something that made her feel safe. The kind of guy who always found a solution — he had proven that by bringing her the meds in the middle of the night. They chatted until closing and, when leaving, Judy offered him a seat for the Palace. Michael attended the performance but did not go to see her backstage. There was another woman in his life…

It was late 1968, and Charlie Cochran was again passing through New York. He stayed with Mickey, who was now free of any female attachments. He and Judy were seeing each other again. An incident would hasten fate: John Meyer got sick. A bad flu. Stuck in bed, he couldn't accompany Judy to London for her concerts at the Talk of the Town. However, she couldn't imagine going alone.

"Will you go with me?" she asked Charlie and Mickey.

Charlie had prior commitments. Mickey didn't say no: he didn't know London…It was thus that on December 28, 1968 Judy and Mickey arrived in the British capital. She was booked starting from the 30th. Although it didn't come close to her performances in London of earlier years, the concert was rather well received: the Talk of the Town press secretary reported that, out of the eighteen reviews that had been published in the British papers, seven were very favorable, three were excellent, two were good, and six were rather negative.

As the shows went on, Judy arrived later and later, to the point of beginning her performance nearly one and a half hours late. The bosses of the Talk of the Town gave her three days off. Thereafter refreshed, she was able to finish the engagement.

Between Judy and Mickey, everything accelerated. Her career was going downhill, so she hung on to love, as she always had done. Sensing that her time was running out, she asked Mickey to marry her. On January 9, they wed in a religious vow-taking in the St. Marylebone church of London in a small, private ceremony.

"We don't have any witnesses, what should we do?" Judy asked Peter Delaney, the Anglican priest who united them.

"God is our witness," he responded to her.

Upon the conclusion of the Talk of the Town shows, they decided to remain in London and rented, at 4 Cadogan Lane, in the Chelsea area, a nondescript cottage that lacked any and all charm. From the entrance door, one arrived directly into the living room which opened onto a small kitchen and dining room. On the second floor, there was a large bedroom, a bathroom, and two small bedrooms, one of which was used by Judy as a dressing room, the other by Mickey as an office.

Did he take their wedding seriously? Legally, their wedding was worthless in that the divorce with Mark Herron still hadn't been made final. A month later, she and Mickey had already gotten into a fight, and

Mickey left for New York. What's more, was he really interested in a life with Judy? Still, ten days later he was back. They reconciled, swore never to leave each other again, and decided to marry, this time in a civil ceremony at the Chelsea Register Office. British television sent a crew to cover the event. These were pathetic images of a tiny woman of forty-six who looked fifteen years older, destroyed by pills, worn out by life, and who obligingly posed for pictures with a playboy who might have asked himself what he was doing there…

Onstage at The Talk of the Town in London, January 16, 1969. Photo by Arthur Sidney

Judy Garland and Mickey Dean's mews cottage, demolished in 2016, in Belgravia, London.

Mickey Deans and Judy Garland in the living room of her last home.

A reception followed at Quaglino's, a fashionable restaurant in the West End. Judy invited the cream of the show business crop, but no one showed up. No one wanted to lend himself to this masquerade. No one wanted to be present for the downfall of a legend.

One journalist asked her if she had any new projects.

"Yes," she replied: "to be happy."

Had she, the interpreter of "Get Happy," ever been happy?

★

And after?

A race to the bottom.

Judy and Mickey took a short honeymoon in Paris, then flew off for a series of concerts in Stockholm, Gothenburg (which she cancelled) and Malmö, in Sweden, then Copenhagen in Denmark, for $10,000. Following these, Mickey planned a few days' rest in Torremolinos in Spain; but she was so weak that she had to spend the first day there in bed. Early in the morning, Mickey had to break down the door of the bathroom, where she was sleeping on the floor. Urgently called in, a Spanish doctor suggested that she be hospitalized. Mickey refused. He thought that the sunshine of the Costa del Sol was her best remedy.

A few days later, they returned to Chelsea. Judy only wanted to live in England.

"I don't know if London still needs me," she had declared to the *Daily Express* a few weeks earlier, "but I sure need London. I feel at home here. People understand me; there isn't this cruelty that I often feel in the United States. I have come to a point in my life where the most precious thing is compassion. Here, I've found it."

In early June, her state of health had improved enough for them to take the plane for New York together. A movie chain would be game for rebaptizing their theaters in Judy Garland's name, in exchange for a few appearances. The deal, unfortunately, was never concluded, and all the plans Mickey had imagined fell through. One couldn't improvise being a manager in just a few weeks' time.

In New York, her doctor decided to replace the Seconal with Thorazine, a powerful antipsychotic which had earned the nickname of "the chemical straitjacket" for its narcotic effect. Judy went shopping, saw her daughter Liza, visited Mickey's parents in New Jersey; but on June 10, 1969, for her forty-seventh birthday, she never left her bed. Five days later, she attended a gig by Anita O'Day in a jazz club in Greenwich Village. In the jam-session tradition, Anita invited Judy to join her onstage to sing "Day In, Day Out" and "Over the Rainbow."

She would never go onstage again.

Copenhagen airport press reception, March 18, 1969.

Judy Garland leaves for New York from London's Heathrow Airport on May 21, 1969.

The last known photo of Judy Garland taken around June 15, 1969 during her stay in New York from May 21 to June 17, 1969. She died on June 22, 1969.

On June 17, Judy and Mickey flew back to London. She was skeletal, with an emaciated face and bony legs. Mickey's friend Bob Jorgen took them to the airport. Horrified by the state of her health, he took Mickey aside and told him:

"Take very good care of her because she's dying…"

The days were peaceful: the calm before the storm. Judy read, Mickey had appointments in London. Often, in the evening, he took a walk alone in the park near the house. What was he up to? Judy never said a word. In a 2022 interview, John Meyer claimed that Mickey was gay. Mystery. On the 19th, a London doctor prescribed Seconal for her once again.

On Sunday, June 22 at 10:40 A.M., the telephone rang at the little Belgravia cottage. Still half asleep, Mickey answered. It was Charlie Cochran. John Carlyle, one of the star's friends, was with Charlie and wanted to find out how she was doing. But she wasn't in bed.

"I don't know where she is," Mickey said.

"Ok, so go look for her…"

He went towards the bathroom. The door was locked from the inside. He knocked. No response.

Mickey went back to the phone to ask Charlie and John to call back later. He then climbed on the roof to get to the bathroom by the window.

Judy was seated on the toilet, her head leaned forward. She was asleep, he first thought. But her skin was ghostly, her lips had dry blood on them, and her body was cold.

She had died six or seven hours earlier, the medical examiner estimated. Dr. Derek Pacock concluded that she had died of an accidental overdose. Her blood contained 4.9% of barbiturates, the equivalent of eleven-and-a-half capsules of Seconal.

On Judy's night table, the police found a box of thirty pills two-thirds of which had been taken, and another pillbox that hadn't been opened. How could Mickey Deans have left powerful sleeping pills lying around within easy reach of Judy? Carelessness? Indifference? It could be called failure to assist a person in danger. Sid Luft reported that Judy had asked him to never leave more than three pills at her bedside. It was proof that her suicide attempts were more self-destructive compulsions or cries for help than a true desire to end it all.

When she learned about Marilyn Monroe's death, Judy had declared:

"You take pills to sleep, you wake up anyway, but you have forgotten you have taken them. So, you take more…"

Which is probably what happened.

*

Liza, Lorna and Joe needed to be told.

With great courage, Liza took charge of organizing the funeral. London? New York? Los Angeles? For practical reasons, it would be New York. And then, Judy loved the city so much…

On Wednesday, June 25, her body was repatriated to New York, where it was exposed in an open casket at Frank Campbell Funeral Home, on the East Side of Manhattan, at the angle of Madison and 81st Street. She wore the same gray satin dress she had worn on the day of her religious wedding to Mickey Deans. Gene Hibbs, the famed makeup artist, did her face. "I want to be beautiful, perfect," she said one day when talking about one day dying. Between her white-gloved hands had been placed a black prayer book.

Judy Garland's coffin is placed into a hearse after arriving at the John F. Kennedy International Airport in New York on Thursday, June 26, 1969 at 1 A.M.

For one day and one night, more than twenty thousand fans passed in front of her coffin lined with pale blue velvet. The young and the old, the poor and the rich, men and women, Whites and Blacks, straights and gays. Such a funeral had not been seen since that of Rudolph Valentino. Judy was not just a star but part of the national heritage. All of America loved this woman who was weak and strong, discrete and exuberant, funny and desperate, self-destructive and for a long time indestructible.

On Friday, at 1 P.M., the reverend Delaney celebrated a religious service in front of a selected group of people: Mickey Rooney, Katharine Hepburn, Dean Martin, Lauren Bacall, and Lana Turner. James Mason, her costar in *A Star Is Born*, delivered the eulogy. The group then dispersed to the sound of "The Battle Hymn of the Republic."

At the exit of the Campbell Funeral Chapel, the crowd paid its respects one last time to the coffin covered in yellow roses.

Yellow, her favorite color.

The same color she had followed to the land of Oz.

Judy Garland's body leaves the Frank E. Campbell Funeral Home in New York on June 27, 1969.

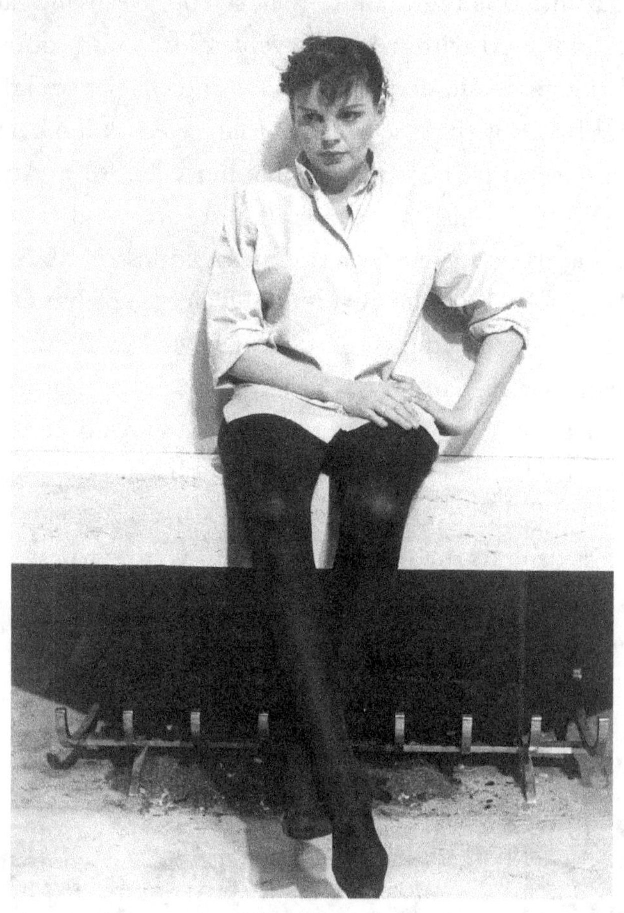

Judy Garland on the set of A Star Is Born, *1954, in a photo by Bob Willoughby.*

Epilogue

Judy Garland was entombed in a crypt at Ferncliff Cemetery in Hartsdale, north of New York. In 2017, forty-eight years after her death, her two daughters and son decided to transfer her coffin to the Hollywood Forever Cemetery in Los Angeles "so they could be closer to her." She now lies in a marble mausoleum inscribed with the inscription: "I'll come to you, smiling through the years," an excerpt from one of her most beautiful songs.

It was in tribute to her signature song, "Over the Rainbow," that the American graphic artist Gilbert Baker designed the rainbow flag in 1978 for the Gay Freedom Day Parade in San Francisco. Since then, the rainbow flag has become the emblem of the LGBTQ community. In 1998, *The Advocate* wrote that Judy Garland was "the Elvis Presley of homosexuals."

In 1973, Liza Minnelli won the Oscar as Best Actress for her performance in Bob Fosse's 1972 *Cabaret*. "If Hollywood were a monarchy, Liza would be the crown princess," Fred Astaire said of her. After the commercial failure of *New York, New York,* she mainly devoted herself to concerts. She most notably did a world tour with Frank Sinatra and Sammy Davis Jr., two of Judy Garland's best friends. Her private life often seems like a carbon copy of that of her mother: Peter Allen, her first husband, turned out to be gay. And she too got trapped in the infernal spiral of pills, drugs, and alcohol.

Lorna Luft became a singer. She has performed in numerous Broadway musicals and has acted in a stage version of *The Wizard of Oz* in England, where she played the role of the Wicked Witch of the West. In 2007, she recorded a record entitled *Songs My Mother Taught Me*.

Joey Luft lives in Los Angeles, away from show business. The victim of fetal alcohol syndrome, he suffers from alcoholism.

David Rose, Judy Garland's first husband, was for twenty years the conductor on the very popular television show of Red Skelton. He also composed countless film scores for the movies and television, including *Little House on the Prairie.* He died in 1990 at the age of eighty.

Vincente Minnelli remarried the French woman Georgette Magnani (with whom he had a daughter, Christiana) in 1954, before divorcing her to marry the Serbian model Danica Radosavljević, then the British actress Margaretta Lee Anderson. He received the Oscar for Best Director in 1959 for *Gigi.* He made his last movie, *Nina,* in 1976, starring his daughter Liza Minnelli. Suffering from Alzheimer's disease, he died in 1986 at eighty-three.

Sid Luft married Patti Hemingway in 1970 and divorced her in 1971, then Camille Keaton, who was the grandchild of Buster Keaton, in March 1993. He died of a heart attack in 2005 at the age of eighty-nine.

Mark Herron lived with Harry Brandon until the latter's death in 1990. Herron died of cancer in 1996.

Mickey Deans died in 2003 at sixty-eight of heart failure. It is today thought that he was bisexual.

David Begelman quit CMA, the agency founded by Freddie Fields in 1973, to take over as president of Columbia, then led MGM, before creating his own production company. Having gone through serious financial scandals in his lifetime, he killed himself in a hotel room in Century City in 1995 at the age of seventy-three. After his suicide, Sid Luft, talking about Begelman's death, told Garland scholar and translator of this biography, Lawrence Schulman, that "he killed the right person."

Arthur Freed remained a producer at MGM until the end of his career, even though the Freed Unit was dismantled at the end of the 1950s. *An American in Paris* and *Gigi,* both directed by Vincente Minnelli, earned Freed the Oscar for both in the category Best Motion Picture, the statuette of which was traditionally handed to the producer in the United States. He died in 1973 at seventy-eight.

After his ousting from MGM, Louis B. Mayer never ran a studio again. He died in 1957 at seventy-two. Samuel Goldwyn said of him: "If there were so many people at his funeral, it was because people wanted to be sure he was really dead."

Filmography

Shorts:

The Big Revue (aka The Starlet Review) (1929, Mayfair Pictures filmed at
Tec-Art Studio)

A Holiday in Storyland (1929 – Vitaphone, filmed late 1929 at the First
National Studio, Burbank, CA)

The Wedding of Jack and Jill (1930, Vitaphone, filmed late 1929 at the First
National Studio, Burbank, CA)

Bubbles (1930, Vitaphone, filmed in December 1929 at the First National
Studio, Burbank, CA)

La Fiesta de Santa Barbara (1935, Metro-Goldwyn-Mayer)

Every Sunday (1936, MGM)

Silent Night (1937, MGM)

Hollywood Goes to Town (1938, MGM)

If I Forget You (1940, MGM)

Command Performance (1944, Program #92, Army-Navy Screen Magazine
No. 20, U.S. Army Signal Corps.)

Feature Films:

Pigskin Parade (1936, 20th Century Fox)

Broadway Melody of 1938 (1937, MGM)

Thoroughbreds Don't Cry (1937, MGM)

Everybody Sing (1938, MGM)

Love Finds Andy Hardy (1938, MGM)

Listen Darling (1938, MGM)

The Wizard of Oz (1939, MGM)

Babes in Arms (1939, MGM)

Andy Hardy Meets Debutante (1940, MGM)

Strike Up the Band (1940, MGM)

Little Nellie Kelly (1940, MGM)

Ziegfeld Girl (1941, MGM)

Life Begins for Andy Hardy (1941, MGM)
Babes on Broadway (1941, MGM)
For Me and My Gal (1942, MGM)
Presenting Lily Mars (1943, MGM)
Thousands Cheer (1943, MGM)
Girl Crazy (1943, MGM)
Meet Me in St. Louis (1944, MGM)
The Clock (1945, MGM)
The Harvey Girls (1946, MGM)
Till the Clouds Roll By (1946, MGM)
Ziegfeld Follies of 1946 (1946, MGM)
The Pirate (1948, MGM)
Easter Parade (1948, MGM)
Words and Music (1948, MGM)
In the Good Old Summertime (1949, MGM)
Summer Stock (1950, MGM)
A Star Is Born (1954, Warner Bros.)
Pepe (1960, Columbia)
Judgment at Nuremberg (1961, United Artists/Roxlom)
Gay Purr-ee (1962, UPA / Warner Bros.)
A Child Is Waiting (1963, United Artists)
I Could Go On Singing (1963, Barbican/United Artists)

Discography

Child of Hollywood: Great Original Performances 1936-1942 (1993, CDS Records Limited)

Swan Songs, First Flights: Her First and Last Recordings (2014, DOREMI/ HALLOW)

Lost Tracks 1929-1959 (2010, JSP Records)

The Best of Lost Tracks 1929-1959 (2015, JSP Records)

Lost Tracks 2 1936-1967 (2019, JSP Records)

The Best of Lost Tracks 2 1936-1967 (2020, JSP Records)

Classiques et inédits 1929-1956 (2008, Frémeaux & Associés)

Creations: Songs She Introduced 1929-1962 (2013, JSP Records)

The Garland Variations: Songs She Recorded More Than Once (2014, JSP Records)

Judy Garland Sings Harold Arlen (2016, JSP Records)

Classic Duets (2017, JSP Records)

The Complete Decca Masters (plus) (1994, MCA/Decca)

Smilin' Through: The Singles Collection 1936-1947 (2011, JSP Records)

Soundtracks: 48 Original Movie Recordings 1929-1961 (2017, Mint Audio Records)

I Can't Give You Anything But Love 1938-1961 (2018, Jasmine Records)

Collector's Gems from the M-G-M Films (1996, Rhino Movie Music/ Turner Classic Movies Music)

Judy Garland in Hollywood: Her Greatest Movie Hits — Original Soundtrack Performances 1936-1963 (1998, Rhino Movie Music/Turner Classic Movies Music)

The Very Best of Judy Garland (2005, TCM Turner Classic Movies Music)

The Story & Songs of The Wizard of Oz (1998, Rhino Movie Music/Turner Classic Movies Music)

Meet Me in St. Louis (1994, MGM Records/Rhino Records/Turner Classic Movies Music)

Easter Parade (1995, Rhino Records/Turner Classic Movies Music)

Summer Stock/In the Good Old Summertime (2001, Rhino Homemade/ Turner Classic Movies Music)

The Two-a-Day Is Back in Town, Closing Night at the Palace, February 24, 1952 (2023, JSP Records)

A Star Is Born (2004, Columbia Legacy/Sony Music Soundtrack)

Miss Show Business (1955/2015, Capitol Records, high-resolution download)

Judy (1956/2022, Universal Japan)

The 1956 "Judy" Sessions - Unreleased Takes, the Final Masterpiece, and More! (2023, High Definition Tape Transfers)

The Lost Vegas Show, New Frontier Hotel, July 16, 1956 (2023, High Definition Tape Transfers)

Alone (1957/2022, Universal Japan)

Judy in Love (1958/2022, Universal Japan)

Judy Garland at the Grove. (1959/2022, Universal Japan)

The Letter (1959/2022, Universal Japan).

That's Entertainment! (1960/2022, Universal Japan)

The Garland Touch (1962/2022, Universal Japan)

Judy at Carnegie Hall (2000, EMI-Capitol Music Special Markets/ DCC Compact Classics)

The Greatest Night in Show Business History, Carnegie Hall, April 23, 1961 (1961/2022, High Definition Tape Transfers)

Judy Garland: Live! (1989/2022, Universal Japan)

Judy Garland and Liza Minnelli: Judy Garland and Liza Minnelli "Live" at the London Palladium. (1965/2022, Universal Japan)

Gay Purr-ee (2003, Rhino Handmade Records/Turner Classic Movies Music)

Judy Garland – The London Studio Recording 1957-1964 (2011, First Hand Records)

The Very Best of Judy Garland: The Capitol Recordings 1955-1965 (2007, EMI Records Limited (EMI Gold)

Judy Garland à Paris, Olympia, 28 octobre 1960 (1994, Europe 1/RTE)

Live in Paris 1960 (2022, Frémeaux & Associés)

The Amsterdam Concert: December 1960 (2012, First Hand Records)

The Show That Got Away: The Judy Garland Show (2002, Hip-O)

At Home at the Palace: Opening Night (1967, ABC Records)

The Final Concert in Copenhagen, March 25, 1969 (2022, High Definition Tape Transfers)

Bibliography

Jeanine Basinger, *The Star Machine*, Knopf, 2007.

Manuel Betancourt, 33 1/3: *Judy at Carnegie Hall*, Bloomsbury Academic, 2020.

Steven Bingen, Steven X. Sylvester, and Michael Troyan, MGM: *Hollywood's Greatest Backlot*, Santa Monica Press, 2011.

Dirk Bogarde, *Snakes and Ladders*, Bloomsbury, 1978.

Patrick Brion, *Joseph L. Mankiewicz*, La Martinière, 2005.

Patrick Brion, *La Comédie Musicale*, La Martinière, 1993.

Gerald Clarke, *Get Happy: The Life of Judy Garland*, Delta Books, 2000.

David Dahl and Barry Kehoe, *Young Judy*, Mason/Charter, 1975.

Mickey Deans and Ann Pinchot, *Weep No More, My Lady*, Hawthorn Books, Inc., 1972.

Richard Dyer, *Heavenly Bodies: Film Stars and Society*, The MacMillan Press Ltd, 1986.

Anne Edwards, *Judy Garland*, Simon and Schuster, 1975.

Christopher Finch, *Rainbow: The Stormy Life of Judy Garland*, Grosset & Dunlap, 1975.

Hugh Fordin, *MGM's Greatest Musicals: The Arthur Freed Unit*, Da Capo Press, 1996.

Gerold Frank, *Judy*, W.H. Allen, 1975.

Will Friedwald, *A Biographical Guide to the Great Jazz and Pop Singers*, Pantheon, 2010.

Walter Frisch, *Arlen & Harburg's* Over the Rainbow, Oxford University Press, 2017.

Serge Glickmann, *Judy Garland*, la pensée universelle, 1981.

William Goldman, *The Season*, Harcourt, Brace & World, Inc., 1969.

Mark Griffin, *A Hundred or More Hidden Things: The Life and Films of Vincente Minnelli*, Da Capo Press, 2010.

Ronald Haver, *A Star Is Born: The Making of the 1954 Movie and Its 1983 Restoration*, Knopf, 1988.

Charles Higham, *Merchant of Dreams: Louis B. Mayer, MGM and the Secret Hollywood*, Donald I. Fine Inc., 1993.

Hedda Hopper, *The Whole Truth and Nothing But*, Doubleday, 1963.

Gerald Kaufman, *Meet Me in St. Louis*, British Film Institute, 1994.

Lorna Luft, *Me and My Shadows: A Family Memoir*, Atria, 1998.

Sid Luft, *Judy and I*, Chicago Review Press, 2017.

John Meyer, *Heartbreaker*, Doubleday & Company, Inc., 1983.

Vincente Minnelli, *I Remember It Well*, Angus & Robertson, 1975.

James L. Neibaur, *The Films of Judy Garland*, McFarland, 2022.

Stevie Philips, *Judy & Liza & Robert & Freddie & David & Sue & Me*, St. Martin's Press, 2015.

Darwin Porter and Danforth Prince, *Judy Garland & Liza Minnelli: Too Many Damn Rainbows*, Blood Moon Productions, 2020.

Mickey Rooney, *Life Is Too Short*, Villard Books, 1991.

Salman Rushdie, *The Wizard of Oz*, British Film Institute, 1992.

Coyne Steven Sanders, *Rainbow's End: The Judy Garland Show*, William Morrow, 1990.

Aram Saroyan, *Artie Shaw Talking*, An Air Book, 2010.

Scott Schechter, *Judy Garland: The Day-By-Day Chronicle of a Legend*, Cooper Square Press, 2002.

Randy L. Schmidt, *Judy Garland on Judy Garland: Interviews and Encounters*, Chicago Review Press, 2014.

Lawrence Schulman, *Garland – That's Beyond Entertainment – Reflections on Judy Garland*, BearManor Media, 2023.

Laurent Valière, *42è rue: La grande histoire des comédies musicales*, Marabout, 2018.

Index